GLOBAL TRANSFORMATIONS OF THE 21ST CENTURY

The Future of Humans, Markets, and Capital

GLOBAL TRANSFORMATIONS OF THE 21ST CENTURY

The Future of Humans, Markets, and Capital

Edited by

Sergey Bodrunov

APPLE ACADEMIC PRESS

First edition published 2026

Apple Academic Press Inc.
1265 Goldenrod Circle, NE,
Palm Bay, FL 32905 USA

760 Laurentian Drive, Unit 19,
Burlington, ON L7N 0A4, Canada

CRC Press
2385 NW Executive Center Drive,
Suite 320, Boca Raton FL 33431

4 Park Square, Milton Park,
Abingdon, Oxon, OX14 4RN, UK

Apple Academic Press exclusively co-publishes with CRC Press, an imprint of Taylor & Francis Group, LLC

Library and Archives Canada Cataloguing in Publication

CIP data on file with Canada Library and Archives

Library of Congress Cataloging-in-Publication Data

CIP data on file with US Library of Congress

ISBN: 978-1-77964-401-5 (hbk)
ISBN: 978-1-77964-402-2 (ebk)

DOI: 10.1201/9781779644022

About the Editor

Sergey Bodrunov

Director of the S.Y. Witte Institute for New Industrial Development (INID), President of the Free Economic Society of Russia, Doctor of Economics, Professor, Corresponding Member of the Russian Academy of Sciences (197101, Russia, Saint Petersburg), Bolshaya Monetnaya St. 16.

Contents

Abbreviations ... *ix*

Preface ... *xi*

1. **Transformations of the 21st Century: Human, Society, Values, Noonomy—Material vs. Ideal, "Physics" vs. "Lyricism"** ... **1**
   Sergey Bodrunov

2. **The Geopolitical Economy of the Current Crisis: The Potential of Noonomy** ... **15**
   Radhika Desai

3. **Quality as the Basis for Development in the Digital Economy** ... **25**
   Vladimir Okrepilov

4. **The Challenge of Noonomy to Global Liberal Capitalism** ... **37**
   David Lane

5. **Economic Development Based on Improving the Quality of Growth** ... **47**
   Aleksandr Shirov

6. **A World Creative Audit: A Research Proposal** ... **59**
   Alan Freeman

7. **Crisis of Global Transition: Noonomy as a Possible Future** ... **101**
   Savvas Michael Matsas

8. **The Transformation of the "Economic Man" into a "Cultural Man"** ... **113**
   Natalia Yakovleva

9. **Re-Thinking the Institutions and Practices for a Better Future World** ... **121**
   Al Campbell

10. **Noonomy: A Platform for Strategic Development (Regional Aspect)** ... **147**
    Svetlana Pyankova

11. The Role of Civil Society in the Transition to a New Economy 157
Leo Gabriel

12. Cognitive Model of the Noonomy Concept in the Author's Discourse 163
Ekaterina Kabakhidze

Index 179

Abbreviations

AI	Artificial Intelligence
ASI	Agency for Strategic Initiatives
BRICS	Brazil, Russia, India, China, South Africa
GATT	General Agreement on Tariffs and Trade
GDP	Gross Domestic Product
IMF	International Monetary Fund
IP	Intellectual Property
ISO	International Organization for Standardization
NGO	Non-Governmental Organization
NIS	New Industrial Society
NOO	Noonomy or Noohuman
OECD	Organization for Economic Co-operation and Development
R&D	Research and Development
RAS	Russian Academy of Sciences
SCO	Shanghai Cooperation Organization
STP	Scientific and Technological Progress
STR	Scientific and Technological Revolution
TNC	Transnational Corporation
UNESCO	United Nations Educational, Scientific and Cultural Organization
UNICEF	United Nations International Children's Emergency Fund
USSR	Union of Soviet Socialist Republics
WIPO	World Intellectual Property Organization
WTO	World Trade Organization

Preface

The 35th session, *Global Transformations of the 21st Century: The Future of Humans, Markets, and Capital*, of the international theoretical seminar of the S.Y. Witte Institute for New Industrial Development was held in Bodrum (the Republic of Türkiye) from August 29 to September 1, 2023. This session continued a series of discussions that have been held over the years by the S.Y. Witte Institute for New Industrial Development at scientific centers in Russia, Europe, and China. Experts from Russia, the Republic of Türkiye, Canada, the USA, China, Greece, Croatia, and the United Kingdom participated in this event.

Based on the discussions held during the international theoretical seminar, this collection of scientific papers from its participants has been prepared. The collection reflects the most striking and interesting points of view of scientists from different countries on current issues of socio-economic development. In our opinion, such discussions are very useful in today's rapidly changing world, where long-held scientific concepts do not always allow for an adequate interpretation of the phenomena observed in the economy and society, necessitating the development of new approaches to their analysis.

At the seminar, the tone of the discussion was set by Sergey Bodrunov, Director of the S.Y. Witte Institute for New Industrial Development and Corresponding Member of the Russian Academy of Sciences, with his plenary paper, *Transformations of the 21st Century: Human, Society, Values, Noonomy—Material vs. Ideal, "Physics" vs. "Lyricism."* His basic ideas develop the methodology of applying the noonomy approach not only to the analysis of the modern socioeconomic system but also to forecasting the prospects for its transformation and long-term development. The scientist drew attention to the fact that it is knowledge, and not scientific and technological progress per se, that is the deep engine driving humanity, society, and civilization forward. At the same time, the long-term development of society must have a humanistic content; therefore, inevitably, along with socioeconomic transformations, changes in humans themselves should be expected.

Vladimir Okrepilov, Scientific Director of the Institute for Regional Economic Studies of the Russian Academy of Sciences and Academician of the Russian Academy of Sciences, presented the paper *Economics of Quality: Scientific Content, Practical Application, and Development Prospects*. As one of the most respected scientists in the field of the economics of quality, he focused not only on the theoretical aspects and basic postulates of this scientific concept but also revealed the applied tools for measuring and managing quality in economics at all levels. The current stage of socioeconomic development, in accordance with dialectical concepts of development, is accompanied by the transition of accumulated quantitative changes into qualitative ones. In this regard, the analysis of the observed transformations from the standpoint of the theory and methodology of the economics of quality seems quite justified.

Alexander Shirov, Director of the Institute of Economic Forecasting of the Russian Academy of Sciences and Corresponding Member of the Russian Academy of Sciences, considered quality issues in a narrower perspective, in relation to the phenomenon of economic growth. His paper, *Economic Development Based on Improving the Quality of Growth*, focused not on quantitative but on qualitative indicators of economic development. Although, from a statistical point of view, measuring growth through GDP dynamics still seems to have no alternative, the acceleration of technological development and changes in the social structure make it necessary to search for new, high-quality indicators of economic growth and development.

The transition to qualitative characteristics of growth and development is inextricably linked with the search for an answer to the question of what the source of these qualitative changes is. Alan Freeman, Professor at the University of Manitoba (Canada), in his paper *A World Creative Audit: A Research Proposal*, put forward and substantiated the hypothesis that human creative abilities should be considered as this source. Accordingly, their stimulation and development, through the formation of appropriate institutions, should be regarded as one of the factors that drive the changes taking place in the socioeconomic system.

Radhika Desai, Professor at the University of Manitoba (Canada), presented the paper *The Geopolitical Economy of the Current Crisis: The Potential of Noonomy* at the seminar. Her paper highlighted that the creative potential of noonomy theory and its explanatory ability are particularly evident under modern conditions of the turbulent development of both the world community as a whole and individual countries and their groups. In this regard, noonomy theory can be considered the basis for the formation of new, complex socioeconomic knowledge that is more adequate to the observed realities than traditional scientific concepts.

These ideas were further developed by Al Campbell, Professor at the University of Utah (USA), in his paper *Re-thinking the Institutions and Practices for a Future Better World.* He also emphasized the weakness of traditional social and economic concepts that fail to adequately explain today's observed transformations, as well as their inability to predict consequences and identify opportunities for effective influence on these transitional processes. Therefore, theoretical rethinking of long-held theories, the introduction of new elements such as noonomy theory, and the inclusion of large amounts of empirical material into scientific discourse are essential.

David Lane, Member of the British Academy of Social Sciences, endorsed the opinions of other discussants. At the same time, his paper *The Challenge of Noonomy to Global Liberal Capitalism* focused on criticizing the liberal model of capitalism, highlighting its imperfections, which require immediate correction. Noonomy theory can serve as a tool for this correction, enabling not only the identification of the shortcomings of the liberal-capitalist model but also the proposal of constructive steps to address them, emphasizing the applied significance of noonomy theory.

Michael-Matsas Savvas, Professor at the National University of Athens (Greece), presented a paper titled *Crisis of Global Transition: Noonomy as a Possible Future.* Along with other discussants, he emphasized the practical importance of noonomy theory. The socioeconomic system is currently in a state of transition to a new phase, and perhaps this transition will be accompanied by a new pathway of long-term development with specific quantitative and qualitative characteristics different from those currently observed. It is precisely in such a transition process that it is important to maintain long-term guidelines, including those of value, which is precisely the opportunity provided by noonomy theory.

Leo Gabriel, Director of the Institute for Intercultural Research and Cooperation at the University of Vienna (Austria), presented the paper *The Role of Civil Society in the Transition to a New Economy.* He paid special attention to the social aspect of the ongoing and expected economic transformations. Moreover, this social aspect was considered not only passively (as the impact of the economy on society) but also actively. The self-organization of society and the formation of civil society institutions make it possible to create an economic model that meets the needs of individuals and social groups. Civil society institutions express these needs; therefore, to achieve balanced development, the support of these institutions is required.

Svetlana Pyankova, Professor at the Ural State University of Economics, in her paper *Noonomy: A Platform for Strategic Development (Regional Aspect)*, focused on the regional features of nootransition. A distinctive feature of Russia and many other large countries is the uneven and asymmetrical development of their constituent regions. This asymmetry is becoming one of the obstacles to the socioeconomic development of the country as a whole. Therefore, increased attention should be paid to the regional aspect of strategizing and implementing new economic management nootools.

Changes in the practice of socioeconomic development, as well as in its scientific understanding, which, in fact, became a prerequisite for the emergence of noonomy theory, are also reflected in language. Ekaterina Kabakhidze, Associate Professor at Lomonosov Moscow State University, in her paper *Cognitive Model of the Noonomy Concept in the Author's Discourse*, drew attention to these aspects. Her research shows that noonomy theory is not only becoming more widespread but also gaining deeper meaning.

Natalia Yakovleva, Leading Researcher at the Institute of Economics of the Russian Academy of Sciences, presented a paper titled *Human Potential in Relation to Noonomy Theory: The Transformation of the 'Economic Human' to the 'Cultural Human'.* She focused on the humanitarian dimension of nootransition. Changes in society and the economy are inevitably accompanied by changes in human beings themselves, which can be both positive and negative. In this regard, it is extremely important to ensure a controlled, constructive approach to the human dimension of ongoing transformations.

All participants in the scientific discussion that took place during the 35th session *Global Transformations of the 21st Century: The Future of Humans, Markets, and Capital* of the international theoretical seminar of the S.Y. Witte Institute for New Industrial Development concurred in the opinion that there was a need for further dialogue and exchange of views on complex modern problems of socioeconomic development. In such discussions, noonomy theory can act as a link, a common platform for discussion.

CHAPTER 1

Transformations of the 21st Century: Human, Society, Values, Noonomy—Material vs. Ideal, "Physics" vs. "Lyricism"

SERGEY BODRUNOV

Director, S.Y. Witte Institute for New Industrial Development (INID); President, Free Economic Society of Russia; Doctor of Economics; Professor; Corresponding Member, Russian Academy of Sciences (Saint Petersburg, Russia)

ABSTRACT

This chapter raises a conceptual problem with both philosophical and socio-economic content: the nature of the interaction between material and spiritual principles in the context of the increasing role of knowledge and cultural values as factors in modern socio-economic development. The author demonstrates that the process of searching for new knowledge has rapidly begun to play a predominant role over the material foundations of production, as it now determines the very nature of these material foundations. This revolution in the relationship between the material and the ideal in the production process itself is based on the transition to knowledge-intensive material production technologies and the creation of knowledge-intensive products. This change also leads to qualitative shifts in property relations and in the nature of humanity. Property relations are gradually eroding, which may eventually lead to their exhaustion. Moreover, in order to ensure the development of society during the modern technological

Global Transformations of the 21st Century: The Future of Humans, Markets, and Capital.
Sergey Bodrunov (Editor)

DOI: 10.1201/9781779644022-1

revolution, a person must transcend the narrow shell of an economic being and become a truly reasonable individual—a noohuman—who relies on the cultural imperatives of human development.

1.1 INTRODUCTION

This chapter is devoted to reflections on problems that, in our opinion, deserve special attention. These are the problems of the transformation of our civilization and the prospects that await us in connection therewith.

The main transformation, no matter what sphere it covers (technology, economic relations, politics), is the transformation of humans. The driving motive here is the need to satisfy growing human needs—satisfying them as they are recognized and depending on objective and subjective prerequisites and possibilities. Let us emphasize two important things: (i) the understanding and recognition of one's needs; and (ii) the recognition of true needs.

Why are these points especially important? Because God endowed humans with minds so that they could: (a) self-discover (*humans have this opportunity*) and thus multiply needs; and (b) develop the need for knowledge. This is what allows them to develop and create tools to satisfy the material and spiritual needs that arise as the desire for knowledge and spiritual development progresses.

The satisfaction of needs leads to the emergence of certain constructs—technical, economic, social, and political. These constructs, reflecting contradictory interests, are also contradictory. In society, too, contradictions arise: on the one hand, there are the particular needs of individuals, which objectively conflict with each other to varying degrees (from zero to complete antagonism); on the other hand, there are the single, common, unifying interests of a given community, more or less recognized by distinct individuals. In the process of resolving this contradiction (*well-known from classical philosophy*) during social development, institutions for harmonizing interests objectively arise. This is a well-known approach to understanding society's historical development.

However, there is one very important aspect. Today, the problem of harmonizing private and public interests is particularly relevant due to the intensification of both global and national problems. Let us reflect on the possibilities of solving this problem through a more fundamental and profound examination. This leads us to the question of the extent to which, and how, the process of transition occurs—from the *"economic" human*, maximizing utilitarian needs, to the *"cultural" human* (a term used by Buzgalin (2018, p. 229)), to the *noohuman* (*our term*), who develops a spiritual world. From a human focused on maximizing private economic benefit as the priority of existence to a human aimed at creating a world where other values prevail—a world of a different, more humanistic culture. This is how we pose the question. Why?

1.2 MATERIALS AND METHODS

Today, this problem has ceased to be exclusively a subject of theoretical, abstract thinking. It has turned into a problem of practical choice, not only moral but also economic and political—and namely in practical terms: who to work as? where and for what to live? whether to orient one's life, and the lives of relatives and friends, toward the goals of human community development as a whole, or to limit oneself exclusively to personal interests—accumulation of wealth, power, etc.?

One could argue that all people are egoistic; they always act in their personal interests. And they agree with this. But a person, having an *ego*-focused need for the immeasurable acquisition of material wealth and not being burdened with morality, is meant to be a robber. Another hypothetical person, on the contrary, gives, satisfying the *ego*, but does so following the need to sow "reasonable, good, eternal" (Nekrasov, 1982, p. 180). One kills, the other defends, and not only oneself and family. In the language of political economy, this distinction is formulated as a contradiction and unity of private and public interests; in the language of noonomy, it is explained as a contradiction exclusively of interpersonal nature, since any *ego*-interest is still the interest of the *ego*; the other question is what lies behind this *ego*. And this depends on the individual's awareness and acceptance of the norms of the noovalue criterion of existence.

Moreover, we should deeply analyze to what extent the interests of the *ego* (individual for a particular person) can reflect the *ego*-interests of other individuals. Only at some point, and in some unknown proportion, can they become "common"—public from the perspective of political economy discourse.

Here, we move into the language of socio-economic theory. Indeed, today, in the space of the economy, a human lives and acts in the world of the market as an actor in the capitalist system: a hired worker, a freelancer, a capital owner—or first, second, and third at the same time. Changes in the essence of humans in a society that remains predominantly economic are closely linked to changes in the market and capital. But before turning to this topic, let us clarify a number of points.

First, there has long been a dispute in the scientific community about whether the market is primarily a socially neutral mechanism of exchange—an objectively necessary tool that ensures the progress of the social division of labor, technology, etc.—or whether the market is a form of special social relations that generate alienation of people, fetishization of goods and money, inequality, and the division of people into hired workers and capital owners. This is the question of whether the market brings people various "evils"—social phenomena with an obvious negative connotation. Professor Alexander Buzgalin belongs to the second group of researchers and constantly criticizes the market (Buzgalin, 2018). We are closer to the first position, which more accurately reflects the real relations.

If we agree with the most reasonable view of the market as a relatively (relatively!) socially neutral mechanism, then the main problem of the future can be emphasized as both the future of humans and the future of capital, considering the market as a certain tool that is necessary at some stages and may cease to be necessary at others—at least in its present form.

Taking this approach, we can conclude that the market will remain, not the only, but an important way of connecting people and firms in the economy. It has served and will continue to serve as a connecting block, an element, a space between humans and capital, but the changes in the relations denoted by the category "capital" will indeed take place. And they have already been taking place—these profound changes.

However (*and this is the second point*), to understand their nature, we must address transformations in the basics of the basics—in technology.

1.3 RESULTS AND DISCUSSION

In social sciences, there is a widespread view that the driver of transformations of humans and society is the development of technology, technological progress, and scientific-technical progress (*we will not argue about the wording*). Indeed, STP is what the progress of mankind stands on. And that of humans! We are sometimes accused of technological determinism, but we do not render absolute the role of technology at all. It is important to realize that technology, in the language of classical philosophy, is just a reflection. Of what? Reflection of knowledge—to the extent that humans: (i) comprehend it; and (ii) learn to apply it to satisfy their needs through social production. Technology is knowledge implemented in the process of social production. Consequently, it is knowledge, and not scientific-technical progress as such, that is the deep driver of human, society, and civilization development. The tool for the progress of knowledge is "cognition" (*let us recall our thesis about the role of need in the recognition of needs*).

By creating new technology with the help of a counting machine or microscope, we are always "improving" the main tool of cognition—our brain. Here, it is very important to realize that technology is also a tool. So, on the one hand, it is a way, a tool to satisfy needs, and not only material ones; on the other hand, it is an implementation of the knowledge obtained in the process of cognition. And, at the same time, a tool for cognition. This is the trick of the technological process—and that of technology.

We often, willingly or unwillingly, assume that there is a basic influence of the material on the process of awareness—on the ideal. And rightly so: "existence" to a certain extent "determines consciousness." Let us not refute Marx; we will only note that we added "to a certain extent" for a reason. Let us explain why. We should not forget that there is a reverse influence. Everything in the world is dual. Using the ideal—new knowledge—we implement it in technology or somewhere else and get new material phenomena. This is fundamentally substantiated by Professor A. Freeman from Canada in his works on "mental objects" (Freeman, 2015).

It is clear to us, but we go further. The theory of noonomy shows that from a certain moment, knowledge rather than material becomes the main factor of production (*creation of material objects!*). "The role of the main resource and the main source of development goes to knowledge, to scientific cognition of the surrounding world by humans" (Bodrunov, 2019, p. 9). Hence, an extremely important fundamental conclusion: the further scientific and technological progress advances, the more the reverse influence of the ideal on the material grows.

This is an important point, perhaps crucial to understanding the fate of civilization! This is where, in particular, all the catastrophic predictions about the threats posed by artificial intelligence, the atomic bomb, viruses, etc., come from. Material things invented by us in the mental, ideal world and realized through technology can so transform this world that "not a stone would be left standing."

Further, the process of reverse influence of the ideal on the material is constantly intensifying. Why? Because there is more and more knowledge discovered by mankind, and its application becomes more and more diverse. The reason is the very process of cognition, its nature, and the nature of knowledge. Increasing and expanding our consciousness, the process of cognition generates new needs in cognition and implementation of the results of this cognition in new technologies. It lures us further, which may lead to both positive and negative consequences. Under what conditions? How can it happen? Our answer: if we don't put this process under "noo"-control. How do we do that?

Let's take a closer look at the details. If there is such a process, the question arises: yesterday, conditionally speaking, the material influenced the ideal, say, in the proportion of 70 to 30, and today, on the contrary, the ideal influences the material more strongly. At what point did a certain "balance" (50/50) arise? This is an important question.

And there is an answer to it: during the period of the economy's transition to noonomy. This answer was provided by us at seminars, in our books, and in articles published in many languages around the world. Therefore, this conclusion is justified and tested.

The coincidence of the transition to noonomy—a qualitatively new way of satisfying human needs—on the one hand, and the achievement of a state where the material influences the ideal as powerfully as the ideal (in particular, knowledge) influences the material, is not accidental.

It is especially important that, by this point, society has utilized for its development some institutions that do not operate spontaneously and within the framework of the "zoo" paradigm of rigid conflict and competition (Bodrunov, 2018), as under the domination of market fundamentalism, but consciously and in solidarity, realizing the true needs of a person who has moved from the "zoo-ego" to the "noo-ego" and the society in which noo-values prevail.

In this way, we come close to more specific issues of the transformation of economic relations—and thus of humans. Technological progress becomes the material basis of these transformations. As it develops, humanity reaches a stage in its growth when the conscious impact of humans on production, the economy, social processes, and other material aspects becomes at least equal to the basic impact of social existence on social consciousness. This state arises when the progress of knowledge, implemented in technology, becomes so powerful that it determines further development by at least 50%. In this case, technology primarily accelerates the process of discovery and cognition.

We are facing not just the acceleration of scientific and technological progress (STP), but an "acceleration of acceleration"—a kind of second derivative of this process. Knowledge is transforming more intensively (also mediated by the progress of technology) into new knowledge, generating this "acceleration of acceleration." The transition to a new quality of technological development is underway—let us call it the seventh technological mode. Recall that the theory of technological modes by Russian academician Glazyev proposes the classification of technologies into six modes (Glazyev, 2018) of different types, which in the context of noonomy have varying degrees of knowledge intensity. We are talking about a new, qualitatively different, seventh technological mode (Bodrunov & Glazyev, 2023, pp. 200–207), based on the "acceleration of STP acceleration," where knowledge becomes the basic factor of production and the key component of the industrial product in knowledge-intensive production of this mode. We call the product itself knowledge-intensive (Bodrunov, 2018, p. 70). Conventionally, knowledge becomes the prevailing component in the social product! It is here that the "border of equilibrium" passes, and at this stage, the bifurcation of civilizational development occurs: either the progressive transformation of human and economic relations, in which the latter gives way to the post-economic way of needs satisfaction, or catastrophic consequences on a global scale.

Before discussing the first scenario, it is essential to note that we do not view these global transformations as a continuation (with some modernization) of the neoliberal model of transnational corporations (TNCs) dominating the countries of the "center" over the periphery, as indicated in world-system analysis by Wallerstein (1982), Arrighi (1994), Frank (1979), and Amin (1973). This type of globalization is in deep crisis (Simonyan, 2018). "…the West (e.g., in the form of the transatlantic community) can no longer dictate its system of perceptions and values as universal. That is why we are talking about the crisis of West-centric globalization" (Kazantsev & Sergeyev, 2020, p. 55).

We are referring to something different: the unity of humanity as a whole and the objective interconnectedness of all changes in time and space. This is not a formal "sameness," but a profound coincidence and interconnectedness of technological, economic, social, and cultural transformations.

Let us first consider the changes in economic relations caused by the progress of technology. As emphasized above, if the market, which links people in the process of exchange, remains a relative constant, then human capital and other forms of capital change fundamentally.

Capital is property, and property is the basic, fundamental characteristic of the economic system. Here, we can identify the beginning of profound changes in the economy.

We have already noted (Bodrunov, 2021) that in recent decades, the process of property diffusion not only continues but also accelerates sharply (in parallel with the acceleration of STP), acquiring new forms associated with the withdrawal from individual private property and the development of various forms of joint use in production and consumption. These include various forms of co-working, co-living, and sharing (the most well-known example being carsharing) (Laurenti et al., 2019; Mosmann, 2019; Torrent-Sellens, 2020).

There are other manifestations of property diffusion, such as the process of *ownership splitting*. Known since the last century and widely researched by scholars of the new institutional direction, bundle set of property rights is becoming more and more diverse: property rights are split into more and more fractional economic-legal "ingredients." The latter, in turn, are also fragmented, and distributed among various private economic actors (natural and legal persons, foundations, etc.)[1].

While mono-ownership used to be typical, today there is a process of blurring mono-rights among persons who hold different elements of ownership of the same object. For example, one actor uses the object in production or consumption (e.g., renting an apartment), possessing certain "branches" of property rights associated with this use. In many cases, a tenant in a private house cannot be evicted even if they fail to pay rent. The second actor manages the property. The third actor receives part of the income, for example, as a landlord; however, even in this case, ownership rights can be split in situations such as sub-rent or the partial transfer of income rights. The fourth actor (the lender who provided a loan to the owner to purchase the house, using it as collateral) receives income and holds

[1]*Symposium*: Property: A Bundle of Rights? (2011) *Econ Journal Watch: Scholarly Comments on AcademiEconomics*, Volume 8, Issue 3.

additional rights associated with the collateral. Another bundle of rights to the same house, including its operation, belongs to the state and society as a whole, which is represented by the state, and so on. Thus, property is subject to diffusion, splitting, and "blurring," all of which have economic, legal, and—more importantly—value-based aspects, as property relations are also tied to human values. As a result, numerous interests of different actors in economic society emerge, and this process is expanding.

However, property remains the foundation of economic society. Its diffusion as an institution indicates that economic society (a society centered on the economic way of satisfying needs) is becoming obsolete. At the same time, the need to satisfy human needs remains! Are there other options for meeting this need? Are they visible?

Yes. And first of all—in the main component. The basic component of future production is knowledge, which will determine the type of future products and their application. But knowledge is intangible. No matter how we define "intellectual property rights," by its nature, knowledge diffuses quickly. This crucial aspect—the accelerating diffusion of knowledge as the basic factor in the production of knowledge-intensive products of the seventh mode—will lead to the development of a new type of need satisfaction, which is non-economic in essence since it is based on a factor not reducible to property: knowledge.

We are witnessing the birth of a different, post-economic way of satisfying needs. The impact of this process on the economy undermines its foundation—property! But this process inevitably affects humans as well. Let us return to the topic of human transformation.

Allow me a brief digression. When I attended a Soviet school as a child, there was a poster in the corridor titled "The Moral Code of the Builder of Communism." Being a diligent student, I read it carefully. Next to the school was a church, which my neighbor, an elderly lady, attended. When I asked her what they discussed there, she answered in such a way that I understood: it was about the same principles found in the "Moral Code."

This is an example of how true values are eternal, given to us as "special knowledge." We continually return to them. And as society objectively transitions away from an economy-centered model, humans will return to true knowledge, to nooessence. This expansion of the sphere of cognition will influence both socialization processes and noo-development, as well as the material foundation of existence—specifically, the methods of satisfying needs. The "economic human" will be replaced by the "cultural human." Let me emphasize: this person will not halt scientific and technological progress (STP), production, or nooproduction but will instead accelerate them further. We emphasize this for a reason.

Another digression: almost all of us have read the exciting novel *Airport* by Canadian writer Arthur Hailey (Hailey, 1971). This is not just a gripping detective story but a true "production novel." It meticulously describes production processes, the operations of a complex technological firm, devices, technology, and more. We are immersed in the buzzing atmosphere created by STP. Yet the novel is also about people—about a human being immersed in the turbulent river of technological progress, whose life becomes increasingly difficult as a result.

At the time, it seemed paradoxical: STP, designed to make life easier, actually makes it more difficult and presents humans with deadly choices. Today, we know for certain that progress can lead to many problems. Hailey's novel profoundly altered my worldview as a 30-year-old "science guy": it became clear that the main problems of technological development and STP are not in the creation of new opportunities—they lie outside the traditional framework of inquiry! As STP evolves into the stage of the scientific and technological revolution (STR), technology becomes so powerful that it starts to destroy its creators. Let us recall Georges-Jacques Danton, one of the leaders of the French Revolution at the end of the 18th century, to whom history attributes the words spoken on the guillotine: "the revolution devours its children."[2] Let us add—any revolution, including the technological revolution.

What is the conclusion to be drawn from it? There are several:

- It is impossible to stop technological progress, but it can and must be brought under ***noocontrol***. For this to happen, humans must change. Only humans have the ability to curb STP—this flow of knowledge implemented in technology—and direct it toward true creation.

  How? In Russia, there is a saying: "One fire drives out another fire." Firefighters extinguish a powerful blaze not with water, but

[2]In the interest of historical accuracy, it should be pointed out that these words are also attributed to the Dantonist Camille Demoulin and the Girondist Pierre Vergneau. However, documenting the first appearance of such a phrase are the notes of Joachim Villat, a former juror at the Revolutionary Tribunal of Paris, written by him in prison and published in 1794: "La révolution, comme Saturne, eut bientôt dévoré ses plus tendres enfants" (The Revolution, like Saturn, soon devoured its most tender children). This phrase is written by him in connection with the arrest of Danton and Demoulin (Vilate, 1794, p. 27).

with fire, by making a "backfire." Humans must oppose the flow of technological knowledge with the flow of knowledge from the sphere of culture—the "culture of life" in the broadest sense. Only by changing consciousness in this way can humans resolve this collision.

- It is paradoxical, but only at first glance. Only a changed human can further stimulate the development of technological knowledge. Humans cannot endlessly drive the technological evolution of the 21st and subsequent centuries while remaining "troglodytes" at the level of the 20th century. To continue increasing the potential to meet needs through technological progress, humans must change. They must evolve to work with higher levels of knowledge.
- It is about the primacy of the ideal. Only through the comprehension of new knowledge can a person create—whether in the sphere of STP, culture, or elsewhere. Ideal knowledge is the starting point of a process that culminates in the creation of material objects to satisfy growing needs. At the same time, it is impossible to "create knowledge"; it exists objectively—outside of us and independent of us. We can only discover it—quantum by quantum, step by step—and "realize" it, including through the use of material objects. For this purpose, humans must become increasingly "knowledge-intensive," expanding consciousness—the receptacle of the ideal.
- It is about society. In the 1960s, there was a heated global debate over what was more important for the development of society: "physics" or "lyricism" (Bogdanov, 2011). The "physics" camp, which prioritized technical progress, won. Today, the lag of "lyricism," which is concerned with sacred knowledge (empathy, kindness, social comfort, cultural and spiritual development, values, social narratives, and much more), has led to the "devouring" of our existence by the "physics of STP." It is time for "lyricism," and our entire society, to catch up. Without alignment and synchronization of society's awareness of the full range of problems during this transition—including seemingly opposing but actually complementary spheres of knowledge—we risk sinking the ship of our civilization.

Let us return to the relationship between humans, individuals, and society. Clearly, all these conclusions strictly dictate the need for the socialization of society, which is both a condition and a consequence of scientific and technological progress (STP) and the development of property diffusion processes. It is through the diffusion of property that one of the pathways for transforming the economy into noonomy, economic society into noo-society, and the "economic" human into a true *homo sapiens—noo-homo sapiens*, or, in short, *noo-homo*, *noo-man*—is formed.

This is only one aspect of the path (note the emphasis on *path*; this is not accidental. In Chinese philosophy, the word *dao* is used as a synonym for a given, chosen, thought-out, and then consistently and persistently implemented strategy. We have much to learn from China in the implementation of long-term strategies). Other components of the path to noonomy include technological progress (the foundation of everything), its material aspects, the socialization processes it generates, and the growing role of solidarity in human relations. I would also like to note that the progress of solidarity relations transforms competition and, consequently, the market. It is no coincidence that we emphasized the relative invariance of the market to global transformations.

The four components of the path to noonomy—STP, the diffusion of property, socialization, and solidarism—form a kind of quadriga, like Apollo's quadriga, that carries us into the future (Bodrunov, 2020, p. 16). And the fact that this future is coming is undeniable. But: what kind of future? What are its invariants? What obstacles await us on this path?

These are the questions—the truly global challenges within the process of the global transformation of society—that the world scientific community faces.

KEYWORDS

- **knowledge-intensive production**
- **material foundations**
- **noohuman**
- **property relations**
- **socialization processes**
- **technological progress**

REFERENCES

Amin, S. (1973). *Le développement inégal: Essai sur les formations sociales du capitalisme périphérique*. Paris: Les Editions De Minuit.

Arrighi, G. (1994). *The long twentieth century: Money, power, and the origins of our times*. London-New York: Verso.

Bodrunov, S. D. (2018). From ZOO to NOO: Man, society, and production in the conditions of a new technological revolution. *Questions of Philosophy*, *7*, 109–118.

Bodrunov, S. D. (2018). *Noonomy*. Moscow: Kulturnaya revolyutsiya Publ.

Bodrunov, S. D. (2019). Noonomy: Ontological theses. *Economic Revival of Russia*, *4*, 6–18.

Bodrunov, S. D. (2020). Noonomy: Basic vectors of genesis. In *Scientific reports of the S. Y. Witte Institute of New Industrial Development (INID)* (p. 23). St. Petersburg: S. Y. Witte INID Publ.

Bodrunov, S. D. (2021). Genesis of noonomy: Scientific and technological progress, diffusion of ownership, socialization of society, solidarism. *Economic Revival of Russia*, *61*(1), 5–14.

Bodrunov, S. D., & Glazyev, S. Y. (2023). *Regularities of the noonomy foundations formation as future social order: To know and operate*. St. Petersburg: S. Y. Witte INID Publ.; Moscow: Tsentrkatalog Publ.

Bogdanov, K. A. (2011). Physics vs. lyricism: To the history of one “stupid” discussion. *UFO*, *111*, 130–154.

Buzgalin, A. V. (2018). A human in the world of alienation: A critique of liberalism and conservatism. Reactualization of Marxist heritage. *Questions of Philosophy*, *6*, 190–201.

Buzgalin, A. V., & Kolganov, A. I. (2018). *Global capital* (Vol. 2: Theory: Global hegemony of capital and its limits, 4th ed.). Moscow: LENAND Publ.

Frank, A. G. (1979). *Dependent accumulation and underdevelopment*. New York: Monthly Review Press.

Freeman, A. (2015). Twilight of the machinocrats: Creative industries, design and the future of human labour. In K. van der Pijl (Ed.), *Handbook of the international political economy of production* (pp. 352–375). Cheltenham–Northampton: Edward Elgar Publishing.

Glazyev, S. Y. (2018). *A leap into the future: Russia in new technological and world economic structures*. Moscow: Knizhnyy mir Publ.

Hailey, A. (1971). *Airport*. In *Foreign Literature* (pp. 8–10).

Kazantsev, A. A., & Sergeev, V. M. (2020). The crisis of “Americanocentric” globalization: Causes, trends, development scenarios. *Bulletin of MGIMO University*, *13*(2), 40–69. https://doi.org/10.24833/2071-8160-2020-2-71-40-69

Klein, D., & Robinson, J. (2011). Property: A bundle of rights? Prologue to the property symposium. *Econ Journal Watch: Scholarly Comments on Academic Economics*, *8*(3).

Laurenti, R., Singh, J., Cotrim, M. C., Toni, M., & Sinha, R. (2019). Characterizing the sharing economy state of the research: A systematic map. *Sustainability*, *11*(20), 5729. https://doi.org/10.3390/su11205729

Mosmann, P. C. (2019). Renaissance of shared resource use? The historical honeycomb of the sharing economy. In D. Wruk, A. Oberg, & I. Maurer (Eds.), *Perspectives on the sharing economy*. Cambridge Scholars Publishing.

Nekrasov, N. A. (1982). *Complete collected works and letters in 15 volumes* (Vol. 3). Leningrad: Nauka Publ.

Simonyan, R. H. (2018). The crisis of the liberal market model of globalization. *Questions of Philosophy*, *8*, 16–25. https://doi.org/10.31857/S004287440000736-4

Torrent-Sellens, J. (2020). Collaborative behavior and the sharing economy: Pan-European evidence for a new economic approach. In B. Orlando (Ed.), *Strategy and behaviors in the digital economy*. London: IntechOpen.

Vilate, J. (1794). *Continuation des causes secrètes de la révolution du 9 au 10 thermidor*. Paris: [s.n.].

Wallerstein, I. (1982). *World-systems analysis: Theory and methodology*. Beverly Hills: Sage.

CHAPTER 2

The Geopolitical Economy of the Current Crisis: The Potential of Noonomy

RADHIKA DESAI

Director, Geopolitical Economy Research Group; Professor, University of Manitoba (Winnipeg, Canada)

ABSTRACT

The chapter explores the concept of international relations in the capitalist world. The results show that, contrary to the widespread tendency to perceive Marx as a theorist of "globalization," he in fact took the existence of nation-states and national economies seriously, believing that the relationships between them arise from the contradictions of the capitalist system. The common features of the phenomena of "noonomy" and "geopolitical economy" are identified, conceptually aligning them with Marx's historical materialism.

My argument today is that the geopolitical economy of capitalism, essentially its contradictory dynamics on the international plane of "the relations of producing nations" (to use Marx's words), is currently amassing historical forces that advance toward Noonomy.

To begin, let us clarify the terms. I take Noonomy, as most recently elaborated in the work of Sergei Bodrunov (Bodrunov, 2018, 2023) and more recently attracting engagement and elaboration from others (Bodrunov, 2022), to be the theory of how to reconstruct society to realize humanity's potential for development—both the development of productive forces and of humans themselves—in harmony with nature

Global Transformations of the 21st Century: The Future of Humans, Markets, and Capital.
Sergey Bodrunov (Editor)

DOI: 10.1201/9781779644022-2

and society. Noonomy's understanding of the development of productive forces is closely aligned with Marx's. Drawing from Adam Smith, Marx also believed that the division of labor, or what he preferred to call the socialization of labor, was central to increasing social productive capacities (see especially Marx, 1867, 1977, Chapters 13–15). To fully develop these capacities, and to continue developing them, society must be organized in a way that unleashes human social creativity and enables it to flow uninterruptedly. While Marx believed that capitalism would develop these forces to an unprecedented extent, he also believed that capitalism would ultimately become an obstacle to their further development. To continue this development, humanity would need to transcend capitalism and adopt a new social form, socialism, so that human productive capacities could continue to improve. Sharing this understanding, Noonomy is, like Marxism, fundamentally concerned with the reorganization of society.

Geopolitical economy, meanwhile, is the term I have given to a historical materialist way of understanding the evolution of capitalism on a world scale (first proposed in Desai, 2013; see also Desai, 2015, 2016, and 2023). This means that Marx's understanding of capitalism as contradictory value production is at its core. Just as class struggles—whether between the capitalist class and the working class or among capitalists and their fractions—arise from the contradictions of capitalism, so too do struggles between nations. These contradictions may be seen in terms of the paucity of demand, the tendency of the rate of profit to fall, or any of the many other realms where capitalism generates contradictions, whether inter- or intra-class (see Desai, 2021). Similarly, struggles among nations also arise from these same contradictions.

These struggles may take the form of competition among major capitalist nations—for markets, technologies, or "economic territory." They also manifest as struggles between imperialist nations and those resisting imperial dominance. Dominant capitalist nations seek to manage the contradictions of capitalism, in part by engaging in imperialism abroad, subordinating many countries and denying them the possibility of development. However, those countries that are able and willing resist this imperialism. At the core of this resistance is the pursuit of the development that imperialism denies its subordinates. While anti-imperialist resistance has often required wars and revolutions to secure the preconditions—national independence and policy autonomy—of the pursuit of development, that pursuit remains the essence of anti-imperialism: autonomous social or national development. The pursuit of development has defined the historical evolution of the world since the onset of capitalism, making it increasingly multipolar (Desai, 2013, Chapter 9). This historical trend toward multipolarity is the chief analytical result of geopolitical economy, and the historic drive toward development is the chief concern of Noonomy (see also Bodrunov, Desai, & Freeman).

It should be clear by now that both Noonomy and geopolitical economy are deeply influenced by and shaped by Marxism, while also drawing on many other compatible perspectives. Two further points are important to note from the outset. First, geopolitical economy places both nations and classes as key agents of history side by side in the same historical frame. Capitalism cannot be fully understood through class struggles alone; international struggles have been and remain equally important in shaping its historical trajectory.

Second, if struggles among both classes and nations originate from the same contradictions of capitalism, then the historical end toward which they tend is also the same: the reorganization of society in ways that liberate its members to cooperatively develop the forces of production in harmony with nature, without limits. This end is what unites Noonomy, geopolitical economy, and Marx's historical materialism. This understanding also explains why socialism first emerged outside the homelands of capitalism, and why, in those contexts, it took—and had to take—the form of national developmental projects.

We are now ready to develop our argument.

2.1 THE CRISIS THIS TIME

The crisis we face today is multifaceted. To many, it recalls the *Thirty Years' Crisis*, as historian Arno Mayer (1981) understood the decades-long crisis from 1914 to 1945. For Mayer, this was not a series of successive crises—the First World War, the waves of revolution, and the Great Depression—but rather a single climacteric embedded in the logic of capitalism's development up to that point.

Today, too, the course and condition of capitalism lie at the heart of the crisis. In a critical sense, the most important element of the current crisis is the crisis of capitalism in its historical homelands and the resulting decline of the capitalist West, which becomes manifest internationally as the changing of the US-and-West-led world order that seemed so secure only two decades ago.

Other elements include the rise of China, and to a lesser extent, other emerging economies; the failure of the West to gain and retain allies; and the success of China and the BRICS countries in doing so. These changes are also associated with shifts in international economic governance, whether through the processes of de-dollarization or the formation of new international economic governance organizations created by the BRICS countries and others, precisely because the West refuses to cooperate in reforming the existing ones.

So, what is the geopolitical economy of this crisis? One important element becomes clear when compared to the *Thirty Years' Crisis*. According to Arno Mayer, that period was an international civil war, involving intense class struggles within countries as well as wars among them. Today, however, the left is largely in abeyance in most major capitalist countries. While the contradictions of capitalism are mounting and reaching crisis proportions domestically, they are manifesting as political upheaval and chaos, not directed toward social transformation but rather toward preventing the sharp deepening of social divides from expressing itself in transformative politics. This is chiefly achieved by framing the choice as one between a neoliberal establishment and an even more neoliberal, authoritarian populist, or even fascist right.

As a result, the international arena seems to be the determining one. It is on the international stage where opposition to the decaying old order and support for the creation of an alternative are emerging. Today, international resistance to a decaying, neoliberal, financialized capitalism is driving the historical momentum of our time.

2.2 THE CRISIS OF CAPITALISM'S SENILITY

Though the current crisis is often termed a "polycrisis," it is not a random mix of unrelated crises. Rather, the second distinguishing element of the current crisis is that it is rooted in the domestic political economy of capitalism's homelands, the imperialist countries, as we may call them. Essentially, the whole world has been cast into crisis because of domestic problems arising from one set of countries. This is a very important point, and the best route to understanding it is through Marx's understanding of capitalism and how it would end.

This point, which is contained in Chapter 27 of Volume 3 of *Capital* (Marx, 1895, 1981), is today largely forgotten. So let us recall it. For Marx, capitalist production in its highest development—that is to say, when it reaches the monopoly phase—is a necessary point of transition towards the transformation of capital back into the property of the producers, though no longer as the private property of individual producers but rather as their property as associated producers, as directly social property. It is furthermore a point of transition towards the transformation of all functions formerly bound up with capital ownership in the reproduction process into simple functions of the associated producers—into social functions (Marx, 1894, 1981, p. 568).

The burden of this chapter is to explain that, when it reached the monopoly phase, capitalism was ripe for socialism. Here, Marx explains how, as capitalist accumulation takes place on an ever-greater scale, it must itself turn social. It is no longer something that can be accomplished by individual capitalists; its ownership is itself socialized in the form of joint-stock companies. All functions bound up with capital ownership become functions of associated producers. They become social functions.

To understand this in terms of the development of the forces of production through the division of labor or the socialization of labor, we understand Marx to be saying that, by the time capitalism had reached the monopoly phase, it had completed its historical work, taking the development of the forces of production as far as it could. Capitalism could take this no further, and the further development of the forces of production would only take place with the establishment of socialism.

And again, the logic was very clear. Capitalism constantly and relentlessly socializes production, albeit it achieves this salutary goal brutally and chaotically. In the competitive phase of capitalism, when production is organized through the formation of a vast sea of competing firms that are, from a historical point of view, small, production is socialized among these competing firms. In the monopoly phase, the socialization of labor takes a quantum leap. As the process of competition, by eliminating all but one or a few of the most efficient firms, leads to monopoly, as production takes place on an ever-greater scale, production becomes socialized in the form of the vast and intricate division of labor within firms.

At this point, as capitalist ownership forms themselves become socialized, as it becomes clear to most that the production is the joint work of associated producers, capitalism would lose its historical justification and give way to socialism.

So, was Marx's expectation belied? Most would answer yes. However, the reality is considerably more complex. Yes, it was belied in the sense that, although capitalism had already reached the monopoly phase in the early 20th century, as the numerous writings on imperialism of the time argued, and although the 30 years' crisis was very much a crisis of that development, the world did not turn socialist in that crisis. However, this point must be heavily qualified.

Firstly, towards the end of the 30 years' crisis, witnesses to the manner in which capitalism could destroy societies and civilizations in world wars and great depressions, witnesses also to what socialism had achieved in the Soviet Union, prominent intellectuals such as Keynes or Karl Polanyi expected that the world would take a decisive turn to the left (see Keynes, 1933, 1936; Polanyi, 1944, 1945). Hayek, fearing the same prospect, wrote his *The Road to Serfdom* (1944), a plea against giving in to socialist temptation, around the same time. Secondly, while the whole world did not turn socialist, the addition of Eastern Europe and China to the ranks of socialist countries meant that a substantial part of humanity had turned towards socialism. At the same time, the countries emerging from colonial rule (largely thanks to the strength of the socialist bloc) were increasingly embarking on projects of autonomous national development that leaned distinctly left and often labeled themselves "socialistic."

Thirdly, in a certain sense, Marx's and these later intellectuals' anticipations were not belied even in relation to the major capitalist countries. The "Golden Age" of growth that followed the 30 years' crisis was made possible precisely because even these countries did turn left. Taking many leaves out of the socialist toolkit—macroeconomic policy aiming at full employment, public ownership, welfare states, encouragement of strong unions, progressive taxation, capital controls, financial repression, and the like (Hobsbawm, 1994, pp. 272–273)—the leading capitalist countries heavily reformed capitalism. These reforms, by creating the broad and deep markets that made investment attractive, were responsible for the legendary growth of the three decades that followed, not any regained vigor of capitalism itself, which it had already lost when it entered its senile monopoly phase earlier that century.

This point was not recognized at the time, and most analysts, including most Marxists, tended to attribute the growth record of the Golden Age to capitalism itself. However, what happened in the decades since the Golden Age ended in the 1970s has made the point irrefutable.

As the underlying system remained capitalist, inevitably, it ran into another major crisis by the late 1960s and early 1970s. This crisis placed the Western world before a major fork in the road. It could take the left alternative and deepen the socialistic reforms of the post-war period that had delivered the Golden Age. Or it could be said, with the neoliberals who were getting increasingly vocal at the time, that they were the problem and had to be rolled back to give capital more freedom, to unshackle it from the burdens that the socialistic reforms had placed on it.

Partly because Marxism and the left were already considerably weakened—intellectually (Desai, 2020) and politically—the second option was taken. Over the four decades since, capital's political power has ensured that, no matter the disastrous consequences for most societies and economies, Western governments have stuck to the neoliberal policy paradigm, with critical help from the nominally left-of-center parties that now subscribed to the same paradigm. This gave rise to a cross-party consensus on economic policy, leaving differences over "culture" to form the main electoral battleground between parties.

The result, 40 years down the road, is increasing concentration of capital, financialization turning investment from productive to speculative, low growth, low productive investment, heightening inequality, an exacerbation of the underlying demand deficit that was a key problem leading to the crisis of the 1970s, the productive weakening of capitalism in its homelands through outsourcing, and a shift in the world economy's center of gravity away from the West with the rising challenge of the BRICS countries, preeminently socialist China. In short, though it was adopted on the grounds that it would revive capitalism, neoliberalism has only revealed the senility of monopoly capitalism, and with the challenge of socialist China combined with the continuing weakness of left forces in the homelands of capitalism, the fate of capitalism now hangs in the balance—not of class power, but of international power.

2.3 THE MOMENT OF NOONOMY

This is the crisis that constitutes the moment for Noonomy. The first half of the 20th century radically changed the world, transforming what was an authoritarian and imperial world into one where there was much greater popular power and national power. This transformation was the result of two interacting forces. The first was inter-imperialist rivalry, in which nearly all the major capitalist powers fought one another to exhaustion, with the exception of the United States, which benefited enormously from this war. The second was the vast groundswell of popular energies, leading to welfare states in the First World, communism in the Second World, and distinctly left-leaning attempts at development in the Third World. It took the combination of these two forces to end the crisis period. Without the contribution of Russia and China in the Second World War, victory over fascism would not have been possible.

Today we are living in a time, as already mentioned, when the left and working people's organizations are in abeyance. This is the context, therefore, in which the power of imperialism, which has been weakening since its peak in 1914, is now weakening at an accelerated pace.

Imperialism is primarily about the denial of development, which is essential, on the one hand, so that the imperial countries can export their excess capital and commodities, and, on the other hand, so that they can import cheap labor and inputs. (These two are mutually contradictory, though we cannot go into that here.) The essence of anti-imperialism, therefore, is development, not war, though its pursuit may sometimes require war.

However, today it is clearer than ever that development cannot be about catching up to what is a decaying and discredited social form. This is where Noonomy, as a way of developing human beings and productive forces together, comes in. It is also important that it promises to do so without ravaging nature or culture. So here is my hypothesis about how Noonomy can advance: today, because the left is weak, the impetus for Noonomy is coming from nation-states. They are the ones who are demanding better terms for development as the minimum requirement for their legitimacy. History is pushing in this direction.

However, this impetus is likely to realize Noonomy lopsidedly, shaped by the imperatives of states as they exist right now. It will reflect their existing class, gender, race, ethnic, etc., character and interests. Some, like China, are committed to policies that are opposed to neoliberalism and financialization and support popular well-being and empowerment, and can therefore be expected to advance Noonomy in a relatively balanced way. Other countries, such as India or South Africa, are ruled by governments that remain too committed to neoliberal corporate capitalist interests, even taking fascist forms in the Indian case.

While they are forced to oppose imperialism here and there because imperialism offers so little to capitalists and demands policies that set back popular well-being, so as to endanger even the minimum of legitimacy that governments must have, they will advance towards Noonomy only when pushed forward by historical circumstances. In these countries, it can only advance in slow and halting ways.

So, popular struggles must be revitalized for Noonomy to be realized in a fuller fashion. In this revitalization, Noonomy is important because it takes the development of the productive forces seriously, unlike much of the Western left, which does not. From a very early point—and I trace it to what Bukharin called the "policy of theoretical reconciliation" (Bukharin, 1914, 1972, p. 163) between Marxism and neoclassical economics—the Western left has sported an understanding of capitalism without contradiction. It is a Schumpeterian rather than a Marxist conception of capitalism in the sense that the Western left believes that capitalism is capable of developing the forces of production infinitely, stabilizing itself spontaneously after crises, and is in no need of imperialism. Many even go so far as to say that imperialism happens—it is very bad and sad, but it has nothing to do with capitalism; it is not necessary for capitalism. This dismissal overestimates the capacity of capitalism to develop the forces of production because it radically underestimates the extent to which Western prosperity is a result of imperialism.

Noonomy's foregrounding of the development of the forces of production in the form of ever-more knowledge-based production is an indispensable component of any progressive politics. It is also necessarily a people-centered conception, one that involves the development of human and social capacities.

KEYWORDS

- **capitalism**
- **geopolitical economy**
- **Marxism**
- **Noonomy**
- **productive forces**
- **socialism**

REFERENCES

Bodrunov, S. D. (2018). *Noonomy*. Moscow: Kulturnaya Revolyutsiya Publication.

Bodrunov, S. D. (2023). *Noonomy: The trajectory of global transformation*. Boston: Academic Studies Press.

Bodrunov, S. D. (Ed.). (2022). *Anthology of noonomy: Fourth technological revolution and its economic, social and humanitarian consequences*. Brill.

Bodrunov, S. D., Desai, R., & Freeman, A. (2022). *Beyond the global crisis: Noonomy, creativity, geopolitical economy*. St. Petersburg: S. Y. Witte INID Publ.

Bukharin, N. (1972). *The economic theory of the leisure class*. New York: Monthly Review Press.

Desai, R. (2021). Capitalism and crises. In P. Bowles & H. Veltmeyer (Eds.), *The essential guide to critical development studies* (pp. 86–109). London: Routledge.

Desai, R. (2022). Noonomy and geopolitical economy: Natural allies. In S. D. Bodrunov (Ed.), *Anthology of noonomy: Fourth technological revolution and its economic, social and humanitarian consequences* (pp. 190–212). Brill.

Desai, R. (2023). *Capitalism, coronavirus and war: A geopolitical economy*. London: Routledge.

Desai, R. (Ed.). (2015). *Theoretical engagements in geopolitical economy*. Bingley: Emerald.

Desai, R. (Ed.). (2016). *Analytical gains in geopolitical economy*. Bingley: Emerald.

Hayek, F. (1944). *The road to serfdom*. London: George Routledge and Sons.

Hobsbawm, E. (1994). *Age of extremes: The short twentieth century, 1914–1991*. London: Michael Joseph.

Keynes, J. (1933). National self-sufficiency. *The Yale Review*, *22*(4), 755–769.

Marx, K. (1997). *Capital* (Vol. 1). London: Penguin.

Mayer, A. (1981). *The persistence of the old regime: Europe to the Great War*. New York: Pantheon Books.

Polanyi, K. (1945). Universal capitalism or regional planning. *The London Quarterly of World Affairs*, *10*(3), 86–91.

Polanyi, K. (1985). *The great transformation*. Boston: Beacon Press.

CHAPTER 3

Quality as the Basis for Development in the Digital Economy

VLADIMIR OKREPILOV

Scientific Advisor, Institute for Regional Economic Studies, Russian Academy of Sciences; Academician, Russian Academy of Sciences; Doctor of Economics; Professor (Saint Petersburg, Russia)

ABSTRACT

This chapter presents the role and importance of quality as a socioeconomic category, which serves as the foundation for social development. The scientific field of *Quality Economics*, developed by the author, is introduced, highlighting its main elements: *metrology*, *standardization*, and *quality management*. Their significance for economic development and improving the quality of life is discussed. The chapter also showcases Saint Petersburg's experience in creating a multilevel system for training specialists in the field of quality.

I believe that supporters of both capitalism and socialism, as well as advocates of the new economy, are always reconciled and united by *quality*. Any statesman, especially during election campaigns, declares their principal mission to be improving the quality of life. Whether they succeed or not is another matter. But the achievement of this objective is considered paramount by the people, and those who succeed in improving the quality of life are the ones who win.

Every country has quality-related legislation: laws on consumer protection, ensuring uniformity of measurements, *standardization*, *certification*, etc. International organizations, which include most of the world's countries, also play a key role. Notably, there are three major organizations: the *International*

Global Transformations of the 21st Century: The Future of Humans, Markets, and Capital.
Sergey Bodrunov (Editor)

DOI: 10.1201/9781779644022-3

Organization for Standardization (ISO) (the youngest, established after the Second World War in 1947); the *International Bureau of Weights and Measures* (the oldest, created in Paris in 1875); and the *International Electrotechnical Commission* (established in the early 20th century), which brings together about 170 countries. All countries adopt uniform rules and standards.

Philosophers, from Confucius and Aristotle to Engels, have offered philosophical perspectives on *quality* (Table 3.1). The most recent definition is provided by the *International Standardization Organization* (ISO): "Quality is the degree to which a set of inherent characteristics fulfills requirements." This is now regarded as one of the primary definitions.

TABLE 3.1 Changes in the Interpretation of "Quality"

Author	Definition of Quality
Confucius (551–479 B.C.)	The idea of quality is creating a harmonious society. A man must positively affect all the life aspects.
Democritus (469–370 B.C.)	People think of things as being white and black, and sweet and bitter, and all the other qualities of that kind. But in truth, properties of bodies are determined by properties of atoms and their combinations.
Aristotle (384–322 B.C.)	Difference between items. Differentiation by the "good-bad" parameter.
Cicero (106–43 B.C.)	Quality is a tangible but unmeasurable sign of animate and inanimate items.
Version accepted in Chinese philosophy (~II c. B.C.)	The hieroglyph designating quality consists of two elements: "balance" and "money" (quality = balance + money). Therefore, quality is identical to the notion of "first class," "expensive."
Hegel (1770–1831)	Quality is, in the first place, the character identical with being: so identical that a thing ceases to be what it is if it loses its quality.
Engels (1820–1895)	There are no qualities but only things that have quality and, at the same time, endlessly numerous properties. Any quality has an infinite number of quantitative gradations, for example, color variances, hardness and softness, durability, etc., and although they are different in terms of quality, they are available for measurement and cognition.
W. Shewhart (1891–1967)	Quality has two aspects: (i) objective physical characteristics; and (ii) subjective side: to which extent the certain thing is perceived as "good."
E. Deming (1900–1993)	Good quality means a predictable degree of uniformity and durability, with quality appropriate for the market.
A. Feigenbaum (1922–2014)	Quality is a totality of marketing, engineering, manufacturing, and service characteristics of a product or service that will conform to consumer expectations in practice.
International standard ISO GOST R ISO 9000–2015	"Quality is the degree to which a set of inherent characteristics fulfils requirements."

Source: Okrepilov (2022, p.78).

I have seen from my own experience that when studying *quality* problems, the interpenetration of sciences is clearly manifested. The higher and more complex the phenomenon that needs to be studied; the more branches of knowledge have to be applied (Figure 3.1).

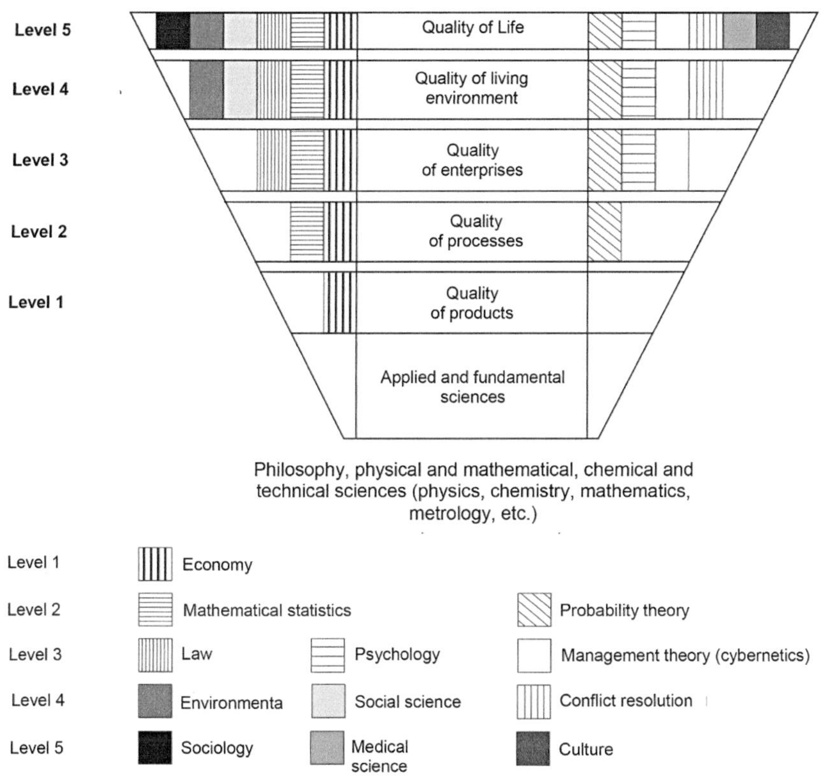

FIGURE 3.1 Application of various sciences for studies of quality.

Source: Okrepilov (2022, p.79).

Quality Economics is a part of economic science that studies the relationship between the qualitative characteristics of items or phenomena and economic indicators. The immediate purpose of *Quality Economics* as a science is to describe, explain, and forecast patterns of the effect of quality on social life processes and events.

Today, *Quality Economics* has already developed into an integral scientific paradigm recognized by the academic community, evolving as an independent area of economic science. The basic elements of *Quality Economics* are *metrology*, *standardization*, and *quality management*.

One of the important programs for the development of *metrology*—the science of ensuring the uniformity and accuracy of measurements—is to improve the reference framework of each country. According to estimates by international organizations, three countries now lead in ensuring the uniformity of measurements within their frameworks—these are Russia, China, and Germany. The USA follows Germany. The most important problem currently facing the whole world is the creation of new reference standards (Figure 3.2). The creation of a new weight reference (kg) in Russia requires 1.5 billion rubles. In other countries, it costs hundreds of millions of dollars or euros.

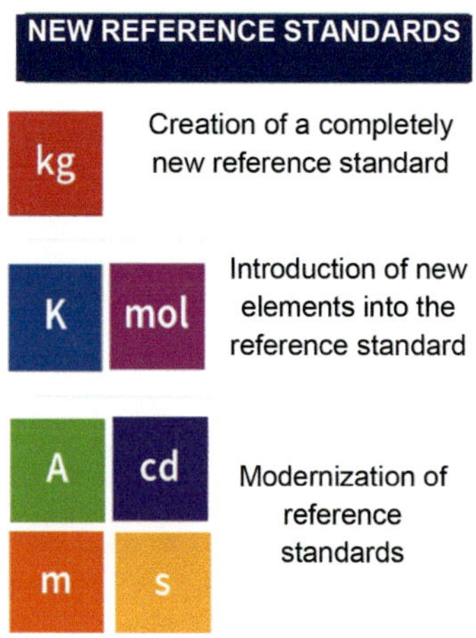

FIGURE 3.2 Combining new reference standards.

As for *standardization*, in WTO member countries, its impact on GDP growth is approximately 27% and up to 30% on productivity growth. Why is the development of *metrology* and *standardization* essential? Because, first of all, these are areas of economic activity, and they provide a colossal economic effect for any country.

When it comes to *quality management*, the contribution of Russian scholars is substantial. In the 1970s, scientists from Great Britain and Russia proposed the creation of international ISO standards. Today, ISO 9000 is implemented in a million enterprises across 170 countries. In the digital economy, this work is also being carried out at the levels of the three main subsystems (Figure 3.3).

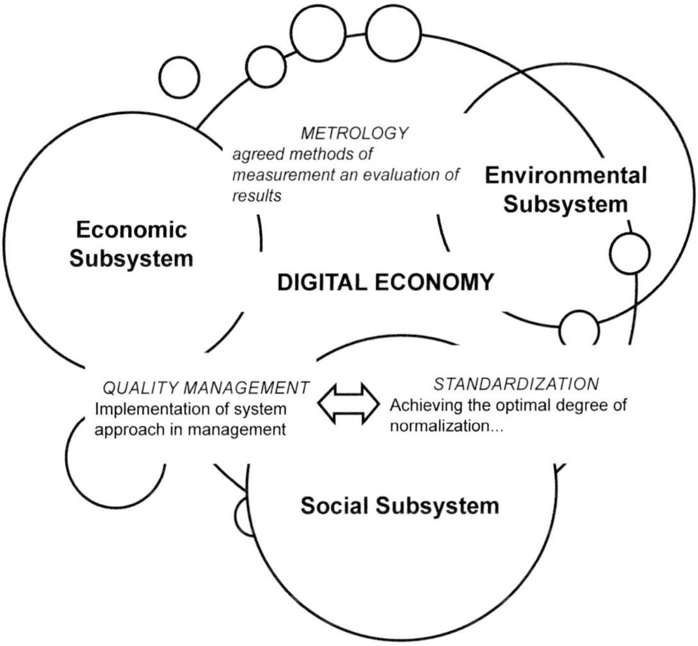

FIGURE 3.3 Quality assurance system in the digital economy.

In *metrology*, all digital formats are formalized in metrological documents necessary for the implementation of new technologies, especially in fields such as artificial intelligence, clinical medicine, robotics, etc. Without this, we cannot move forward. Digital *standardization* has significantly accelerated the development of new standards. For example, in Russia, the required time decreased on average from two years to eight months.

Quality management is undergoing an innovative transformation. Indeed, using quality management methods, we can address almost any economic problem at any enterprise, at any level of management, regardless of the social system, form of ownership, nature and size of production, or number of personnel. *Quality management systems* make it possible to comprehensively solve the problem of managing any entity in all areas—environment, safety, and the social sector (Figure 3.4).

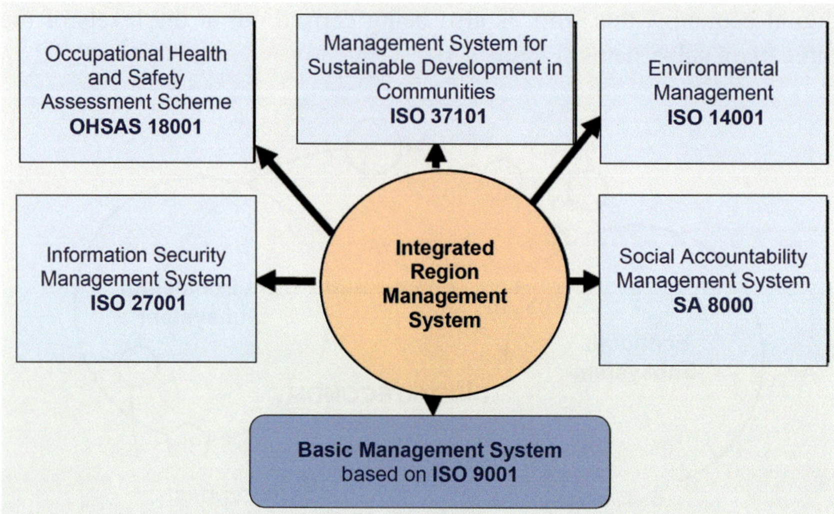

FIGURE 3.4 Management system based on quality management systems.

Now let's look at *quality of life*. Very often, *quality of life* is identified with the general standard of living. However, differences in understanding the quality of life can exist not only among different generations but also within the same generation. We conducted a survey among high school students about how they feel about the quality of life (Figure 3.5). Eighteen percent of respondents linked quality of life to material wealth, but the majority recognized that this concept encompasses not only the material aspect but also spiritual well-being.

There is a UN methodology for assessing quality of life. It includes three indicators: life expectancy, education, and gross national income per capita. At the end of 2021, Switzerland ranked first in these indicators, while Russia ranked 52nd, mainly due to the lag in life expectancy. Although in the 1960s, Russia ranked 5th or 6th in this indicator. Today, our task is to improve the quality of life in other areas (Figure 3.6).

There are many different rankings for assessing the quality of life in regions across different countries. For example, Russia has two well-known rankings. One is administered by *RIA Rating*, which uses 67 indicators, and the other is a ranking by the *Agency for Strategic Initiatives*, which uses 141 indicators (Figures 3.7–3.10).

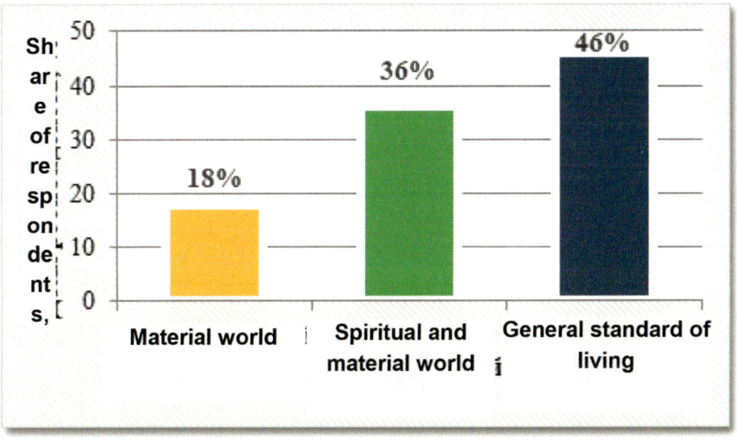

FIGURE 3.5 Meaning of the "Quality of Life" notion in respondents' answers.

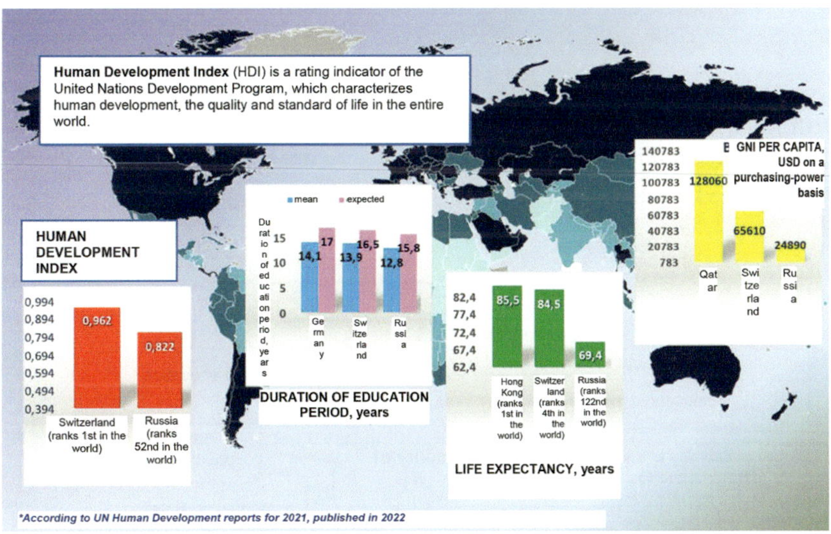

FIGURE 3.6 Global Rank of the Russian Federation in terms of quality of life.

3.1 QUALITY OF LIFE RATINGS AT THE REGIONAL LEVEL OF THE RUSSIAN FEDERATION

In turn, we sought to create a system of indicators that would correspond to the current global situation regarding quality and international ISO standards for quality management. We developed a database, patented by the *Russian Federal Service for Intellectual Property*. It contains just 32 indicators and allows for computational operations, including the use of supercomputers. We published a monograph on this topic, *Scientific Solutions to Complex Economic and Social Problems with the Help of Supercomputers* (Makarov, Okrepilov, & Bakhtizin, 2023).

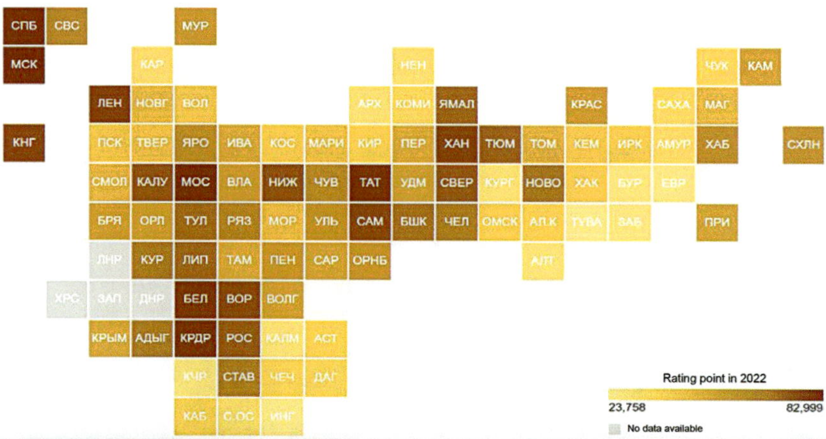

FIGURE 3.7 Map of regions of the Russian Federation, tinted in accordance with the level of quality-of-life rating in 2022.

Source: According to RIA rating (2022).

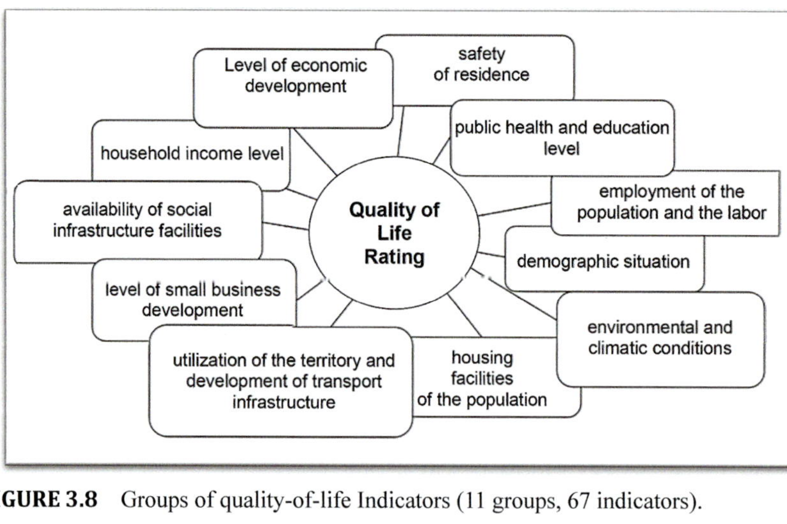

FIGURE 3.8 Groups of quality-of-life Indicators (11 groups, 67 indicators).

Source: According to RIA rating (2022).

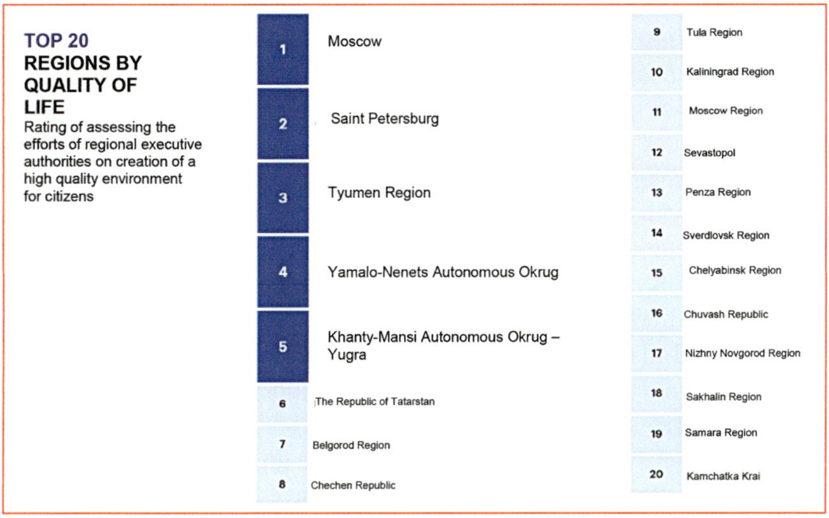

FIGURE 3.9 Top 20 regions of the Russian Federation by quality-of-life.

Source: According to ASI rating (2021).

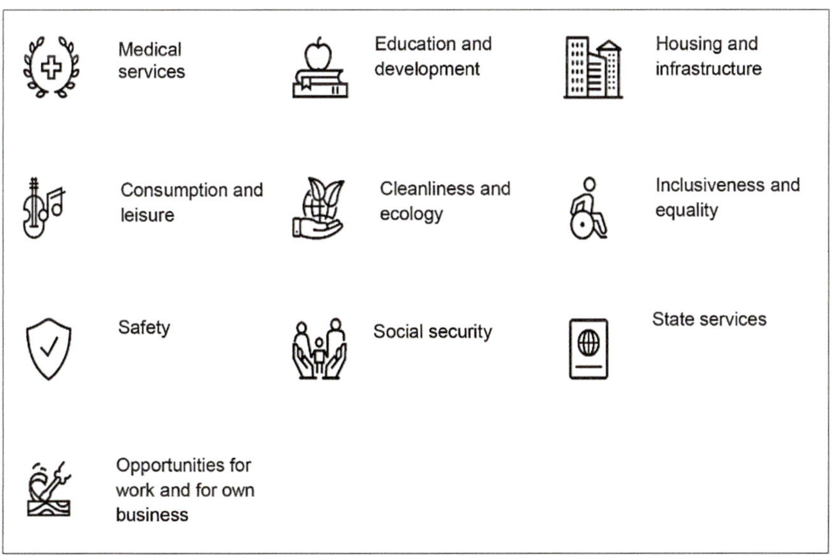

FIGURE 3.10 Areas for measuring quality-of-life (10 areas, 141 indicators).

Source: According to ASI (2021).

It is necessary to conduct *quality-of-life* modeling. Since all sets of significant living conditions in a region can be calculated, with our methodology, it is possible to assess changes in the quality of life.

Indicators of quality of life were recorded in the Development *Strategy* of St. Petersburg[1], which is based on the *development of advanced sectors of the knowledge economy*. Our considerations were adopted in its preparation, with the active involvement of members of the Free Economic Society, including academicians Aganbegyan, Makarov, foreign member of the RAS V. Kvint, and corresponding member of the RAS S. Bodrunov. According to their proposal, the knowledge economy became the pillar of the Strategy. Today, in St. Petersburg, the share of the knowledge economy is 25%. We are catching up with developed economies, and the goal is to bring it to 35%—I believe it will be achieved.

A multilevel system for training personnel in the area of quality has been created in St. Petersburg (Figure 3.11). We have already started offering quality lessons in schools, and there are three basic universities focused on these issues, with specialists trained in 30 universities. The Economic University has a specialized academic council, where more than 30 doctoral and 250 master's theses have been defended. Peter the Great Polytechnic University has a UNESCO Chair in Educational Quality. Advanced training courses are also offered at the Institute of Quality Management, where two thousand specialists have completed training in recent years, helping address this issue in various sectors of the economy and social sector.

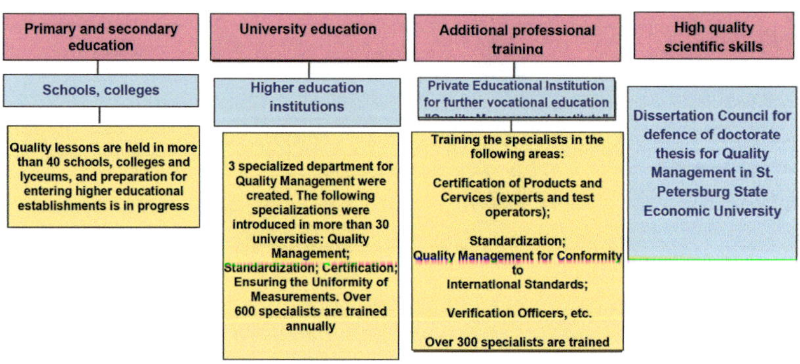

FIGURE 3.11 Multi-level system for training personnel in the area of quality (using the example of St. Petersburg).

[1]Strategy for Socioeconomic Development of St. Petersburg until 2035. Appendix to Law of St. Petersburg No. 771–164 dated December 19, 2018 "On the Strategy for Socioeconomic Development of St. Petersburg until 2035."

The Russian Academy of Sciences has established a Scientific Council for Metrological Support and Standardization, which includes economists, philosophers, lawyers, and technical experts. I would like to note that we published the first textbook on digital metrology in Russia and prepared a textbook on digital standardization. For children, we published the books *Standardization for Fun* and *Metrology for Fun*, which clearly explain what these areas involve.

KEYWORDS

- **digital economy**
- **metrology**
- **quality management**
- **Quality Economics**
- **standardization**
- **training system**

REFERENCES

Makarov, V. L., Okrepilov, V. V., & Bakhtizin, A. R. (2023). *Scientific solutions to complex economic and social problems with the help of supercomputers*. Moscow: Lenand Publication.

Okrepilov, V. V. (2008). *Evolution of quality*. St. Petersburg: Nauka Publication.

Okrepilov, V. V. (2019). *Development of the science of quality: Selected works*. St. Petersburg: Polytech-Press Publication.

Okrepilov, V. V. (2022). Economics of quality: The most important direction in the development of economic science. *Studies on Russian Economic Development*, *33*(5), 78–90. https://doi.org/10.47711/0868-6351-194-78-90.

CHAPTER 4

The Challenge of Noonomy to Global Liberal Capitalism

DAVID LANE

Member, International Committee of the Free Economic Society of Russia; Member, International Union of Economists; Fellow, Academy of Social Sciences (UK); Emeritus Professor of Sociology; Emeritus Fellow, Emmanuel College, University of Cambridge (Cambridge, UK)

ABSTRACT

The latest phase of post-socialist global integration has led to conflicts between the hegemonic core and rising states, which are moving from a competitive, interdependent semi-core to a challenging economic formation. The rise of a hybrid world system gives opportunities to the semi-core states to enhance their own economic, political, and civilizational institutions. Global ideational norms, principally neoliberalism, are confronted by national civilizational ideologies. *Noonomy* proposes a shift to reindustrialization, greater social solidarity, and statist as well as market forms of coordination. The chapter calls for further developments of *noonomy*, particularly an ideational vision of the future.

The modern form of capitalism, which arose in the last quarter of the 20th century, was a step beyond the imperialism of the early 20th century. Capitalism and life in general became globalized. Underlying the shift to capitalist globalization were three major interconnected economic and political advances that occurred in the late 20th century.

Global Transformations of the 21st Century: The Future of Humans, Markets, and Capital.
Sergey Bodrunov (Editor)

DOI: 10.1201/9781779644022-4

First, economic corporations, headquartered in the hegemonic Western countries, which had always had an international reach, became transnational companies with subsidiaries transferring profits to the home country. Finance, media, transport, pharmaceutical, and energy companies consolidated as global corporations. These corporations became geographically spread through subsidiaries in the world economy, though their ownership and control remained principally in the USA, Western Europe, and Japan. The capitalist class shifted from a national to a global base.

Secondly, a qualitative shift took place in the spatial relationships between countries and regions, consequent on the globalization of economic and social relations. Borders between countries became porous as electronic communications facilitated instant and spontaneous financial and personal linkages. Many positive developments ensued: knowledge, information, goods, people, capital, and services moved with minimum restriction across national borders. The flow of knowledge and information is crucial for the development of societies, and this was furthered by globalization (Bodrunov, 2023).

Thirdly, these economic developments resulted in parallel social and political changes. There were major changes in the control and coordination of capital. The structure of capitalism transformed from segmented, territorially based capitalist classes to transnational political and economic classes. Economies of advanced nations experienced the growth of industries with a non-manual workforce: transport, trade, electronic communications, insurance, education, banking, health, recreation, and research. Knowledge became a more important component in the production process. Industrial production continued, though in an attenuated form, with a smaller technically based workforce supervising machines and robots to perform industrial and commercial tasks.

The financial system enabled the immediate transfer of funds across country boundaries, and the international political system enforced the payment of debts and profits on a global scale. For example, in 1982, total world foreign direct investment (FDI) outflow was $28 billion, which rose to $1,216 billion in 2006. Between 1986 and 1990, the annual growth of FDI inflows was 21.7%; between 1996 and 2000, it rose to 40% (UNCTAD, 2007). These flows had an enormous impact on national economies and led to deindustrialization in the core economies of the world system. Production took the form of outsourcing and offshoring, creating global value chains: by 2013, 453 million jobs, approximately 20% of world employment, were involved in global value chains, which accounted for approximately half of world trade (World Bank, 2020). From the 1960s to the 1980s, the largest FDI flows took place between the core regions (Harris, 2006). By 1997, three-fifths of FDI took the form of mergers and acquisitions. Neoliberal capitalism developed as a global capitalist system technically in advance of its 19th-century national form.

4.1 THE MOVE TO BIFURCATED WORLD CAPITALISM

The advantages of global capitalism as a world system were strongly advocated at the end of the 20th century, when the dismantling of the European state socialist societies and the "opening up" of China enabled their economies to adopt markets, private enterprise, and to shift from state to private ownership. Politically, they joined the international economic coordinating framework provided by the IMF, the World Bank, and the WTO. The post-socialist Central and Eastern European states joined the EU and NATO. Indeed, it appeared that a global political class was well under construction. By the late 20th century, media commentators, academia, and politicians projected a picture of a world constituted by a dominant core of states, politically led and economically sustained by the USA, surrounded by interdependent, competing rising states.

However, the rising states were never accepted as full members of the hegemonic core. Russia and China were excluded from military alliances, such as NATO, and from leadership groups, such as the Group of Seven. Despite the "right of establishment" promoted by the WTO, members of the core and some rising states imposed restrictions on the purchase of assets by each other within their respective blocs. The post-socialist states in Europe and the Commonwealth of Independent States, such as Russia, became economically retarded as a consequence of neoliberal economics, particularly through the application of the theory of comparative advantage in international trade. By the 21st century, growing divisions between the hegemonic states, led by the USA, and rising states, led by China and followed by Russia, became apparent. The world system of states moved from competitive interdependence to adversarial political blocs. Consequently, the post-socialist European states suffered significant deindustrialization and social underdevelopment.

China and Russia have emerged from a state socialist political formation and retained features of state ownership and control quite distinct from those of the advanced capitalist countries of Europe and the USA. They can no longer be referred to as "semi-peripheral" or subaltern states to the hegemonic West. As components in the world economic system, the rising countries form an ascendant counterpoint to the hegemonic countries. These countries exchange with the Western core but are not part of it politically or militarily. They constitute an interdependent but separate semi-core of countries (Sbragia, 2010, pp. 368–382). Moreover, contemporary China and Russia are devising their own civilizational ideology, their own economic institutions and forms of property relations, and they retain independent military power. Conflict arises when the rising states are reluctant to accept the rules of the international economic order, which have been set by the economic and political core under the leadership of the USA.

4.2 MOVING TO THE NEW INDUSTRIAL STATE

Sergey Bodrunov's work highlights the negative consequences of neoliberal policies, which have weakened the Russian Federation. He contends that a more independent form of state provision and regulation is necessary for economic development. Such economic changes could lead to a new type of social system predicated on a "second generation of the new industrial state" (Bodrunov, 2023, p. 217). Here, he envisages not only reindustrialization but also a greater diffusion of property rights and a different kind of social structure. His work is illuminating and policy-oriented, and I would suggest further development in political and ideological terms. A more positive outcome could be a civilizational alternative embodied in a developmental state.

Reindustrialization, modeled on robotization and information-networked enterprises, high-tech development, and a rising GDP, should be at the "very heart" of an economic development model (Bodrunov, 2023, p. 140). This kind of technological revolution has been achieved under state guidance by countries such as South Korea and China. Bodrunov calls for a long-term time span for investment (Bodrunov, 2023, p. 257) through a developmental state. However, *noonomy* is much more than what the industrial development achieved by these states represents. There is a vision of a new type of society. *Noonomy* entails a complex transformation based on technological developments and changes in the social organization of society. It is a new and higher level of civilization, based on an industrial economy of an advanced cultural type. Human work activity occupies less time, while self-development, creativity, communication, and leisure become more important to human beings.

But how do we move from here to there? In Bodrunov's approach, there appear to be drivers in the forces of production, but it is unclear just who or what constitutes these drivers: individuals, civil society associations, state institutions or political factions, or supra-state forces? Other major theorists identified the agents of change: for Marx, social classes; for Lenin, socialist-led political parties; for Friedrich von Hayek and Milton Friedman, the utility-maximizing individual. Or do we assume that there will be a spontaneous metamorphosis—a series of developments inherent to the production process itself, not driven by conscious human objectives?

At the level of economic policy, we have proposals that indicate the way forward. One must replace institutions that have had deleterious effects on the Russian economy. "Financial speculators now dominate the economy, placing virtual reality and fictitious needs over the interests of material production" (Bodrunov, 2023, p. 233). Sergey Bodrunov advocates a power shift "from the financial elites to the technocrats, enabling the technological elite to mobilize sufficient social resources for its growth" (Bodrunov, 2023, p. 343). Earlier writers, such as Daniel Bell, John Kenneth Galbraith, and Joseph Schumpeter, took a similar position but in a different context. They argued that the development of a capitalist industrial society would lead to the rise of a technologically based class structure and to the growth of the state. However, Schumpeter concluded that these developments would lead to the rise of a bureaucratic class, which would diminish the bourgeoisie's propensity for entrepreneurship, thus retarding higher-level technical progress. One way out of this dilemma is for markets and areas of economic activity not directly controlled by the state to continue, thereby preserving an area of autonomous innovation. We can agree that the state has to "create a socioeconomic and political atmosphere" that eliminates bureaucratic control (Bodrunov, 2023, p. 198). The problem here is that corporate bureaucracies (both state and private) can create just that. This dilemma calls for new forms of authority in large industrial and commercial enterprises in order to safeguard the initiative of the creative classes under a developmental state.

The technological elites alone have too narrow an economic focus and will not necessarily promote wider social welfare. There has to be a more inclusive political leadership. In my view, one needs to look to actual social and political structures to find interests that will move economies in a developmental direction. To achieve the desired changes, one could search for allies in the structure of ruling elites or counter-elites. Crucial for national security is knowledge transformation and the integration of science, production, and education. Thus, the military-industrial-security complex could be an important component in moving toward industrial development and could be a crucial instrument to support national innovation (Bodrunov, 2023, p. 150). Ironically, Western sanctions may strengthen the Russian military-industrial-security complex. The sanctions policy of the Western states is a two-edged sword. Sanctions can be utilized positively, and, as Bodrunov (2023, p. 145) has pointed out, import substitution would be a positive way to promote reindustrialization. The danger here is the utilization of the industrial infrastructure for the enlargement of unjustifiable military ends. Excessive production for the American military-industrial-security complex is a good example of how security issues can divert a disproportionate amount of resources away from social welfare. This leads to a wider discussion of democracy and the role of civil society. The participation of employees and other stakeholders on the boards of state and private companies might be adopted to ensure support for, and control of, production. This line of thinking is developed by writers such as Nick Srnicek and Alex Williams (2015).

Non-economic factors, particularly civil society institutions, are important means of change. As Sergey Bodrunov points out, "the quality of sociopolitical institutions largely determines the quality of economic institutions and the conditions in which they are formed" (Bodrunov, 2023, p. 81). We need more discussion of how civil society can be organized to achieve the kind of synthesis proposed. What drives civilizational development? It is not clear whether economic institutions propel sociopolitical ones, whether it is the other way around, or whether there is interaction between both. Clearly, the market, planning, and civil society are interrelated. But in what respects? Who, and what processes, are going to decide the priorities, and when and how priorities should change?

All industrial transformations have costs, which have been particularly high in the transition from state socialism to a market society. It is recognized that, while the new industrial economy is capable of creating a world of plenty, transformation can result in economic depression and unemployment, causing "social tensions" (Bodrunov, 2023, p. 235). One must prevent the fate of the Luddites by ensuring control over the rate of change, and that innovation and technical advancement lead to benefits for the entire population. Politicians must address the social consequences of economic development to strengthen national security and provide work and employment. One can endorse Bodrunov's view that cumulative reforms are the most probable and acceptable way forward (Bodrunov, 2023, p. 227). Policy must facilitate the recalibration of the relationships between planning, market, and civil society, particularly through changing forms of ownership. Welfare state provisions and the introduction of a universal basic income are real possibilities, given the higher levels of material production. Such positive policies have immediate benefits and political support.

However, there are institutional barriers to the propositions advanced in this transformative approach. While Bodrunov recognizes the weaknesses of liberal economic theories and quotes Glazyev's positive view of a "collapse of liberal theory" (Bodrunov, 2023, p. 99), neoliberalism should not be prematurely dismissed. There are two sets of elites in the capitalist global political order that need to be contextualized in the *noonomy* framework: the elites of international economic coordination (the WTO, IMF, and World Bank) and current Western internationalized political leaders in the core states (such as President Biden, Ursula von der Leyen, and heads of states of the European Union and Japan). These elites are strongly committed to neoliberal economics. How do they fit into the *noonomy* framework, if at all? As long as the USA remains a hegemonic state, the economic coordinating bodies are unlikely to endorse the kinds of statist industrial policies entailed by *noonomy*. Indeed, the charters of international economic institutions are currently predicated on neoliberal principles, which severely limit the policies of nation-states. This being the case, rising states like Russia might have to find a niche, not as part of global neoliberalism, but in a global economy with its own boundaries and dynamics. One has to think of globalization that does not prioritize Western capitalistic political and economic interests. The rise of China as a world economy and the BRICS and SCO associations point in the direction of a bifurcated world system. However, competitive relations between the two blocs might spiral into adversarial conflicts and seriously compromise world peace. A serious current question of world politics is how a hybrid form of economic globalization can maintain harmony and cooperation between states.

4.3 PROBLEMS OF TRANSITION

I would highlight the need for greater attention to the ideational aspects of *noonomy*. Whereas material structures are defined by economists and sociologists, the ideational prescriptions endorse and legitimate their application. Ideological constructions exist in people's minds to make sense of and interpret material institutions and legitimize economic and political policies. The proposed economic changes to be implemented have to attract popular political appeal. Neoliberalism has been successful in creating a popular image of itself. It promises to give people "what they truly deserve," what "they have earned by their own efforts." It has captured the idea of individual freedom for itself. Similarly, Soviet socialism created an ideational image: it promised a future of social equality with security and peace; the assurance of a "classless society." A youth could dream of being a teacher in the morning, a footballer in the afternoon, and a philosopher in the evening. Not everyone agreed with these sentiments, but both worldviews had a significant public resonance. How can *noonomy* develop such a public appeal?

Certainly, the idea of a new industrial state has had a major impact, placing the development of real production in a socially oriented and state-regulated market economy. In the concept of *noonomy*, there is also a utopian vision. Sergey Bodrunov, for example, mentions many positive aspects of the new industrial society: the ideals of a "new type of humanity," a "higher level of culture" (Bodrunov, 2023, p. 231), the "potential for endless employment" (Bodrunov, 2023, p. 232), and the "potential [of] a conflict free society" (Bodrunov, 2023, p. 225). A synthesis of planning and market regulation is proposed (Bodrunov, 2023, p. 221). These ideal forms of economy would surpass the moral order of the present post-socialist societies which, in the Russian Federation, is a fusion of neoliberal market ideas and Russian statism.

There has to be an appeal for a more popular form of advanced industrial society in the context of globalization and consumerism. Globalization is not only a political mechanism extending the control of the hegemonic powers but also a higher form of technology, which shrinks time and space and has the capability of substantially increasing the level of human knowledge. The elites articulating the values of consumerism cannot be ignored; they must be tempered to meet human needs. Aaron Bastani is moving in a similar direction when he envisions a future of Fully Automated Luxury Communism (FALC), in which automation, energy resources, health, and food technologies cohere into "a society beyond scarcity and work" (Bastani, 2019, p. 12). Not only is the advance of technology, consequent on competition, leading to innovation, thus bringing about the end of capitalism, but it also echoes the basis for the kind of civilization order implied in *noonomy*. In the post-scarcity society, brought about by advanced technology and artificial intelligence, human labor is replaced by machines. The rise of an economy with free goods will diminish the market and significantly modify the contemporary capitalist form of production and exchange.

However, we have to avoid what Bodrunov calls "empty fantasy" (Bodrunov, 2023). Counter-developments are to be found in the powers of transnational corporations and hegemonic states. There is growing commodification of innovation through intellectual property rights; universities, publicly and privately financed centers of research and learning, assert their rights to income from their services and products. Monetarization and financialization have increased the commodification of goods and services. The "creatosphere" is an important part of culture, which is globalized, commercialized, and monetized. It makes profits. Financialization has formed a "new mode of economic regulation" (Bodrunov, 2023, pp. 110–111) and these institutions cannot easily be dismantled.

Reindustrialization has to contribute positively to a consumption-based society, not obliterate it. One has to show how "real human needs" can be met in ways that people can understand. Yesterday's extravagances are today's accepted needs. People now have "needs" for foreign holidays, for their own motor carriages, and the need to own their own homes. Consumer society has arrived and requires an industrial base. But *noonomy* envisions more than that: it has a civilizational concept. To be influential, it needs an ideational appeal. To be accepted politically and put into practice, it has to fulfill the perception of people's needs. Remember Margaret Thatcher. After her election as Prime Minister, she addressed the leaders of the British

Conservative Party. She pulled out a book from her famous handbag and triumphantly declared, "This is what we believe." That book was Friedrich von Hayek's *The Constitution of Liberty*. The next task for *noonomy* is to capture the minds of political leaders. "The Coming New Industrial State, Mark II" must have an ideational appeal. The ideational beliefs people hold about the economic system are as important as the economic theorizing.

KEYWORDS

- **bifurcated world system**
- **globalization**
- **neoliberalism**
- **Noonomy**
- **reindustrialization**
- **state-led development**

REFERENCES

Bastani, A. (2019). *Fully automated luxury communism*. London: Verso.

Bodrunov, S. (2023). *The coming new industrial state: Reloaded.* Boston: Academic Studies Press.

Bodrunov, S. D. (2016). *The coming of new industrial society: Reloaded.* St. Petersburg: INID Publication.

Enright, M. J. (2000). Globalization, regionalization, and the knowledge-based economy in Hong Kong. In *Regions, globalization and the knowledge-based economy* (pp. 381–406). Oxford University Press.

Harris, J. (2006). *The dialectics of globalisation: Economic and political conflict in a transnational world*. Newcastle: Cambridge Scholar Press.

Lane, D. (2023). *Global neoliberal capitalism and the alternatives*. Bristol: Bristol University Press.

Sbragia, A. (2010). The EU, the US, and trade policy: Competitive interdependence in the management of globalization. *Journal of European Public Policy*, *17*(3), 368–382.

Srnicek, N., & Williams, A. (2015). *Inventing the future*. London: Verso.

CHAPTER 5

Economic Development Based on Improving the Quality of Growth

ALEKSANDR SHIROV

Director, Institute of Economic Forecasting, Russian Academy of Sciences; Corresponding Member, Russian Academy of Sciences; Doctor of Economics; Professor (Moscow, Russia)

ABSTRACT

This chapter analyzes the main problems faced by countries moving along the post-industrial development model. The key contradictions between economic growth and development are considered. It is noted that in some cases, economic growth is not accompanied by development, but it is extremely difficult to ensure development in the absence of economic growth. The qualitative and quantitative components of economic growth in the Russian economy over the last decade are analyzed. It is shown that economic growth in Russia between 2011 and 2020 was mainly driven by the involvement of primary resources in production, rather than by increasing the efficiency of their use. One of the key directions for the development of the Russian economy should be the diversification of its structure, based on the expansion of demand for goods and services in high-tech sectors and the development of industrial cooperation. Requirements for a new model of economic development are formulated, ensuring a balanced development of the real sector and the service sector, as well as employment, which would contribute to a more equitable distribution of income across the population.

Global Transformations of the 21st Century: The Future of Humans, Markets, and Capital.
Sergey Bodrunov (Editor)

DOI: 10.1201/9781779644022-5

5.1 IMBALANCES IN THE GLOBAL ECONOMY

The world economy is now at a crossroads: further sustainable development based on the globalization model seems impossible, and the contours of a new global model have not yet been fully formed. Globalization has enabled the world economy to grow steadily over the past 30 years, generating significant income growth for both developed and developing countries through increased trade, cooperation, and the exchange of research and development results. However, the liberalization of global trade and economic relations has reached its natural limits.

A number of imbalances have accumulated in the global economy, and perhaps the most important is that the model of post-industrial society, the effectiveness of which has been widely discussed in recent decades (Bell, 1973; Tsvetkov, Morgunov, & Illarionov, 2008; Ivanov & Makhosheva, 2011), has proven vulnerable to the slowdown in global economic growth and trade.

5.2 CHALLENGES OF ECONOMIC GROWTH WITHOUT DEVELOPMENT

What are the main problems associated with the development of post-industrial society? First, there is a restriction on the possibility of moving production from developed to developing countries, which is most clearly manifested in the decline in the number of jobs with wages at or above the average level of the economy. Second, there is the growing importance of secondary income redistribution and the insufficiency of state revenues under the current system of corporate taxation to solve this problem, particularly in developed countries. Third, there is the declining return on research and development (R&D) expenditures. Despite the fact that R&D spending in OECD countries increased from 2.3% of GDP in 2000 to 3.0% in 2020, there has been a steady downward trend in per capita GDP growth throughout this period.

However, one may wonder whether economic growth is still a goal that ensures the sustainability of development in societies where basic needs have been largely satisfied, as is the case in most developed countries (Van den Berg, 2016; Bobylev, 2023). This raises the question of whether development is possible without economic growth, which is primarily understood as an increase in the quality of life. Many researchers answer this question positively. However, it is equally important to note that the opposite situation is often encountered, where economic growth is not accompanied by development.

5.3 THE ROLE OF THE REAL SECTOR IN ECONOMIC DEVELOPMENT

The most striking example is the United States, where substantial GDP growth in the last two decades has been driven by the revenues of large transnational corporations (TNCs). At the same time, middle-class incomes have stagnated. Despite the overall efficiency of the American economy growing, the quality of life for a significant portion of the population has not improved, and the transformation of the job structure has not contributed to uniform income growth (Wolff, 2017).

In Russia, one of the most persistent macroeconomic problems remains the static structure of household incomes (Shirov, 2022). Despite significant economic growth from 2000 to 2008, there has been no qualitative change in the consumption structure of the population. The share of expenditures on food and other primary goods and services (housing and utilities, public transport) remains at a very high level and has hardly decreased over the last 20 years, which hinders the development of new businesses focused on consumer demand (Shirov & Potapenko, 2020). This example of the stagnant consumption structure shows that in the absence of effective income redistribution between economic agents, even in developed and developing countries, societal development can be limited, despite the formal preservation of economic growth.

However, if we return to the original question about the possibility of development in the absence of economic growth, we face significant difficulties in answering it positively. Let us attempt to illustrate this with a simple diagram (Figure 5.1).

If development and economic growth are at the extreme poles of this scheme, then a prerequisite for development is the expansion of human capital and the improvement of production efficiency. This, in turn, requires that the incomes of the population, businesses, and the state be directed toward addressing these tasks and increasing the sustainability of the economy.

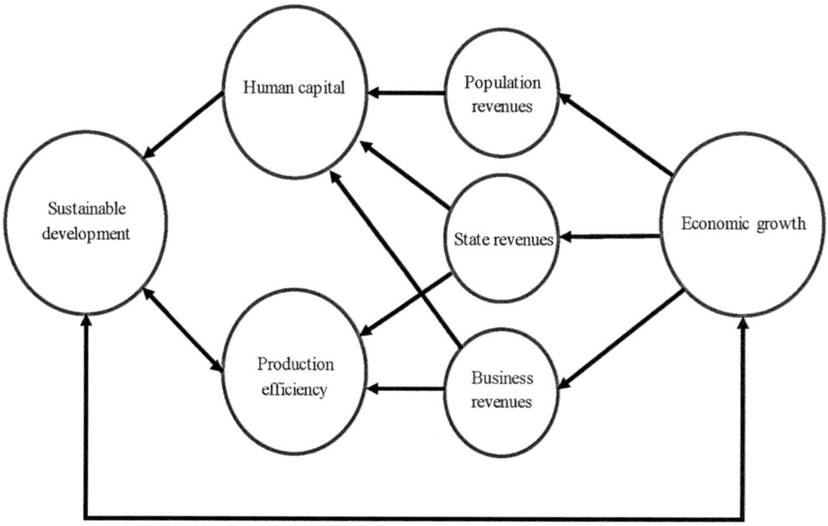

FIGURE 5.1 Interaction between growth and economic development.

The revenues of businesses, the population, and the state are formed no other way than through economic growth. This closes the loop: it becomes clear that ensuring sustainable development in the absence of income from economic growth is extremely difficult. While it may be theoretically possible in some cases, on the scale of the entire economic system, it is highly unlikely. Thus, economic and income growth remains necessary. Otherwise, budget constraints will become the main obstacle to economic development. At the same time, it is evident that the type of growth required must ensure an appropriate redistribution of revenues, forming a positive impetus in terms of quality of life and overall economic development.

In recent years, significant constraints have emerged that hinder the effective development of the established model of global trade and economic relations, which has been based on the outpacing growth of trade relative to economic growth (Voytolovsky, 2019). After the global crisis of 2008–2009, the share of exports in world GDP stopped growing. The absence of outpacing growth in world exports indicates that the globalization model has ceased to function as effectively as it did over the past three decades. Simultaneously, there has been a gradual decline in the return on investment in research and development (R&D),

particularly in developed countries. While the volume of such expenditures has been growing substantially in recent years, the growth rates of labor productivity and other efficiency parameters have been steadily declining.

The gradual reduction in the medium-term economic growth potential of developed countries, against the backdrop of increasing expenditures on R&D, prompts a rethinking of the causes behind this trend and the possible transformations necessary for forming a new, sustainable model for global economic development.

One possible hypothesis is that developed countries have reached the limits of reducing the role of the real sector in the formation of GDP and employment. The "easing" of developed countries' economies, observed over the last 20 years, appears to have reached certain limits. It is impossible to reduce the real sector in the American or French economies to zero. Under such conditions, the economy will not be able to function properly. This is primarily because the absence of primary income generated by the real sector creates conditions for social instability. On one hand, the transfer of production to developing countries and control over value chains provides a steady flow of income. On the other hand, the job structure deteriorates, requiring increasing state intervention in the secondary redistribution of income (Gimpelson & Kapelyushnikov, 2023). The lack of a sufficiently robust real sector that demands medium- and highly-qualified specialists has become one of the key limitations of the post-industrial development model.

Of course, we are not advocating a return to the industrial model characteristic of the post-World War II period. Rather, we envision a real sector built on new principles, emphasizing more knowledge-intensive products and environmental sustainability (Bodrunov, 2018). Nevertheless, the need for a balanced economic structure in terms of income distribution and job creation is one of the key requirements for an effective development model in today's context. This applies equally to both developed and developing economies. It should also be noted that, due to automation and robotization, advanced industries will have lower labor intensity, potentially reducing the number of jobs. However, through a more complex system of cooperation than other sectors, manufacturing industries can serve as an important element in balancing the economic system—particularly by contributing to the formation of balanced incomes for working citizens.

5.4 QUALITATIVE VS. QUANTITATIVE GROWTH

In the new environment, the qualitative component of economic growth should be seriously enhanced (Uzyakov, 2011). The quality of growth can be considered a specific indicator that can be measured. In this case, it becomes possible to decompose a country's economic growth rate into qualitative and quantitative components. One key characteristic of growth quality is the efficiency of primary resource utilization.

The qualitative component of growth occurs when more income and value-added are generated from the same amount of resources. Conversely, if growth is not accompanied by an increase in the share of value-added in output, it can be said that the growth is driven by the quantitative rather than the qualitative component. Growth based on the quantitative component leads to increased demand for primary resources, reducing the efficiency and competitiveness of the economy. Unfortunately, over the last 10 years, there has been no significant increase in the efficiency of the Russian economy. If the share of primary resource expenditures in gross output was 39% in 2011, it was only slightly lower, at 38.7%, in 2020 (Figure 5.2).

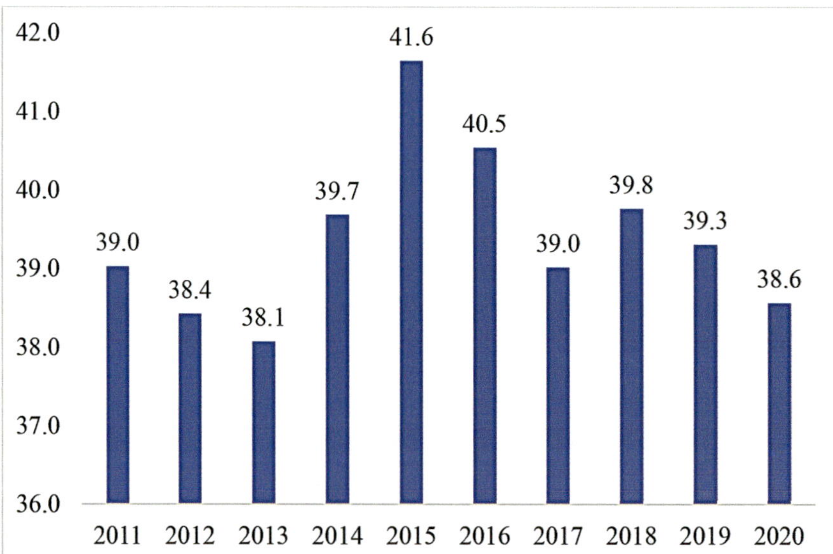

FIGURE 5.2 Share of primary resources expenditure[1] in gross output (in %).

Source: OECD, INP RAS calculations.

[1]Primary resources in this case are understood as the products of agriculture and forestry, mining, oil refining, metallurgy, chemical production, production and distribution of electricity, gas, and water.

The cumulative increase in GDP between 2011 and 2020 amounted to only 8.6%. Of this growth in the Russian economy, just 5.8% was due to the qualitative component, while 94.2% was attributed to the quantitative component. Unfortunately, in the Russian economy, quantitative growth still far outweighs qualitative growth. This is undoubtedly one of the key problems hindering economic development and limiting the competitiveness of the national economy.

In general, the retardation in primary resource efficiency is one of the most visible distinctions between developed and developing countries. Despite the major leap China's economy has made in the last two decades, it still lags significantly behind almost all developed countries in terms of efficiency, including the utilization of primary resources. In particular, China trails developed countries by a factor of about two in terms of material intensity of production (Figure 5.3). This efficiency gap is associated not only with technological lag but also with the policy, pursued over the last three decades, of shifting the most material- and labor-intensive industries from developed to developing countries. Nevertheless, it is the high productivity in primary resource utilization that determines the leading positions of developed countries in the world economy. However, this technological lag also presents growth potential for developing countries, offering opportunities for modernization in the basic sectors of the economy and industry.

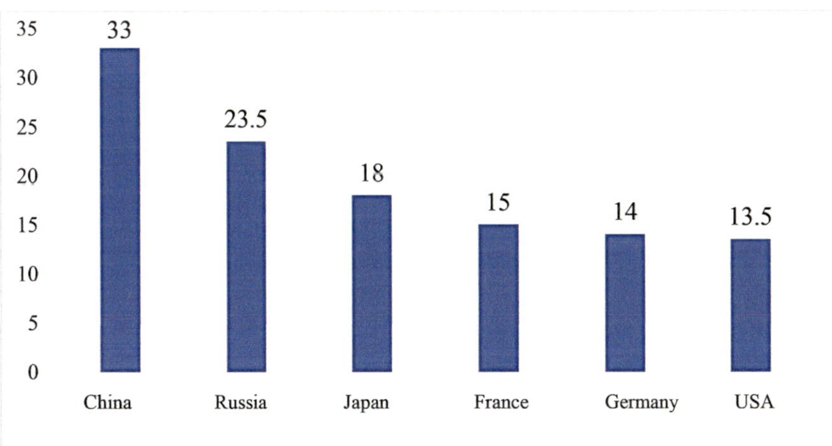

FIGURE 5.3 Material intensity of gross output (in %).

Source: OECD, INP RAS calculations.

5.5 REQUIREMENTS FOR A NEW ECONOMIC MODEL

The current situation in the global economy will contribute to the acceleration of efficiency growth in large developing economies (Fituni & Abramova, 2022). In the context of increasing global competition, developing countries will be compelled to increase expenditures on research and development, which will positively impact the growth of production efficiency[2]. According to our estimates, in order to compete with developed countries, BRICS nations should increase their total R&D expenditures by about $200 billion per annum. Through industrial digitalization processes and the use of new construction materials, the rate of growth in production efficiency can be significantly accelerated. The new situation of increased competition between developed and major developing countries may reverse the trend of steadily declining returns on R&D investments.

For Russia, the key issue is the structure of the economy, particularly when compared with other countries (Gusev, 2023; Nekipelov, 2021). Economic competitiveness is influenced by many factors, but the way a country utilizes its most important resources is crucial. When considering the Russian economy from this perspective, we can state that, in terms of trade services, transportation, electricity, and oil refining products, Russia is not inferior to developed countries.

However, the Russian economy has significantly lower aggregate demand for financial services, engineering products, scientific research, and even IT services compared to developed nations. While the IT sector is rightly regarded as one of the most competitive sectors of the economy (Belousov et al., 2021), demand for its services from the broader economy, particularly the manufacturing sector, remains insufficient. As a result, the potential multiplier effect of IT industry development is reduced due to the modest level of intersectoral interactions.

The level of intersectoral interactions required for the transition to a new qualitative level of economic development implies a significant increase in the complexity of the Russian economy, driven by higher domestic demand for knowledge-intensive products. Only in this way can additional revenues be generated, ensuring an acceptable growth rate in efficiency. Based on this, a new reproduction model can be formed, which

---

[2]On the long-term scientific and technological development of Russia / ed. by Belousov D.R. and Frolov I.E. Moscow: Dynamik Print, 2022. 168 c.

implies the diversification of income sources and a substantial increase in the share of sectors responsible for the development of human potential.

Thus, while further increasing the role of the service sector may encounter significant limitations, this does not negate the necessary structural shifts within the economy. Expanding the real sector through increased economic complexity is essential to ensuring the flow of primary income, which is necessary to address challenges in the social sphere, infrastructure, and technological development. Therefore, increasing economic complexity is a vital step in structural and technological transformation.

Particular attention should be paid to increasing the number of highly skilled jobs in sectors of the economy with a high level of technology application (Edinak, 2022). However, there is a contradiction here. While high technology can lead the economy to a new level of growth and generate new income, the most high-tech activities, including the IT industry, indirectly generate more low-skilled jobs in the economy than traditional sectors like machine building. For example, according to our estimates, one job in the IT sector in Russia now supports about 3.5 low-skilled jobs in areas such as hotels and restaurants, transportation, and services. Similar estimates for the US economy are even higher—up to 4 low-skilled jobs per new job in the IT industry.

Thus, the goal of increasing technological development cannot be achieved by instantly replacing obsolete industries with new ones or by drastically reducing the real sector's share in the economy. The real sector, which generates primary income, must evolve in such a way that the balance between high-, medium-, and low-tech jobs is maintained. Unfortunately, this balance is often overlooked, and we believe this presents a serious problem in forming a new concept of economic development.

What are the requirements for this new model of economic development? First, a balanced ratio of the real sector to the service sector is essential. This represents a fundamentally new requirement compared to the ideology of the post-industrial development model. Second, increasing R&D expenditures while improving their efficiency is necessary to address the issue of deteriorating returns on investment. Third, as the economy becomes more efficient, there must be an increase in corporate taxation to address the hollowing out of jobs with acceptable wages, requiring compensation through secondary income redistribution. This is a problem that the tax system must address. Fourth, there is a need to account for the indirect effects on employment development.

In this case, we are discussing a new industrial model of development, in which reproduction mechanisms ensure the sustainability of economic development, and the structure of employment does not place excessive pressure on the budget system. It is also important to note that the formation of this model can be equally effective for both developed and developing countries.

KEYWORDS

- **economic growth**
- **post-industrial development**
- **primary resources**
- **qualitative growth**
- **real sector**
- **structural transformation**

REFERENCES

Bell, D. (1973). *The coming of post-industrial society: A venture in social forecasting*. New York: Basic Books.

Belousov, D. R., Mikhailenko, K. V., Sabelnikova, E. M., & Solntsev, O. G. (2021). The role of digitalization in the target scenario of Russian economic development. *Studies on Russian Economic Development*, *187*(4), 53–65. https://doi.org/10.47711/0868-6351-187-53-65.

Bobylev, S. N. (2023). In search of sustainability measurement. In *State regulation of the economy and increasing the efficiency of business entities: A collection of scientific papers of the XVII International Scientific and Practical Conference dedicated to the memory of Professor S. A. Pelikh* (pp. 15–19). Minsk: Academy of Public Administration under the aegis of the President of the Republic of Belarus.

Bodrunov, S. D. (2018). *Noonomy*. Moscow: Kul'turnaya revolyutsiya Publishing.

Edinak, E. A. (2022). Labor market and non-economic shocks. *Social and Labor Research*, *48*(3), 56–66. https://doi.org/10.34022/2658-3712-2022-48-3-56-66.

Fituni, L., & Abramova, I. (2022). Developing countries in the new equation of the post-crisis world order. *World Economy and International Relations*, *66*(11), 5–13. https://doi.org/10.20542/0131-2227-2022-66-11-5-13.

Gimpelson, V. E., & Kapeliushnikov, R. I. (2023). Job structure evolution in Russia: Polarization, upgrading, stalemate? *Problems in Economy*, *1*, 59–85. https://doi.org/10.32609/0042-8736-2023-1-59-85.

Gusev, M. S. (2023). Russian economic development strategy – 2035: Ways to overcome long-term stagnation. *Studies on Russian Economic Development*, *197*(2), 18–29. https://doi.org/10.47711/0868-6351-197-18-29.

Ivanov, P. M., & Makhosheva, S. A. (2011). Improving the management of economic processes of post-industrial development at the meso-level. *Economic and Law Issues*, *42*, 72–76.

Nekipelov, A. D. (2021). On economic strategy and economic policy in Russia under current conditions. *Scientific Works of the Free Economic Society of Russia*, *230*(4), 76–89. https://doi.org/10.38197/2072-2060-2021-230-4-76-89.

Shirov, A. A. (2022). *Potential for growth of the Russian economy: Analysis and forecast.* Moscow: Artique Print.

Shirov, A. A., & Potapenko, V. V. (2020). The Russian consumption paradox. *ECO*, *552*(6), 8–25. https://doi.org/10.30680/ECO0131-7652-2020-6-8-25.

Tsvetkov, V. A., Morgunov, E. V., & Illarionov, N. V. (2008). Innovative economy as a form of post-industrial development. *Industrial Policy of the Russian Federation*, *1*, 24–42.

Uzyakov, M. N. (2011). Efficiency of use of primary resources as an indicator of technological development: Retrospective analysis and forecast. *Studies on Russian Economic Development*, *125*(2), 3–18.

Van den Berg, H. (2016). *Economic growth and development*. World Scientific Publishing Company.

Voytolovsky, F. G. (2019). Changes in external environment affecting Russia's national security. *Herald of the Russian Academy of Sciences*, *89*(4), 393–399. https://doi.org/10.31857/S0869-5873894393-399.

Wolff, E. N. (2017). Household wealth trends in the United States, 1962 to 2016: Has middle class wealth recovered? *National Bureau of Economic Research*, *24085*, 74.

CHAPTER 6

A World Creative Audit: A Research Proposal

ALAN FREEMAN

Researcher, Geopolitical Economy Research Group, University of Manitoba (Winnipeg, Canada)

ABSTRACT

This chapter examines the need to develop an international research program on creative work as a prerequisite for the new forms of social structure required for *noonomy*. The study has two goals—qualitative and quantitative. Qualitatively, it aims to establish objective standards for defining creative labor and related forms of mental productive activity. Quantitatively, it seeks to obtain statistical data on the creative production resources of five or more key countries.

6.1 CREATIVE LABOR, NOONOMY'S DEFINITIVE RESOURCE

I propose nine principles. Since I expect them to be controversial, I will set out and address the debates surrounding them. That said, my concern is to chart a practical course of action for collaborative research. Agreement with every principle is not a requirement; they can be thought of as postulates to be critically assessed during the research process.

6.1.1 THE PRINCIPLES

- The relation between Noonomy and creativity is dual and symmetric. Creative labor is the primary resource of Noonomy's

Global Transformations of the 21st Century: The Future of Humans, Markets, and Capital.
Sergey Bodrunov (Editor)

DOI: 10.1201/9781779644022-6

emerging new technologies but only Noonomic principles can develop it into a generalized productive resource, restoring creativity to its rightful place as a universal human capacity and a universal human right.

- Creative production is an industry: it is a branch of the division of labor with a common resource, common methods of production, and common products.
- Creative production is a sunrise industry: it is absorbing labor and its output is rising, in contrast to sunset industries such as agriculture and manufacturing.
- Creative labor is a cooperative human activity. The precondition for its efficient and beneficial use is the universalization of creative cooperation.
- The co-operative organization of labor in creative production is complementary to, but also superior to, the socialization of ownership on which Marx and Engels laid stress when assessing the prospects for transition from monopoly capitalism to socialism.
- Information and Communication Technology (ICT) is central to this new phenomenon. It constitutes a means of production for the creative industries. In particular, software production is its 'cell form,' comparable to the factory in the mechanical age.
- The proper management of creative production, unlike that of machinery, requires a different model of social organization based on the rounded development of the human; this is why Noonomy is central to its proper utilization.
- Central to this process is creative innovation: the development and rapid deployment of new discoveries. This shares, with all previous waves of innovation, the superficially paradoxical prerequisite of standardization, the irreducible basis of all human cooperation.
- It may seem paradoxical to treat standardization as necessary for creativity (Hofstadter, 1986), whose essence is variety. However, it takes a distinctive form in creative production; it seeks to maximize variety in human life by minimizing the obstacles to creation.

The primary standards required in the age of creation are, in conclusion, those governing its primary resource: creative human labor. Devising such socially-managed standards would be a major achievement for Noonomy. The research should provide an evidence base for this goal.

6.1.2 THE PROGRAM OF RESEARCH

Before embarking on a discussion of the issues, I outline a suggested program of work. This will both focus our minds and increase the probability of achieving something while the discussion unfolds. Thus, we should aim at a dialectic between theory and practice.

The program does not claim to be the totality of research required; rather, it sets out objectives that are both possible on the basis of existing research and a foundation for future research.

The focus is on the characteristics and extent of the creative labor force in the world economy as at present constituted. It has a qualitative and a quantitative aspect, corresponding to the intensity method developed jointly by researchers in the UK, Australia, and France, which has been adopted by the UK's Department of Culture, Media, and Sport (DCMS) as the basis for the UK's statistical reporting on the creative industries.

- The qualitative aspect requires us to define the *occupations* that should be considered creative and the *industries* that should be considered creative.
- The quantitative aspect requires us to measure, in each of the nations under study, the size of the creative and non-creative labor force within that economy's industries and so identify those that make particularly intensive use of this creative labor force.
- Estimate the wealth created by these industries, and hence the use and results of productive creative labor.

This method has been set out in a number of places: we refer the reader in particular to Bakhshi et al. (Bakhshi, Freeman, & Higgs, 2013) and Freeman (Freeman, 2002) for a more detailed account.

The results lead to a creative *Trident* (Higgs & Cunningham, 2008) which allows us to focus on those specific industries that make intensive use of a creative labor force, which are those that we designate creative, and in addition allows researchers to examine the growing role of creatively-occupied workers in the other industries and hence, in the economy as a whole.

This has not been done before except for the UK, France, and Canada. Moreover, even for Canada, the method employed, though useful as a source of preliminary information, was limited in that it did not base itself on a detailed examination of Canada's occupational structure – which, as will be explained, is required for full comparability. The study of this structure (which would open the way to a comparable treatment of the US and Mexican economies) would be a subject of the research.

The intensity method admits a number of choices so that the definitions and hence magnitudes it yields depend on these choices. Our aim is to create a flexible system in which different hypotheses regarding which activities are creative can be scrutinized.

On the one hand, this is rooted in existing practice and hence has a body of past work on which to draw rather than inventing *ab ovo*, but on the other, it develops this practice and thus extends the results beyond the boundaries established in the mechanical age which we are leaving behind.

The prerequisite for effective and practical governance in the post-mechanical age is, in consequence, a proper re-structuring of the categories used to describe human productive activity, which are derived from a study of how this activity is *now* conducted and *now* organized.

This is not counterposed to the necessary discussion of how it should in the future be so managed and organized, which is a specific field of enquiry of Noonomy. All social transformation other than mere utopianism starts from what is and exists actually, and enquires how we may consciously manage to change it into what we as humans desire it to be. This does not commit us to accepting what is; it is however a necessary point of departure. Dealing with this basic rationalist problematic, dating (in Western thought) to the disagreement between Kant and Hume on the relation of 'is' to 'ought' remains a necessary foundation of practical proposals for change.

6.1.3 WHAT IS A BRANCH OF PRODUCTION? THE CASE FOR THE STUDY OF COOPERATION IN MODERN INDUSTRIAL DEVELOPMENT

The basis for the current practice of industrial classification dates back to Adam Smith: it is the concept of a branch of the division of labor—a collection of enterprises or production sites connected by specialization. The centrality of this notion can be gauged from the fact that, according to Smith, this is the foundation of *The Wealth of Nations*.

It behooves us to consider why this is the case, as it is so commonplace that it is easy to overlook. Since the more exciting advent of mechanical production has been the focus of most subsequent research into the sources of productivity advances, the temptation to ignore specialization has evolved into a near obsession. In the machinocratic rush to identify the machine, the factory, and the entrepreneur's property as the true sources of wealth, specialization—which is a social, not a private, achievement—has become one of the many orphaned children of modern economic thought.

The reason for this is that specialization is the primary basis by which labor can be made more productive. Any fool can place a waterwheel in a stream, but to transform it into a technological paradigm, it is necessary to create an entire system of labor around it. It is this system of labor—not the wheel, nor the machinery it powers—that constitutes the essence of the technological advance it represents.

At the center of any such system of labor lie two achievements:

- The development of a skilled labor force capable of dedicating itself to making some particular system of machinery work; and
- The cooperative engagement of this skilled labor force in this enterprise, in turn imposed by specialization.

Marx offers the analogy of an orchestra: there are many different instruments, but only when they coordinate their efforts do they produce a symphonic sound. Indeed, if we were to examine more closely the under-examined category of skill—often taken for granted and distinguished from knowledge in the literature, yet in many senses preceding it and constituting its material foundation—we would almost certainly find it in an intimate relationship with the category of specialization. Beyond tool use, which is often postulated as the *genus specificus* of humanity, a significant evolutionary characteristic of humanity is the separation of function. A society in which certain people hunt while others perform different roles will inevitably perform better if its hunters focus on improving their hunting skills. This is a skill, not reducible to the acquisition of knowledge. On the contrary, knowledge, if it even exists in such a context, would best be described as a means for the social generalization of skills.

Co-operation is the orphaned twin of specialization in modern economic thought, which simply assumes the market will coordinate between a variety of specializations. This leads to the peculiar paradox that within the enterprise, the coordination between its parts is meticulously planned and entirely insulated from the disruptive effects of the market, whilst in society as a whole, planning is anathematized.

The chief productive function of the modern nation is, in consequence, twofold. It is to introduce, into the nation, those specialist skills which make for the effective use of machinery and, by virtue of this division of labor into a bewildering range of distinct activities, to arrange for them to cooperate in a common national framework of regulation and communication: a system of railways, a system of road usage, a system for the production of interfacing engineered components, a system for the production and consumption of electricity, for the construction of units of habitation (as in Sweden) on scales that create a mass market in reproducible units of installed furniture, laying the basis for the world domination of IKEA, for the interoperability of the means of warfare down to the dimensions of shells, for the standardization of such humble components as the screw and the nut, all the way down to the specification of a system of weights and measures, one of the first and technologically fundamental achievements of the French Revolution. To any economist who neglects standardization as a minor frippery rather than a fundamental principle of industrial production, I always pose two questions:

- Have you ever tried to fit a metric bolt in a BSI nut?
- Why drive on the right?

The joint and dialectical relation between specialization and cooperation, and the mediative role of standardization that arises from this contradiction, is, we suggest, a primary concern if not the primary concern of Noonomy. It is also, we will argue, central to any meaningful understanding of how the modern creative economy, with software at its center, really functions.

It is a common misconception that the analysis of cooperation and specialization constitutes some kind of intellectual prehistory to Marx's analysis of the true source of value—human labor. This arises from the mistaken belief that social labor consists merely of the amalgamation of the activities of individual laborers, achieved by the market. Anyone familiar with the realities of industrial production would recognize this notion as a fable.

Marx not only accepted Smith's concept of specialization as the foundation of capitalism's superior productive capacities but also developed it, placing it at the center of his theory of how capitalist society reproduces itself and accumulates. It is central to the famous Schemes of Reproduction in Volume II of *Capital* and to his discussion of the infamous Transformation problem, both of which attempt to specify the quantitative relations governing the exchange of commodities produced by distinct branches of production.

This concept was strongly developed by Victorian economists worldwide when they established a kind of "map" of industrial production, categorizing and subcategorizing it into sectors such as agriculture, mineral extraction, construction, and manufacturing (which was further subdivided into mechanical and civil engineering); transport and communication; utilities; retail; finance; and other services such as education and health. In fact, industrial classification became one of the earliest international standards on which practical economics reached a general agreement, serving as the basis for the systematic management of production and development.

The concept reached its highest form in Wassily Leontief's Input-Output Analysis, which traced how supply chains transferred products through various stages of production from one branch of industry to another. It also appears in a cruder form in the distinction that permeates the National Accounts, made by Keynes, Kalecki, and others, between industries whose final collective output consists of sales to "final demand" and the remainder—essentially Marx's Departments I and II.

Crucially, thanks to Leontief, this notion became a planning instrument not only in the Soviet Union but also in wartime America, where his "economic technology" was used to organize the US economy for war, calculating precisely how much each industry would need to produce and employ to fulfill the goal of becoming the workshop of the Western war machine.

Thus, the notion of a branch of industry is not some abstract or academic frippery but arguably one of the most fundamental discoveries of economic theory, and certainly one most in need of preservation and extension in the theory of *noonomy*.

However, it cannot be accepted in the form in which it was developed during the age when the mechanical production of physical objects was the dominant employer of human labor. What is therefore required is a fundamental adaptation of the concept to meet the practical requirements for governing a society organized on the principles of *noonomy*—a society in which the production of intangible objects (of which mental objects are a subcategory) is the primary and overwhelmingly dominant form of productive human labor.

The standard definition of an industry is well established and is explained in the internationally accepted manuals governing the classification of industries[1]. At least one of three characteristics defines the activities comprising an industry:

- They specialize in the use of some common resource, for example agricultural land, a specific type of mineral or other raw material, a specific source of energy (steam, oil, electricity).
- They specialize in some particular type of process (e.g., spinning and weaving in the early stages of the first industrial revolution, the modern assembly line, chemical plants, etc.).
- They produce some particular product – for example cars, aeroplanes, cookware, buildings, transport services – or, in modern times software, broadcasts, newspapers, and so on.

Some industries are defined more by one of these characteristics than others, but the definitive rule of thumb, dating from Smith's original conception, is that a group of activities comprises a branch or sub-branch of production if productivity is increased in these industries by specialization within enterprises and cooperation between them.

This leads us to pose what is, in effect, the fundamental issue facing the governance (which includes self-management) of a service-based, mentally productive economy—*Noonomy*: what leads to the enhancements due to specialization? Conventional economics is focused on—indeed, one might reasonably say obsessed with—the individual producer. From this standpoint, technological innovation consists of developing new types of machines, new products, and new processes. Indeed, the innovation literature is rooted in this notion of technological change—so, for example, it treats the transistor or the electronic component as the foundation of the putative *Fourth Industrial Revolution*. Nothing could be further from reality. What has transformed modern production is not electronic components, but the social use made of them. This is not simply a mode of changing the individual components of a productive system; it is the means of cooperation employed by society in integrating these components into a productive system.

[1]ISIC. 2008. International Standard Industrial Classification of All Economic Activities Revision 4. United Nations Department of Economic and Social Affairs, Statistics Division. URL: unstats.un.org/unsd/ publication/seriesM/ seriesm_4rev4e.pdf

Of course, cooperation and specialization, which are in a certain sense the dialectical opposite processes at work in capitalist productive progress, have always worked with, and against, each other: thus, the real basis of the second industrial revolution is as much the railway system – a prototype, along with the postal system, of modern industrial cooperation, as it is the use of steam power as such. Similarly, electrification and the power system are as much the foundation of what Christopher Freeman terms the 'age of steel, electricity and imperialism' as are the generation and use of electrical power. Indeed, when one studies the close relation between the classical 'originators' of capitalism such as the spinning Jenny and the Loom, from the standpoint of their relation to the world economy, we see that they owe as much to a revolution in clothing and the supply of raw materials from the colonies – that is, the shipping and military systems on which this supply depended – as to the genius of Hargreaves or Arkwright.

Yet for the exponents of modern innovation or the history of invention, the drivers of this process are the Jenny, the Loom, the Steam Engine, the Dynamo, and the Electric Motor.

This focus is not only outdated in the post-mechanical age but downright misleading. The basis of modern, mental specialization is cooperation; it is therefore on systems of cooperation, both nationally and internationally, that a future science of innovation must rest.

We propose the software industry and ICT in general as the carrier and archetype of this revolution precisely because it is the single industry in which cooperation is the fundamental basis for specialization. We propose the creative industries as the archetypal drivers of this revolution precisely because, by migrating to this carrier and its archetypal models of production, they have become its drivers.

6.1.4 THE NOONOMIC CONJUNCTURE: THE CURRENT STATE AND TREND OF DEVELOPMENT IN TODAY'S NATIONAL PRODUCTIVE SYSTEMS

What do we mean by "now"? This concept has been the subject of philosophical discourse, particularly in Western thought, since the time of Heraclitus. It is one of the most fundamental issues of science, heavily emphasized in Desai's work on *Geopolitical Economy*, where the historical dimension of all categories of political economy is stressed, allowing us to situate them in the appropriate geographical context.

To take just one example central to the analysis of this section: what does it mean to "be industrialized"? Is this a historically absolute or historically relative concept? Was Japan during the Meiji Restoration already an "industrialized" society? By the standards of the day, it was not. Yet, Japan delivered a rude shock to the short-lived Eastern aspirations of Count Witte by defeating a supposedly superior Russian military force in the war of 1905.

As any physicist or indeed, biologist or chemist can testify, the scientific concept of the 'state' of a system is a dialectical unity of two aspects: the current position of the system and its direction of motion. Thus, we do not understand what a particle is unless, along with its position in space, we include its momentum. We do not understand the ecology of animate entities unless we understand their evolution. Most importantly, we do not understand a society by supposing it to be frozen in time, as does all equilibrium – that is to say, mainstream neoclassical – economic theory.

Consequently, a Noonomic understanding of the future requires a study of the trends of industrial specialization which in turn must arise from the study of their historical past. This notion is encapsulated in the notion of conjuncture.

The notion of conjuncture was, and rightly remains, a principal object of attention for Russian and Soviet social science. Kondratieff consciously named his research group the 'Conjunctural Institute.' Varga, arguably the most eminent Comintern statistician (if possibly also the most controversial), regarded his role as the study of the 'economic conjuncture.' Kuznets to my knowledge did not use the term, but his entire method is conjunctural; that is to say, it is devoted to the study of economic dynamics.[2] The Oxford *Dictionary of Sociology* defines conjuncture thus: "A term used by so-called structural Marxists (*see* Louis Althusser) to refer to the concrete state of political-economic and especially class relations, in a specific society, at a particular point in time (as in 'specific historical conjuncture')."

Any treatment of industrial conjuncture necessarily embarks on abstractions, such as agriculture, industry, or services, which are both universally applied and widely questioned. For example, trees are not a food product

[2]Consider thus 1965 *Modern Economic Growth: Rate, Structure, and Spread.* New Haven: Yale University Press, 1966 *Economic Growth of Nations: Total Output and Production Structure.* Cambridge: Belknap Press of Harvard University Press, 1965. *Economic Growth and Structure: Selected Essays.* New York: Norton.

but a construction material. So, is modern forestry best placed within the agricultural, construction, or manufacturing sectors? This makes it easy to pick holes, or make fun, of any system of industrial classification.

Such superficial criticism should not be undertaken lightly. The only currently available alternative to a systematic approach to classification is nihilism – anything goes. This opens the door to individualistic modes of interaction between theoreticians, in which anybody can adopt any definition that suits their purpose. This erodes and ultimately dissolves the fundamental principle that we are attempting to establish, namely, the necessary cooperative basis for human advancement.

However, the dialectic of specialization and cooperation inevitably confronts the basic dilemma of cognition. Every specialist encounters reality via a distinct practical engagement with it. For a theoretical physicist, the molecule is an unbelievably complex set of quantum-level interactions. For the chemist, it is the mere basis for the study of compounds. For the biologist, these compounds are the elementary basis of the biosphere. For the sociologist, the biosphere is nothing but the unexamined precondition of human social existence. For the astronomer, human social existence is but a means to examine the cosmos. For the cosmologist, nothing matters more than integrating the study of matter in all its iridescent glory with the theory of particulate existence which is the special provenance of the physicist. All 'knowledge' therefore depends ultimately on the cooperative relations that these specialized researchers establish with one another.

Indeed, this is the basis for the parable of the elephant. But ultimately, the specialists in Elephant tails, the specialists in Elephant feet, and the specialist in Elephant trunks, each 'blinded' by ignorance of the special cognition that her collaborators have acquired by virtue of their own particular interaction with Elephants, all have to work together and agree on some description of the whole Elephant. In short, cognition itself, the very foundation of knowledge, is pre-conditioned by specialization, the earliest evolutionary characteristic of human productive labor.

It is for this reason that we insist on the necessity to standardize what we regard as creative labor, and how we should measure it. Whether or not we agree with the 'merely conventional' national rules of traffic that apply in any nation, such as driving on the left or the right, a nation that attempts to govern road traffic with no rules at all is not a national productive system but a national collision Centre. The critique of industrial definitions cannot be equated to the abandonment of such definitions.

In fact, the contradictions in thought – such as whether tractor driving is an agricultural or industrial activity – arise from contradictions in the material system itself, and therefore, the method of critique should be materialist in character, that is to say, it must study what are the material conditions which give rise to the paradoxes of thought, not the other way round.

For the above reasons, we begin with the conventional broad classification of productive activity into agriculture, industry, and services.[3] Data have been collected on this basis from as early as 1870 but modern standardization dates from the establishment of the postwar International System of Industrial Classification[4] which has gone through four revisions at the time of writing, with a number of national variations – notably the NAICS system of North America and the NACE system of the European Union. Thus, it is possible, with some manipulation, to produce comparable historical statistics over a substantial historical period. The importance of this is that it allows us to distinguish genuine trends from both accident and cyclic variation.

Following the inductive principles of all true science, we start by simply presenting some facts, in the shape of a set of charts, which we will then attempt to interpret. Of course, other interpretations are not only possible but positively invited; these counter-interpretations may extend to critiques not only of the methods by which the data are collected, but the system by which they are classified. We make only one proviso, based on the preceding discussion of the principles of classification. This proviso however imposes a strict discipline: dismissal does not constitute critique. The task of a scientific critique of current knowledge consists of the construction of alternatives. Therefore, the critic should be obliged not merely to point to the defects of the current or proposed system, which are many, but to propose a different practical way of presenting the facts along with a different theoretical analysis of the said facts (Figure 6.1).

---

[3]Note that 'manufacturing' *per se* is treated, within the industrial classification system, as a subsector of industry - albeit a large one – since 'industry' includes other spheres of material production such as construction. Similarly, as we hope to discuss in this paper, 'services' comprises a syncretic medley of activities ranging from transport and communication to financial speculation. One of the principal tasks of the *reconstruction* of the classification system we propose is a systematic *deconstruction* of the category of services, a term whose etymological origin in the feudal concept of personal service betrays both its antiquity and its inadequacy.

[4]ISIC. 2008. International Standard Industrial Classification of All Economic Activities Revision 4. United Nations Department of Economic and Social Affairs, Statistics Division. unstats.un.org/unsd/publication/ seriesM/seriesm_4rev4e.pdf.

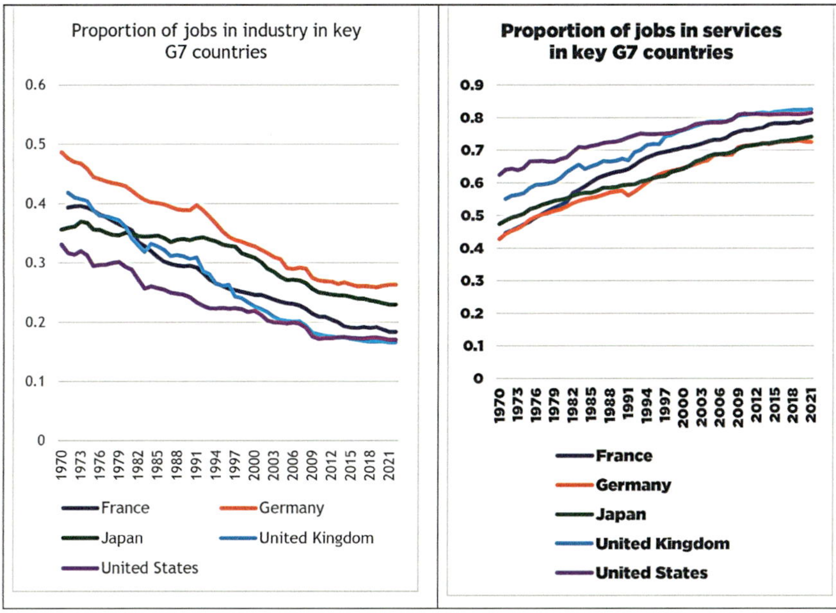

FIGURE 6.1 Some basic facts of the current industrial conjuncture.

Source: International Labor Organization, Bureau of Labor Statistics, Author Calculations.

The first point is the absolute trend towards the displacement of all other sources of employment by the production of services. This has been more or less completed in the countries of the global North, aka the 'advanced' countries of the IMF or more accurately, the imperialist countries. In no such country does service employment fall below 70% today, and in no such country does industrial employment rise above 30%.

The second point is a differential trend for the displacement of agriculture by the combination of industry and services, which does not contradict the first trend as we shall see. It is different both geographically and historically. 'Industrialization' is a geographically specific point in the conjuncture that varies from country to country, even among the non-Northern countries. Thus from 1990 to the present, industrial employment rose sharply in China, India, and Brazil,[5] but from 2010 (though it is early

[5]South Korea having been singled out for a role as a buffer state as an outcome of the Chines and Korean wars of liberation, was obliged – at considerable social cost – to industrialize rapidly in the 1950s and 1960s and was allowed join the select club of 'advanced' nations. As a result, it now exhibits the pattern of displacement of industry by services characteristic of this club.

to be certain) have joined the general pattern which is thus becoming a world pattern, in which industry is being displaced absolutely, not just relatively, by services (Figure 6.2).

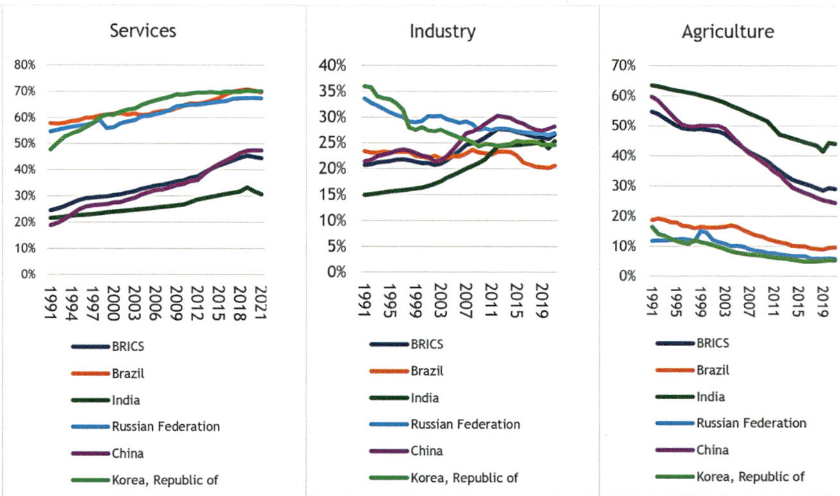

FIGURE 6.2 Proportion of jobs in services, industries, and agriculture in key countries and regions outside the Global North (shorter timescale).

A general hypothesis thus arises, on which this paper and much of our previous work (Freeman, 2014) are based: the conjuncture is one in which services are displacing industrial manufacture absolutely as well as relatively, throughout the world.

6.1.5 HOW NOT TO MISUNDERSTAND THE FACTS: TANGIBILITY, SERVICES, MENTAL OBJECTS, AND THE CONCEPT OF PRODUCTION

To the naïve observer, the conclusions above may seem counterintuitive. Surely, we live in a world of industrial abundance, surrounded by marvelous mechanical and electrical devices and factories of all kinds. Surely, the world is producing more industrial products than ever before. How, then, can "industry" be in decline? And what exactly are America's 150 million "service workers" doing?

This misunderstanding leads to many frivolous conclusions (Elliott & Atkinson, 2007) notably the notion that service labor is in some sense unproductive. This false notion, which originates in Smith's attempt to define production as the creation of 'tangible objects' was corrected in the Nineteenth Century by Marx. He rightly pointed out that a teacher, in a private school, is creating value for the school owner, who functions as a capitalist, selling his services to the parents of its rich pupils. This is a straightforward wage relation in which the private teacher creates surplus value and hence profit for the owner. There is thus no difference in principle, as regards its productive character, between service production and manufacturing. The true difference resides in the social relations governing the production process.

Indeed, a worker in a state manufacturing concern, insofar as it is run not on the basis of profit but of need (as for example in a non-privatized public transport system) is unproductive in capitalist terms because the owner does not retain and accumulate the surplus in a capitalist manner. This is why in the Soviet economy, where the surplus was allocated by the state, instead of the mechanism of the migration of capital in search of profit, most 'production' was, in the strict sense required for the analysis of market economies, unproductive: it did not create capital.

However, there is a second basis for the intuitive confusion arising from an unreflective absorption of the above facts. This does not require us to embark on the difficult discussion of 'what constitutes production' as applied to intangible objects, which is the topic of the next section but requires us only to recognize a paradoxical fact to which Marx, again, was the first to draw attention and indeed, he qualified as a Law of Motion of capitalism: namely, the more productive a branch of industry becomes, the fewer people are required to work in it.

This social law is part and parcel of the basic Law of Value, which is that as productivity increases, fewer people are required to make the same thing. This is reflected in a steady decline in prices. The price of the product of any industry, in which innovation is taking place and therefore productivity is rising, tends despite ups and downs to follow a historical trend governed by the number of laborers needed to make that product. This is the reason for the very long-term decline in agricultural prices which is accompanied by, and causes, the equally long-term decline in employment in the agricultural sector. These are merely mirrors of each other.

Therefore, and hopefully trivially though we can argue about it if necessary or useful, the decline in industrial employment, a long-term trend of all modern society whether capitalist or socialist, is in no way to be confused with a decline in industrial production. The contradiction is that industrial output has risen more or less in tandem with the decline in industrial employment. This is merely the social expression of the private Law of Accumulation of a capitalist market economy, namely, in a succession of branches of industry, as productivity rises, employment falls.

Noonomy is therefore the natural conclusion of this process in which the limits of increasing industrial productivity as a mechanism for social progress express themselves in the inability of industry to furnish the means of life to the majority of the population by means of the wage relation. Put simply, it no longer employs enough people to do so.

Finally, the clarification of this illusion, required for an adequate factual analysis of the tendencies to which Noonomy is called on to respond, obliges us to return to the taboo subject of *value*. The underlying phenomenon at work, in the tendencies charted above, is a decline in the value of the products of industry, which their prices merely track. But what is this value, and how should it be measured? Neoclassical economics falls back on the notion of so-called 'real value' which purports to be a measure of physical quantity but is, in essence, a disguised attempt to construct an aggregate measure of their use-value. But for Marx and his predecessors, value in its most general sense is a measure of Smith's 'difficulty of obtaining a thing,' that is, the human effort or labor required in order to bring it into existence.

Modern economic statistics are more or less paralyzed by the obvious fact that the *quantity* of a mental product is impossible to measure *per se.* It can be ingeniously quantized in the market, for example by the sale of tickets or (as in the modern software industry) by selling 'software as a service' but this does not resolve the difficulty of stating, in objective terms, 'how much' of a musical performance the ticket entitles the user to, or 'how much' software the subscription entitles the subscriber to.

This does not place mental production beyond scrutiny, as conservative art advocates like Tusa (Tusa, 2014) maintain in the case they make for 'art for art's sake.' Society is entitled to ask, of its mental producers, what benefits it is getting from them, and to thereby allocate resources rationally and indeed, democratically, to the various competing demands placed upon it by these producers. It does tell us, however, that the standard measures of output employed in the production of economic statistics, irretrievably rooted in the notion of physical quantity as the ultimate measure of usefulness, are increasingly unfit for purpose. Therefore, a legitimate goal of enquiry is the construction of measures of *social* usefulness over which humans can exercise democratic control.

6.1.6 FOUNDATIONS OF THE MACHINOCRATIC ILLUSION

Now the man that invented the steam drill
Thought he was mighty fine
But John Henry made fifteen feet
The steam drill only made nine, Lord, Lord
The steam drill only made nine
John Henry hammered in the mountains
His hammer was striking fire
But he worked so hard, he broke his poor heart
He laid down his hammer and he died, Lord, Lord
He laid down his hammer and he died

US folk song

The illusion that production consists of making material products permeates modern thought. This constantly recreates the illusion, characteristic of commodity fetishism, that the only true form of a commodity is a physical object and the only true source of its value is machinery. This is an anti-human idea: in denies the contribution of human labor to production, elevating capital, which is to say property, above all property in machinery, over the labor that vitalizes it.

Historical materialism explains that the origin of this illusion is the characteristic of machine-age products, namely they are the most eminently suited of all commodities to be converted into private property. They enjoy the characteristic that neoclassical microeconomics recognizes as 'excludability,' ultimately a function of the mode of use of a physical object. The archetypal form of an excludable product is food – only one person may eat the same thing. Actually, after that it gets murky so that, for example, houses are occupied by many people who share their use on the basis of non-market principles such as patriarchy. Cars, in theory, can only be 'used' by the driver, but most cars carry a variable number of people. Indeed, carpools constitute a fundamental and significant measure towards the socialization of transport, whilst it would be lunatic to confine the use of a bus, just as physical as the car, to a single person.

Neoliberal thinkers ridicule this with frankly puerile critiques, such as the idea that only one person can use a toothbrush. This misses the point: it is in the nature of a physical object that its properties restrict the number of possible users, which is what allows the capitalists to enclose and alienate this use, as when they sell tickets to a football match or a train journey.

Is this true for services? In some cases yes, and in some cases no, which is why the category of service production has to be deconstructed. The archetypal excludable service is essentially an extension of the feudal category of personal serfdom, which is why domestic servitude not only survives into the modern age but even proliferates and has a constant tendency to degenerate into forms of patriarchal slavery. Transport is an intermediate category in that the use of all logistical systems is restricted ultimately by physical capacity. If transport was a non-excludable service, there would be no need to build railways, roads, or aircraft, let alone impose international standards for their delivery.

In contrast, at the extreme opposite end of the spectrum of excludability come those objects that Professor Buzgalin assigns to the 'creatosphere' (Buzgalin, 2017, Buzgalin & Kolganov, 2013), which also belong more generally to Vernadsky's (Vernadsky, 1945) and Chardin's *Noösphere*. These are what Freeman (Freeman, 2021) designates 'mental objects' – traditionally the products of artistic, scientific, or other ratiocinatory activity, but today becoming far more widespread as the true product of the Creative Industries.

A mental object may be thought of, approximately, the 'content' of a product. It consists of any usable entity that exists independent of its material form. Thus, a poem, or a scientific theorem, may exist on paper, in spoken form, in the brain of the poet or of her audience, in the skills of the technicians, or – crucially in modern production – in a digitalized form.

Ray Bradbury's *Fahrenheit 451* was an early deep examination of this phenomenon in which all books were burned, yet communities of rebels preserved them by memorizing them. A *Fahrenheit 451* for the 21st century is by no means an irrelevant possibility, when censorship becomes the norm of online availability and suppression the norm of online production. All that has happened is that silicon and fiber have taken the place of paper and ink.

Independence from material form is taken by Freeman (2021) to be the characteristic of a mental object. Today, the 'film' is no longer a reel of celluloid, any more than the book is a bound ream of paper or a musical piece an imprint on a CD or a tape. This has two consequences central to this paper and the entire enterprise of Noonomy. Both must be understood together.

First, the market relation is fundamentally inimical to the production and widespread access to mental objects. This is precisely because in order to sell an object, access to it must be restricted. This is experienced by social critics in the first place in the sphere of consumption: it contradicts and is rightly criticized, as a denial of right: mathematical theorems are freely available, and it would be as absurd as it would be impractical to penalize the use of Pythagoras's theorem without payment to his estate. Yet this absurdity is freely practiced when it comes to scientific methods of production or literary or musical products.

However, in the post-mechanical era is increasingly eclipsed by the yet greater and more fundamental contradiction in the sphere of production. It was first noted by von Mises and remains a canonical feature of Austrian economics in its pure form, that Intellectual Property constitutes a restraint of trade, which is why the most consistent neoliberals are actually opposed to it. Undeterred by this contradiction, the USA in the 1990s, with the Uruguay Round of the GATT negotiations, the construction of the World Intellectual Property Organization (WIPO) and the imposition of its terms on the newly-minted World Trade Organization (WTO), not only underwent but imposed on the world, the reconstruction of Intellectual Property as a Monopolistic Institution. It unified the institutions of patent and copyright. It established a life term of 70 years.[6] Most importantly, it legally sanctioned the key use of IP in American capitalism, which is not the dissemination of knowledge or ideas, but the prevention of dissemination in order to maintain a technological monopoly.

It might reasonably be argued that at the heart of the current conflict between China and the US there lies a key difference in the use to which knowledge is put which leads in turn to a key ideological difference in the conception of Intellectual Property. For the USA, IP is fundamentally private, and society should allow its private owners unrestricted monopoly rights. For China, IP is a form of social ownership, which private owners enjoy at the discretion of the state, on several conditions of which the most important is that they demonstratively disseminate the knowledge.

[6]No coincidence that 'threescore years and ten' is the Abrahamic and biblical lifetime of a human – this ensures that IP is owned by corporate entities in the place of humans.

From the Trumpist viewpoint, therefore, China is 'stealing' US technology whenever it commits the crime of allowing its own producers to use it.

This 'stealing' takes place in a kind of intellectual Sherwood Forest. China is the Robin Hood of the creative age: it seeks only to ensure that the poor have enough of what the rich have too much of, at one and the same time relieving the rich of the burden of wealth whilst relieving the poor of its absence. But in the age of mental production, there is no contradiction, or rather, the contradiction is illusory. The rich can have their intellectual cake and eat it: nobody is proposing they should stop using their technology, only that they should cease denying others, equally deserving of this cake, their rightful place at the potlach.

But this brings us right back to the question we asked at the start of this section. In what sense is the creation of a mental product an act of production? The critics of this notion may feel and argue that an intangible and infinitely reproducible thing cannot be treated as a product, because – ultimately – they do not see such things as having a use. But if technological knowledge is useless, how can China be using it and why should the USA seek to monopolize it? Why is the world threatened with world war over a useless thing?

The above points, I argue, in a single direction: the necessity to deconstruct the category of service production and reconstruct it on the basis of a concept, or concepts, of social rather than private usefulness. Central to such a reconstruction is the idea that we must evolve a useful conception of the usefulness of the products of mental activity.[7]

6.1.7 MENTAL PRODUCTION AND THE STRUCTURE OF SERVICES

[7]In all discussion of utility or use value from Bentham to Marx, it is supposed that the use of a thing (unlike its exchange value) is a characteristic of the thing itself; otherwise, Marx could not write "Let us consider two commodities, a coat and 10 yards of linen, perhaps. Let the first have twice the value of the second, so that if 10 yards of linen = w, the coat = 2w." Here, the coat is the unit of use-value of the *genus* coat whilst the yard is the unit of the use-value of the genus linen. Any distinction between more desirable coats and the rest, or high-quality and low-quality linen such as tendency to break and so interfere with production, is abstracted from. This is a legitimate abstraction but the issue 'who determines what is useful?' hangs over it and comes to the fore in the sphere of culture. Bourgeois society generally imposes a specific concept of what constitutes 'good art' (Belfiore and Bennet 2008). But this is moot: was Impressionist Art, prior to its general acceptance, without use value because the galleries refused to exhibit them?

What does 'service' labor consist of? Its main distinguishing feature, as already discussed, is that its results are intangible – they do not consist of material objects. But this does not mean all service labor is the same, which is why the category has to be deconstructed and reconstructed. A preliminary attempt at so doing suggests three distinct forms of activity:

- **A 'Department I of Services': These produce the mental means of service production. Sometimes called 'B2B or 'Business to Business' services, including:**
  - Software *per se*;
  - Communication and logistic services to industry;
  - Commercialized Business Services in general. This is really quite a large sector and is often wrongly confused with Finance. It includes, for example, architecture, design services, and much of the STEM industries, including that part which sells and develops methods and technologies.

- **A 'Department II of Services': These produce or transform services sold to consumers. Sometimes called 'B2C' (Business to Consumer) activities:**
  - A significant sector, notably transport, which is closest to manufacturing and other forms of material production, in that by moving goods and storing them, it functions as an 'extension of industrial production into commerce.'
  - A large mass of 'drudge' low-paid and low-skilled labor which is, in essence, commercialized labor of servitude. Here we find office cleaning, Amazon, Starbucks, and many enterprises at the forefront of the New Unionization.
  - A growing mass of essentially high-skilled labor to provide high-value services to households, notably education and health. This is subject to continuous pressure to lower wages and worsen working conditions being organized in an industrial manner but has some bargaining power because of the essential skills involved.
  - A rapidly growing sector selling products that are purchased for their content rather than their physical form. This is one part of the Creative Industries

- **The Unproductive Labor of Commerce, Finance, and Real Estate:**
    - This includes almost all banking and almost all retail but includes productive elements detailed below. It is unproductive not because its results are intangible but because they are not bought and sold as commodities.
    - In the case of finance this is clear, since financial profit arises from a kind of levy (interest or rent).
    - In the case of retail, it is less clear in that the output is sold to consumers. However, the mere act of charging a consumer for a product purchased elsewhere does not create new value, but yields a profit arising from the general equalization process because it is cheaper for the productive capitalists to sell to a specialized intermediary than engage in selling to the public.
    - The rental and real estate sector is almost entirely speculative and unproductive in character (Figure 6.3).

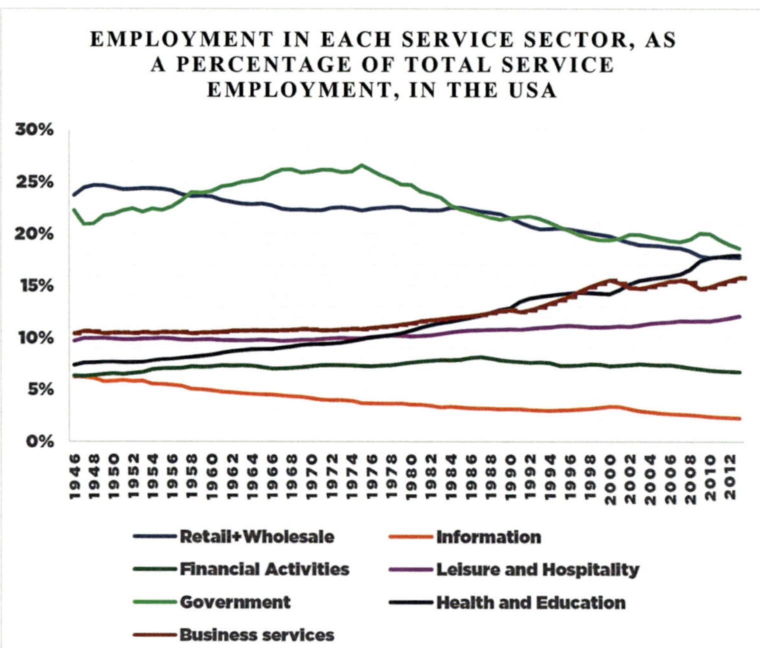

FIGURE 6.3 Employment in each service sector, as a percentage of total service employment, in the USA.

In the present service sector accounts these are all mixed up together in a semi-inchoate fashion, but the underlying reality may be dug out by descending deep enough into the subcategories of the accounts to see what is really going on. Some notion of the relative scope of these various activities can be gleaned from the detailed statistics provided by the USA and shown above. Actually, these are not very informative because of the confusion described above, but they do serve to dispel some illusions and inspire some thought.

First, it is clear that the growth of services can in no way be identified with the growth of the financial and retail sectors, in employment terms. Both reached an employment peak in the mid-1970s and have been declining ever since. Again, this may appear counter-intuitive because finance occupies a much more dominant role in the US economy today than in the 1970s – this has been, after all, a phase of history in which 'financialization' has played an enormous role.

Again, the distinction between output and employment is relevant and fundamental. The profits and income of the finance and retail sectors, precisely because they are divorced from the circuit of productive capital, bear little relation to the work they put in. A financier can raise, essentially, whatever interest he can squeeze out of his creditors – and when these creditors consist not only of Ninja mortgage holders but entire debt-ridden countries such as Argentina, this is huge. The relation between value and revenue asserts itself, in these industries, only in crisis, when vast volumes of overrated fictitious assets, constructed on the assumption that the creditor can be squeezed without limit, collapse in these moments to something approximating the real surplus value they can realistically levy.

But at the very same time, precisely because of the lucrative character of this type of activity, the financial and commercial sectors are at the forefront of innovation – for example, jointly with the military, they were the drivers of the information revolution right up to, and beyond, the arrival of the internet and the world wide web.

This leads to further confusion: enterprises, such as the makers of computers, or the suppliers of software, which sell goods to the banks or retail sector, are productive of value. A computer sells for real money that corresponds to the real labor of making it, as does a computer application. This is not altered by the fact that this product is used unproductively by the bank to which it is sold.

In this respect, the apparent decline of employment in the 'information' sector is a classification error. It arises because most of the labor of the information revolution is classified as a business service.

This leads to a second observation: the rapid rise of business services employment cannot be identified with the growth of the unproductive financial sector. Any close examination of it reveals it is just not the same thing. The temptation to dismiss this growth as a mere parasitic outgrowth should therefore be resisted.

Thirdly as regards the consumer-facing service sector, two facts stand out: the striking growth of health and education, and of 'leisure and hospitality.' The latter comprises the bulk of the consumer-facing Creative Industries. Neither should the former be neglected since it constitutes, as we will see, part of the 'infrastructure' of Creative production, namely it provides the human means for creative workers to function creatively – it lets loose what Blake termed the 'Tigers of Wrath' and which he counter-posed to the 'Horses of Instruction.'

Fourth, finally, and most decisively, a division imposes itself that is not recognized in the accounts: the mental component of service labor is systematically confused with its manual component and is consistently underrated by the employing classes.

The 'labor of teaching' is, for example, indissociable from the incorporation of 'knowledge' in the specialized practice of the educator, as indeed is the labor of health provision. Yet our societies systematically underestimate the attention that needs to be given to the process by which this knowledge lodges itself in the brains of the teachers, the nurses, and the doctors,[8] and attempts to depress both the wages paid to them, and the resources devoted to their education, to the minimum possible given the labor relations in their respective industries.

Indeed, the very notion of branches of 'manual' and 'mental' production, expressed in the Fabian notion of 'workers by hand or brain' ignores the basic facts of what labor consists of, namely the coordination of the hand with the brain. All labor is purposive, and all labor therefore contains an

[8]As noted, what is really meant by the 'transmission of knowledge' is providing the benighted recipients of this 'knowledge' with the time and means to absorb it, which actually amounts to the very simple act of giving them the time to do it. That is to say, the real issue is the labor of the acquisition of skill. This has as much to do with the transmission of 'knowledge' as swimming has to do with the academic study of aquatics. To be sure, a champion athlete can learn much from psychologists, linguists, and anatomists. But the human who can swim without getting in the water would indeed be a miracle to behold.

indissociable mental component. Indeed, in earlier times than the present mechanical age, the mental capabilities of artisanal workers were widely recognized and formed the foundation of the guild system. Shakespeare makes fun of his 'rude mechanicals' for attempting to perform theatrical plays but the mere fact of making the attempt constitutes a thespian recognition of their creative aspirations that vanished with the coming of modern industrial production.

The contemporaries of the manufacturers, at the dawn of the mechanical age, fully understood that the separation of mental from manual labor was not biologically given and indeed, did not really exist prior to that age. It was imposed by the manufacturers. Thomas Carlyle (Carlyle, 1829) puts it thus:

> *Were we required to characterize this age of ours by any single epithet, we should be tempted to call it, not an Heroical, Devotional, Philosophical, or Moral Age, but, above all others, the Mechanical Age.*
>
> *It is the Age of Machinery, in every outward and inward sense of that word; the age which, with its whole undivided might, forwards, teaches and practices the great art of adapting means to ends.*
>
> *Nothing is now done directly, or by hand; all is by rule and calculated contrivance. For the simplest operation, some helps and accompaniments, some cunning abbreviating process is in readiness.*
>
> *Our old modes of exertion are all discredited, and thrown aside. On every hand, the living artisan is driven from his workshop, to make room for a speedier, inanimate one. The shuttle drops from the fingers of the weaver, and falls into iron fingers that ply it faster. The sailor furls his sail, and lays down his oar; and bids a strong, unwearied servant, on vaporous wings, bear him through the waters.*
>
> *Men have crossed oceans by steam; the Birmingham Fire-king has visited the fabulous East; and the genius of the Cape, were there any Cameons now to sing it, has again been alarmed, and with far stranger thunders than Gamas.*
>
> *There is no end to machinery. Even the horse is stripped of his harness, and finds a fleet firehorse yoked in his stead. Nay, we have an artist that hatches chickens by steam; the very brood-hen is to be superseded! For all earthly, and for some unearthly purposes, we have machines and mechanic furtherances; for mincing our cabbages; for casting us into magnetic sleep.*

The category of 'manual labor,' in short, is not a biological distinction but is imposed by a specific form of production, namely mass repetitive or mechanical production. The means by which capitalist industrial production drove revolution after revolution in productivity was by using machinery in order to produce *many identical things*. In the self-created war of men against their own machines, if conducted on the battlefield of mere quantity, the machines cannot but win. John Henry will always lose his epochal and mythical battle with the steam hammer.

6.1.8 THE CONCEPT OF MENTAL OBJECTS

Precisely for the same reasons that 'Manual Labor' is a construct of industrial mechanization, not an innate biological function of labor, 'Mental Labor' is also a construct. Because it is a construct, it is not analytically useful, because it is not innate in the nature of labor to be thus divided. All labor combines manual and mental aspects and indeed, Engels characterizes tool-using as the driver of the development of the brain. Cave painting dates to the earliest times of human existence and the notion of some 'period of history' when humans were obliged to devote themselves to the purely biological or 'Zoo' aspects of their existence, is historically false. In fact, the separation of Mental from Manual is not only artificially imposed, but recent: it dates from the mechanical age.

It follows, therefore, that a more fundamental analytical construct is required. This is achieved by asking what the result of the labor is. The rational kernel in the notion of "mental and manual labor" is a distinction not in the nature of the labor, but in the results—in the product. For most of human history, these products have been tangible in character. This allows us a more accurate characterization of the present stage of technological development, which we prefer to the notion of a "knowledge economy" for many reasons too detailed to go into: its decisive character is the rapid growth, and indeed massification, of the production of intangible objects.

As noted, the category of "service" does not adequately capture this distinction. The critical issue is whether the object produced by the labor exists independently of its material form—as is the case most notably with a software component, but also for earlier examples of mental products or objects, such as the book, the theorem, the scientific discovery, and, in fact, the objects that live in the "Creatosphere" of Buzgalin and Kolganov.

Not all mental labor is creative and indeed, creative production lives in a wider sphere of distribution and reproduction, which engages much of the significantly larger labor force that is responsible for the material aspects of its reproduction. It is all very well to say that the content of a book lives independently of the printed book, but try to read a book that is out of print, unavailable online, and not on the shelves of your local library, and you will be made rudely aware that this 'content' is a somewhat elusive magical beast. Independence from a specific material form cannot be identified with the illusion that a mental object has no need of incarnation in some material form.

It is for this reason that I personally am suspicious of the notion of a 'knowledge economy' – because, pace Neoclassical Growth Theory, knowledge does not exist independently of knowledgeable human beings. It is the human beings and their activity – specifically, the character of what they produce – that defines the technological state of the economy.

To put it another way, the precise definition of the present age that is most suited to our purpose is that is an age of the mass circulation of mental objects, whereby 'circulation' we mean not only their production, which is the specific function of creative labor, but their reproduction and application. The term we suggest to describe this totality is 'mental economy,' which (in distinction from 'Noonomy' refers to the purely technical state of the economy, not to the modes of its usage. We do however suggest it is used in the place of 'knowledge economy.'

The labor of creation exists side by side with the labor of reproduction and application. It is co-dependent with them and engages in a profound cooperative relation with them. In order to cater to this interdependence, we must recognize it, and measure it.

For that reason, we propose the research project widen the sphere of existing enquiries, to define and measure the labor engaged in the reproduction and application of mental products. This would then include, for example, much scientific labor which is not in general engaged in discovery, but in the technical application of existing discoveries.[9] This would then extend the labor force thus defined to around 30% of the workforce of a so-called 'advanced' country (Bakhshi et al., 2015), which demonstrates just how central this resource is in the existing society, never mind the role it could play in a society organized according to the principles of Noonomy.

[9]No 'hierarchy' is implied and of course, much if not most new discoveries arise in the course of applying old ones. The question as indicated from the outset is always 'what is the specialization of the labor?' The fact that orchestras employ people to play its pianos does not these players from composing orchestral works but to the contrary, facilitates it. Nevertheless, the 'occupation' of such a player is 'pianist,' not 'composer.'

The cultivation of this resource should be the primary objective of any serious modern industrial policy. For this very reason, it is essential to clarify who the laborers are engaged in producing and reproducing such objects, how their capabilities are developed and sustained, and how to apply this huge modern resource to the benefit of humanity.

6.1.9 CREATIVE LABOR: WHAT IT IS, AND HOW TO MEASURE IT?

Creative production is, nevertheless, a specific component of mental production, concerned primarily with origination, meaning, and bringing new mental objects into existence. As such it is classified by the statisticians in current practice as a component of service labor. However, it is 'buried' in the accounts, which do not classify it separately. We now turn, finally, to the deconstruction of this specific component of what is now classified as service production.

Research projects attempting to classify mental production date back as far as the very notion of a "knowledge" or "post-industrial" economy (Bell, 1976). In parallel, at various times, a vast literature has attempted to analyze the "service" economy, and an even earlier tradition of attempts to measure the "value of art" dates back to Victorian-era controversies. These controversies divide the socialist John Ruskin, who proposed that the value of an art product should be rooted in a social evaluation of the artistic capabilities of the artist's labor, from the equally socialist Oscar Wilde, who insisted that any true measure of an artist could not rest on social approbation.

Modern work on the Creative Industries can be distinguished from all the above in that it is driven by the goal of identifying the wealth-producing capacity of mental production.

A somewhat discredited, but nevertheless famous, such attempt is the work of Florida, who developed the notion of the "creative class"—a very broad category comprising managerial workers, artistic workers, scientific workers, and many more, extending to almost half the working population in some cases. The difficulty with this scattergun approach would be analogous to the idea that, in the physiocratic era, all town-dwellers constituted productive laborers.

A second, much-neglected work is that of Richard Caves (2000), in a seminal study of contractual relations in the creative industries that sheds crucial light on how they create wealth, above all on the co-operative character of collaborations in them.

The origin of what we may term, without wishing offense to Florida, the scientific study of the Creative Industries is to be found in the Australian "Creative Nation" project and the research it generated at Queensland University of Technology (QUT). This inspired the work of the UK Minister Chris Smith, who caused his department to produce a "mapping" of the UK's creative industries comprising a list of the occupations and industries considered creative.

Freeman, working at the Greater London Authority, then produced at the request of the Mayor of London a document entitled *Creativity: London's Core Business*, which led to a long collaboration between him, Peter Higgs of QUT, and Hasan Bakhshi of the UK think tank NESTA (National Endowment for Science, Technology, and the Arts). They developed the so-called intensity method for defining and quantifying the Creative Industries. This was subsequently adopted by DCMS and a range of European institutions (Table 6.1).

TABLE 6.1 Intensities in the DCMS Sectors, 2011 Estimates

		Creative	Other Occupations	Total Occupations	Intensity
1.	Advertising	45,900	69,400	115,300	40%
2.	Architecture	67,300	36,200	103,500	65%
3.	Art & Antiques	500	8,300	8,800	6%
5.	Design	56,400	42,100	98,500	57%
6.	Designer Fashion	3,700	2,900	6,600	56%
7.	Film, Video & Photography	28,700	29,500	58,200	49%
9&10.	Music & Visual and Performing Arts	138,400	52,800	191,300	72%
11.	Publishing	71,300	111,500	182,700	39%
8&12.	Software/Electronic Publishing	900	22,300	23,200	4%
8&12.	Digital & Entertainment Media	2,000	11,200	13,200	15%
13.	TV & Radio	61,700	34,200	96,000	64%
	Total	476,800	420,500	897,300	53%

The core notion of the Intensity method was explained in NESTA's seminal *Dynamic Mapping of the Creative Industries* (Bakhshi, Freeman, & Higgs, 2013) and can be explained quite simply with the use of a table taken from that document and reproduced below.

Researchers in the field therefore isolate specific sub-sub-industries, such as 'the production of craft jewelry,' calculate the employment in each of them, and then add them up.[10] Thus, for example, most writers define the 'video industry' as the sum of the following three SIC components:

SIC code 9211: Motion picture and video production
SIC code 9212: Motion picture and video distribution
SIC code 9213: Motion picture projection

In addition, however, the 'Intensity' definition also and indeed, first, calculates employment in a set of creative occupations. The 'intensity' of employment in any given industrial subsector is then simply the proportion of its workforce that is creative when defined in this way. The Creative industries are then defined to be those in which this intensity is especially high – typically greater than 30%, which is 12 times higher than in the non-creative industries.

When we define both the creative occupations and the creative industries, in this way, we can produce a summary 'map' of the productive potential of the creative labor force which, as mentioned, by researchers in this field (Higgs & Cunningham, 2008) designate a 'Trident.' The first row exhibits the size of the entire labor force engaged in creative production, and the distribution of creatively occupied laborers within that sphere. The second row exhibits the size of the non-creative industries, which are also employers of some creative occupations, and again reports the distribution of the creatively-occupied and non-creatively-occupied workers in those industries (Table 6.2).

---

[10]See for example DCMS. *Creative Industries Mapping Document 1998.* URL: webarchive.nationalarchives.gov.uk/+/; http://www.culture.gov.uk/reference_library/publications/4740.aspx; DCMS. *Creative Industries Mapping Document 2001.* URL: gov.uk/government/publications/ creative-industries-mapping-documents-2001; Bakhshi H., Davies J., Freeman A. The Geography of the UK's Creative and High-tech Economies. London: Nesta.Belfiore, 2015; Bakhshi H., Freeman A., Higgs P. A Dynamic Mapping of the Creative Industries in the UK. London: NESTA, 2013. URL: https://www.academia.edu/5538116/A_Dynamic_Mapping_of_the_UKs_Creative_Industries

TABLE 6.2 Employment in the Creative Industries

Industry	Occupation			Intensity (Creatively Occupied/Total Employment in the Industry)
	Creative Occupations	**Other Occupations**	**Total in this industry**	
Creative Industries	476,800	420,500	897,300	53%
Other Industries	600,900	27,622,800	28,223,700	2%
Total in this occupation	1,077,700	28,043,300	29,121,000	4%

Source: Creative Industries Economic Estimates Full Statistical Release, 8 December 2011, Page 28.

6.1.10 WHAT IS SPECIFICALLY CREATIVE LABOR?

Creative labor, in this framework, is a resource, not a branch of the division of labor but an aggregate of a group of specialized occupations. It is to be distinguished from a creative Industry, which is a branch of the division of labor that makes intensive use of creative labor. How do we define a creative occupation? The above analysis shows that it must be distinguished by its non-mechanical character, which is to say its non-repetitive character.

The modern discussion on mechanical and repetitive activity is actually quite old—it starts with turing and his famous "test"—but has been revived lately with the irruption of Artificial Intelligence (AI) into popular consciousness. In fact, by the 1970s, it was well underway; indeed, in 1968, I was already working with Donald Michie's Artificial Intelligence unit at Edinburgh University.

The reason is that computation itself is a mechanical process. It simply translates the achievements of the mechanical age from world of the physical to the world of the electronic. It achieves a simulacrum of intelligence essentially by speeding up the repetition to such an extent that it becomes possible, essentially, to imitate the thought processes of human reasoning, which are of a different and non-repetitive character, and which I term 'predicative' as opposed to the algorithmic methods of the computer.

This distinction is the basis for our definition of a creative occupation, which is specified in Peter Higg's 'grid' of the characteristics of a creative occupation. This 'grid' is not immutable, and part of our research should consist of revisiting it in the light of modern resources now becoming available, which include detailed statistical and qualitative accounts of the nature of modern work. However, our aim is to provide a comparative account of the mental productive capacity of a representative set of countries: it is therefore essential that whatever definition is adopted, it is applied universally (Table 6.3).

TABLE 6.3 The Creative Grid

Novel Process	Does the role most commonly solve a problem or achieve a goal, even one that has been established by others, in novel ways? Even if a well-defined process exists which can realize a solution, is creativity exhibited at many stages of that process?
Mechanization Resistant	The very fact that the defining feature of the creative industries is their use of a specialized labor force shows that the creative labor force clearly contributes something for which there is no mechanical substitute
Non-Repetitiveness or Non-Uniform Function	Does the transformation which the occupation effects likely vary each time it is created because of the interplay of factors, skills, creative impulse, and learning?
Creative Contribution to the Value Chain	Is the outcome of the occupation novel or creative irrespective of the context in which it is produced; one such context being the industry (and its standard classification) of the organizational unit that hosts or employs the role? For example, a musician working on a cruise ship (a transport industry) is still creative while a printer working within a bank is probably operating.
	printing technology and hence would be considered mechanistic and not creative.
Interpretation, Not Mere Transformation	Does the role do more than merely 'shift' the service or artefacts form or place or time? For instance, a draughtsperson/CAD technician takes an architect's series of 2D drawings and renders them into a 3D model of the building. While great skill and a degree of creative judgement are involved, arguably the bulk of the novel output is generated by the architect and not by the draughtsperson.

6.1.11 THE OUTPUTS OF CREATION: WHO BUYS CREATIVE PRODUCTS AND WHY?

> "You are a clever, generous man, Dymov," she would say, "but you have one very serious defect. You take absolutely no interest in art… That's awful!"

> "Why? Your friends don't know anything about science or medicine, but you don't hold it against them. I don't understand landscapes and operas, but the way I look at it is that if one lot of sensible people devote their lives to them, and another lot of sensible people pay immense sums for them, they must have a use. I don't understand them, but that's no reason to disbelieve them."
>
> —Anton Chekhov, *The Grasshopper,* 1891

6.1.12 SIMULATED BENEFITS

We cannot leave this subject without some reflection on the important question: what is the output of creative production? We have addressed this at greater length elsewhere (*see* for example Freeman, 2014), but some short explanatory remarks are in order here also.

We can approach the issue by interrogating what is commonly known as 'Baumol's law' which is said to show that productivity in services cannot be expanded because the quantity of a service cannot be altered by the very nature of a service activity. Baumol, who advances this thesis to advocate for public support for the arts, gives the example of an orchestra. It can only play a designated musical piece at a certain pace that is set by the composer and the conductor. It therefore appears nonsensical to raise the orchestra's productivity by having it play more pieces, or play them faster.

This, I term the 'Baumol fallacy' rather than the 'Baumol theorem' since a theorem is generally supposed to be a true proposition, but this thesis is in fact false, on two grounds: first, the measure of delivery of any service is the number of people that receive it, not the output of the producers. But secondly, the measure of a service is not independent of who produces it, or how well they do it. Its quality, in some sense to be defined by a mixture of empirical study, theoretical refinement, and indeed, social regulation of standards, also must be taken into account.

Both these points shed important light on the question 'what is the nature of a mental product?' because they highlight the point that the 'quantity' of any immaterial product cannot be supposed to reside in its physical properties alone. A fundamental revision of modes of thinking derived from the mechanical age is thus called for.

To take the first and simplest point, even if we suppose that the service delivered by an orchestra is uniform (that is, independent of the orchestra and how well it performs), its productivity is obviously higher if it reaches more people. Indeed, this is the reason for the transition from chamber music, performed as its name suggests to the small company of listeners in a private room, to Symphony Orchestras performing in large specialized venues.

But once we accept this point, we can see that any measure that raises the number of listeners, increases the orchestra's productivity. The earliest such development was the gramophone record, followed by broadcasting. These in turn raised the productivity of orchestras merely by growing the size of the audience, as electronic reproduction developed into a mass industry, and radios followed by televisions became ever cheaper and more widely available. As the digital age dawned, all these were one by one subsumed into the modern world wide web which can deliver live performances across the globe into either households or Cinemas and other venues in which the visual effect of the performance is at least as good as the original and in some respects better.

Now this brings us to the second point. The critical reader will have noticed, or even energetically remarked, that one cannot compare the experience of a high-quality orchestral performance with that of listening to a scratchy vinyl record, or indeed, that a live performance is an altogether different, and higher 'quality' experience than a recorded or broadcast one. But as soon as this point is made and gladly accepted, it must be recognized that all orchestral experiences are not equal – indeed, this is exactly why some orchestras are more sought-after than others – by and large, because they perform better.

In other words, the use-value of an orchestral performance is not identical for all orchestras and all types of performance. An orchestra can therefore indeed 'increase its productivity' without playing more or faster music. It can get a better performance venue with superior audio quality It can hire better musicians. It can practice more, which is an underrated means of raising productivity that is nevertheless fundamental to the life of any musician or body of musicians. It can, finally, gain recording contracts with recognized labels, secure richly-paid broadcast contracts, or simply release musical pieces on the Web.

In short, the Baumol 'theorem' is a fallacy, pure and simple. It is an assertion that does not accord with the evidence, based on a fallacious analogy between material and service production. It is for this reason that a specific theory of the use-value of a service is required, which, crucially, takes into account differences in the quality of what is consumed.

It may be though that this provides a license for any seller to establish an arbitrary value to a service determined simply by finding a small gaggle of rich consumers who will pay whatever the market will bear, and this is a real problem. It is raised, in particular, in the notion of 'simulated benefit' to which Professor Bodrunov and Professor Buzgalin rightly refer in their works, and place centrally in the critique of conventional economics, to which Noonomy is a response.

However, the purely negative criticism that something is wrong is an insufficient basis to establish what is right. If something is not correct in a theory, the job of the scientist is to propose something better, based first and foremost on the observation of the facts and secondly on a theory that accounts for the facts. Thus, Professor Buzgalin has provided the example of a Gucci bag costing $5,000. He does not actually state, however, what that bag should in fact be sold for – whether in the society of today, or in the Noonomic society of the future, or (if this is different) in the socialist society of the future.

The current, machinocratic answer is, in essence, that all bags are the same. There is no objective difference between them – they are all simply implementations of the social genus 'container of things.' If therefore the price of a Gucci bag differs from that of a sack, this is merely a reflection of some kind of Orwellian principle that 'all bags are equal, but some are more equal than others.'

The answer that could be given by an extended Noonomic audit is that the value of the bag, like the value of any other produced commodity, is given by the socially necessary labor time required to produce it. We would then have to investigate not merely the occupation and industrial location of creative workers, but the value chain that leads from their work to the final product. This is not at all impractical, and indeed, a proper labor accounting system is actually a further, necessary requirement of a Noonomic system of management. It is, however, well beyond the scope of the present proposal.

It moreover goes some way to dealing with the problem but does not solve it, because it contains the awkward phrase 'socially necessary.' In reality, the production of a Gucci bag does use up actual labor – that of the bag's makers, its artists, of Gucci's adroit team of designers, of the considerable labor of branding and marketing, and so on. This is real labor, not fake labor. It is performed by real people who spend real hours doing these things. And they are really paid for so doing. It is not some kind of con-trick in which the company keeps Gogol-like dead souls on the payroll who are already dead and buried, pretends to employ them, and pretends pay them, before presenting to society a bill of accounts padded out with fictitious costs.

One could of course argue that these real costs are not necessary, and Gucci should be forbidden to employ these workers, while the purchasers should be forbidden to obtain them, put things in them, or flaunt them in public.

But this is moral definition, not a definition derived from the reality of production relations in actually existing capitalist society. By Marx's definition, the labor of Gucci's designers is indeed socially necessary, because society uses it. Marx's definition, like that of Chekhov's Dymov in the opening quotation of this section, is strictly confined to ascertaining whether society actually uses the labor concerned and contains no element whatsoever of moral approbation.

It is sometimes highly paid, but generally speaking labor in the fashion industry (Freeman, 2011) – to which Gucci belongs – is no better paid than any other, and sometimes, except for a small number of high-flyers – a lot worse. Nor does Gucci charge an especially monopolistic price or a resource rent, as for example the oil industry, and many food industries do, when goods are in short supply. But we do not call these high prices simulated benefits. We call them monopoly rents.

Perhaps, then, Gucci maintains the high price by restricting the supply of its product? To some extent, this is true, in that the brand serves to create a scarcity value. But this does not resolve the problem either since it leads to the conclusion that every seller of artistic prints, who restricts the number of prints on offer by creating a sought-after 'special edition' is a monopolist creating a simulated benefit, and that the only true producers of artistic value are those who create unlimited quantities of every article that they put on the market.

The real substance of the argument is hence that the labor of Gucci's army of designers and marketers is not, in some sense 'socially necessary.' Very well, but who should determine what is necessary, and how? One answer is 'the state.' This is, to say the least, problematic. A more sophisticated answer is 'delegated associated bodies of producers' such as the Soviet Writers' Guild, or in the UK, the Society of Foot and Mouth

Artists, an excellent organization to which insufficient attention is paid. A solution proposed, interestingly, by Lenin in response to the cost of advertising, was to provide state funding in place of market allocation, so that a newspaper or journal with a certain number of readers, say 500, would be allocated $10,000 per year, whilst one with a higher circulation, say 50,000, would get more, but not on proportion – say $50,000 per year.

A third solution proposed by the art critic John Ruskin was to evaluate the labor of artists in proportion to their artistic merit, that is to treat it, in the terms defined by Ricardo and Marx, as 'more complex' labor and therefore productive of more value. Note that this is not a proposal for determining the wage of the artist, but for determining the value of her product. It leads to the conclusion, for example, that if the artist is employed by a capitalist entrepreneur, this entrepreneur is socially entitled to a higher profit than her or his rivals. Of course, a socially-minded such entrepreneur would then pay the artist more, and indeed a capitalistically-minded one might also, though empirical investigations into the fashion and art industry suggest this is not so – essentially because the supply of creative labor currently greatly exceeds the demand for it, which is cramped and restricted by the constant tendency of capitalism to restrict the right of the public to enjoy and consume creative and cultural products.

But we have now come full circle. The problem for Noonomy is to systematically raise the entitlement of the consumers to diversify access to the fruits of creative labor – the range of artistic and designed immaterial products that they enjoy. Is this to be done, then, by restricting the range of what 'we' (whoever 'we' are – the state, some mind of clerisy, or associations of producers and consumers) determine to be socially necessary? The problem here is that all regulation consists, to a greater or lesser degree, not just of enabling what is deemed good, but disabling what is deemed bad. Any proposal to abolish 'simulated benefits' carries with it the implication that we will deny the buyers of expensive Gucci bags the right to consume them, and deny the right of Gucci's army of designers the right to create them. Who will do this? How? On what lofty principles will this new and in all likelihood self-appointed clerisy dictate to the population what they are entitled to enjoy, and to its artists what they are entitled to produce?

The answer which I propose is the standard answer of science: we must first determine the facts, and then construct a theory that explains them. Why do consumers pay $5,000 for a bag, or for that matter, $500 for a ticket to attend a live performance by an acclaimed orchestra – not to mention

$5000,000 for a Damien Hirsch sculpture that consists of little more than an assembly of baubles with the artist's certificate of authenticity attached?

My answer is that it is because society is a class society. It is the existence of classes, above all classes with great differences in wealth and purchasing power, that gives rise to the seemingly extortionate prices of fripperies and baubles. Indeed, any attempt to solve the problem by regulating what is artistically acceptable, without addressing the root problem of social inequity, is doomed to failure because actually, it will elevate the price of elite products, creating black markets in the shape of the mania for Western-made blue jeans that prevailed in the late stages of Soviet society. It will migrate into other spheres such as the demand for luxury tourist resorts, expensive dwellings, yachts, and everything we today associate with mafia culture. But it will not go away until the class inequities that sustain it are either abolished by measures regulating income and wealth, or wither away by measures bring the great mass of the population up to the standards hitherto available only to a restricted portion of society.

Gucci bags sell for $5,000 because society contains privileged elites who pay for them. The question is then 'why do they pay for them'? The very brief explanation that I have given in other writings is that it is because they convey distinction – a concept fully developed by Bourdieu (1979) and others.

The value of creative products consists in the fact that they are different from each other; Henry Ford once enunciated the machinocratic principle that 'you can have any color you want as long as it is black.' The more technology evolves to include the creative labor of design in its products, the less acceptable is this answer and the more it enables its consumers to choose from a variety of products. What is the basis on which these choices are made? It is the dissolution of uniformity. Consumers of bags are no longer reduced to the users of gunny sacks, of mere objects used to carry other objects. Bags are distinguished, moreover, not merely by functionality (large, small, lots of pockets, different straps, and handles, etc.) but by appearance – color, pattern, contours, and so on. They thereby extend the capability of humans for varieties of experience, which is the obverse of the creative differentiation of varieties of creative production.

In particular, therefore, the demand for the variety of experiences arising from the expansion of creativity, which I term 'horizontal distinction' is entirely healthy and merely consists in the self-realization of the humans who enjoy them. It should be, I would argue, a major goal of Noonomy.

But in class societies, above all those containing a substantial but restricted layer of social-climbing middle classes, a different kind of distinction emerges which I term 'vertical distinction.' This arises from the need for the aspiring wealthy to demonstrate their superiority in order to obtain access to the means of actually becoming wealthy. Hierarchic social differentiation leaks out of every pore of middle-class consumption patterns: they live in 'nice places,' send their children to 'nice schools,' enjoy 'superior art,' read 'quality newspapers' (for which read 'socially-recognized nonsense' in place of 'socially disreputable nonsense') wear clothes that demonstrate 'superior taste,' and so on. The Gucci bag is just the tip of this vast iceberg composed of a multitude of crystallized 'little objects of desire,' to cite Bunuel, each of which is, to give it the correct name, a signifier of social status.

In conclusion, the object of research, much of which is already being conducted and is too vast to summarize, should be to identify the adverse effects not just of the use of "simulated benefits" but the absence of genuinely superior alternatives. The solution to the excessive price assigned to high-priced products that manifest design or creative inputs not widely available is to make such products widely available: to make creative, design labor an intrinsic and recognized part of all production. This, finally, brings us back to the fundamental requirement of a Noonomic system of workforce management—the massive expansion of creativity and its transformation of the creative potential that is currently only latent in most human production, into a universal human right by transforming the nature of production.

KEYWORDS

- **creative labor**
- **creative production**
- **Noonomy**
- **social cooperation**
- **standardization**
- **technological innovation**

REFERENCES

Amarel, S. (1996). On the mechanization of creative processes. *https://stacks.stanford.edu/file/druid:zv585py2131/zv585py2131.pdf* (accessed on 7th October 2024).

Bakhshi, H., Davies, J., & Freeman, A. (2015). *The geography of the UK's creative and high–tech economies*. London: Nesta.

Bakhshi, H., Freeman, A., & Higgs, P. (2013). *A dynamic mapping of the creative industries in the UK*. London: NESTA. https://www.academia.edu/5538116/A_Dynamic_Mapping_of_the_UKs_Creative_Industries (accessed on 7th October 2024).

Bell, D. (1976). *The coming of post-industrial society*. New York: Basic Books.

Bennet, E., & Belfiore, O. (2008). *The social impact of the arts*. Palgrave Macmillan.

Bodrunov, S. D. (2018). From ZOO to NOO: Man, society and production in the conditions of a new technological revolution. *The Questions of Philosophy*, *7*, 109–118. https://doi.org/10.31857/S004287440000232-0.

Bodrunov, S. D. (2023). *Noonomy: The trajectory of global transformation*. New York: Academic Studies Press.

Bourdieu, P. (1979). *Distinction: A social critique of the judgement of taste (La Distinction: Critique sociale du jugement)*.

Buzgalin, A. V. (2017a). Creative economy: Why and how private intellectual property can be limited. *Sociological Studies*, *8*, 20–30. https://doi.org/10.7868/S0132162517080037.

Buzgalin, A. V. (2017b). Creative economy: Private intellectual property or ownership by everybody of everything? *Sociological Studies*, *7*, 43–53. https://doi.org/10.7868/S0132162517070054.

Buzgalin, A. V., & Kolganov, A. I. (2013). The anatomy of twenty-first century exploitation: From traditional extraction of surplus value to exploitation of creative activity. *Science and Society*, *77*(4), 486–511.

Buzgalin, A. V., & Kolganov, A. I. (2016). Critical political economy: The 'market-centric' model of economic theory must remain in the past—Notes of the Post-Soviet School of Critical Marxism. *Cambridge Journal of Economics*, *40*(2), 575–598.

Carlyle, T. (1829). Signs of the times [The mechanical age]. *Edinburgh Review*, *xlix*, 439.

Cheng, E., Wang, G., & Zhu, K. (2019). *The creation of value by living labour: A normative and empirical study* (Vol. 2). New York and Beijing: Canut Press.

Darnall, T. (1994). *Artificial intelligence and creativity*. Springer-Science+Business Media.

Elliott, L., & Atkinson, D. (2007). *Fantasy island: Waking up to the incredible economic, political and social illusions of the Blair legacy*. London: Constable.

Freeman, A. (2002). *Creativity: London's core business*. London: GLA. https://ideas.repec.org/p/pra/mprapa/52548.html (accessed on 7th October 2024).

Freeman, A. (2011). *The value of fashion*. British Fashion Council.

Freeman, A. (2014). Twilight of the machinocrats: Creative industries, design, and the new future of human labour. In K. Van Der Pijl, B. Cohen, & M. Watson (Eds.), *The international political economy of production* (pp. 207–265). Cheltenham: Edward Elgar.

Freeman, A. (2021). Mental objects as a productive force: Towards a critique of noonomy. In S. D. Bodrunov (Ed.), *Anthology of noonomy: Fourth technological revolution and its economic, social and humanitarian consequences* (pp. 207–265). St. Petersburg: INID Publishing.

Higgs, P., & Cunningham, S. (2008). Creative industries mapping: Where have we come from and where are we going? *Creative Industries Journal*, *1*(1). https://www.tandfonline.com/doi/abs/10.1386/cij.1.1.7_1 (accessed on 7th October 2024).

Hofstadter, D. R. (1986). On the seeming paradox of mechanizing creativity. In *Metamagical themas* (pp. 525–546). London: Penguin.

Kuznets, S. (1965a). *Economic growth and structure: Selected essays*. New York: Norton.

Kuznets, S. (1965b). *Modern economic growth: Rate, structure, and spread*. New Haven: Yale University Press.

Kuznets, S. (1966). *Economic growth of nations: Total output and production structure*. Cambridge: Belknap Press of Harvard University Press.

Tusa, J. (2014). *Pain in the arts*. I.B. Tauris.

Vernadsky, V. (1945). The biosphere and the noösphere. *American Scientist*, *33*(1), 1–12. https://monoskop.org/images/5/59/Vernadsky_WI_1945_The_Biosphere_and_the_Noosphere.pdf (accessed on 7th October 2024).

CHAPTER 7

Crisis of Global Transition: Noonomy as a Possible Future

SAVVAS MICHAEL MATSAS

Professor, National University of Athens (Athens, Greece)

ABSTRACT

Following the still unresolved, spiraling global post-2008 crisis of capitalism, the configuration of the world is changing. A turbulent transition is underway but it seems to evolve lacking direction. The transition itself is in crisis. Mainstream economics fails to comprehend its nature and find a way out from a historic impasse. The dangers for the survival of humanity and of life itself on the planet are immediate and dramatic. They become obvious with the climate catastrophe and the ongoing global hybrid war waged by the collective imperialist West. The existential threat of an anthropological crisis of the social metabolism between nature and human society arises from the historical decline of global capitalism. The decline is not only the manifestation of the exhaustion of a dominant principle of social organization but also, as Hegel stressed, a negative expression of the rise of a new higher principle of organization of human relations. The concept of Noonomy advanced by Bodrunov for a transition beyond the homo economicus to a *homo culturalis* superseding the division between mental and manual labor by a knowledge-based material production could trace a possible outline of a future socialist society.

The tectonic shifts, following the spiraling global crisis from the 2008 world crash onwards, have changed and continue to dramatically change the configuration of the world. A turbulent transition is underway although

Global Transformations of the 21st Century: The Future of Humans, Markets, and Capital.
Sergey Bodrunov (Editor)

DOI: 10.1201/9781779644022-7

it seems to lack directionality, evolving without orientation, in darkness. At every moment of this transition, it clashes with new obstacles and contradictions, obstructing further movement forward as well as a return to the past, or even to just stagnate at the same stationary point. The transition itself is in crisis (Matsas, 2023).

New questions arise with every new, unexpected, world-shaking shock of the unresolved, ongoing crisis spiral – from the Global Financial crisis and Great Recession of 2008–2009, through the global pandemic shock in 2020 to the notorious *Zeitenwende,* the inflection point of history marked by the US-led NATO military conflagration with Russia over Ukraine.

After 40 years of finance capital globalization, is globalization ended? Has global economic interdependence been replaced by increasing fragmentation?

After the demise of the Soviet Union in 1991, the greatly exaggerated fake news of an "end of history" as well as the short-lived "uni-polar" moment of US world hegemony were the dominant *Zeitgeist*. It is ended now. How is the world today shaken by the violent convulsions of America's decline and fall from the hegemon's throne?

Is this decline affecting the US dollar as global reserve currency? Is it initiating a process of de-dollarization and the rise of rival international systems of exchange?

The growing geopolitical conflicts and socioeconomic rivalries between the US-led West with China and Russia drive irreconcilable clashing blocs not just into a "New Cold War" but towards World War III.

The absence of global cooperation urgently needed to resolve global problems, including the threat of a climate catastrophe and the nightmare of a nuclear Armageddon, brings humanity at the brink of the abyss. Is there a way out from the historic impasse and the impeding catastrophe? Is there an alternative road to human history? Can the contradictions of the real world be theoretically comprehended and resolved in practice?

7.1 CRISIS AND FAILURE OF MAINSTREAM ECONOMICS

During the first decades of the 21st century, it has become clear again and again that mainstream bourgeois economics, and Western think tanks have no answer to these pressing questions. This failure is openly acknowledged even by the most authoritative voices. Esther Duflo, a Nobel prize of economics stressed in 2017 that economists should give up on the big ideas and instead just solve problems like plumbers(!) "lay the pipes and fix the leaks." The current IMF deputy managing director Gita Gobinath has admitted in 2022 that mainstream economic theory "does not work in the real world."

The so-called "international rules-based liberal system" is breaking apart as the rulers themselves, the ruling classes of the West that imposed these "rules" to the rest of the world, had to admit, without being able to fix it. More the failure becomes obvious, more aggressive becomes the imposition by force of the "rules" of the failed "rules-based system."

In Hiroshima – where the proverbial criminals returned to the site of the crime – the 2023 G7 Summit turned into a War Council against Russia and China as well as a bad theater of the absurd.

The G7 Summit issued a long 19,000 words Statement covering any problem on the earth, a pretentious Manifesto of world governance when "the G7 must accept that it cannot run the world," as Martin Wolf, the chief analyst in Financial Times, has rightly stressed. "Today," writes Wolf in the same article, "hopes of a co-operative global economic order, which reached their zenith at the G20' s London Summit of April 2009 have evaporated. […] The earlier world of G7 domination is even more remote than that of G20 co-operation. Neither global co-operation nor western domination look feasible. What might follow? Alas, "division" might be one answer and "anarchy" another."

The dominant contradiction in today's world capitalist economy manifests itself in the form of two clashing polar impossibilities: from one side, the impossibility to dissolve arbitrarily global interdependence; from the other side, the impossibility of global cooperation in today's historic conditions, Powerful centrifugal forces threatening indeed with disintegration global interdependence. More the integration of the world economy is advanced by globalizing capital, more it clashes with its own external and internal limits driving to more disintegration – which, in its turn, at each step, it finds that there is no escape from world economic integration.

The implosion of finance capital globalization in 2008 – the "mother of all crises"– immensely intensified the dynamic of centrifugal and centripetal forces expressing the law of combined and uneven development according to Leon Trotsky, leading to the current impasse.

7.2 HISTORICAL DECLINE OF US AND GLOBAL CAPITALISM

> "*...[B]oth the "uni-polar" moment of the US and the economic dominance of the G7 are history,*" Martin Wolf again reminds us. "*True the latter is still the most powerful and cohesive economic bloc in the world. It continues, for example, to produce all the world's leading currencies. Yet between 2000 and 2023, its share in global output (at purchasing power) will have fallen from 44 to 30%, while that of all high-income countries will have fallen from 57 to 41%. Meanwhile, China's share will have risen from 7 to 19%. China is now an economic superpower.*"

It is an understatement. In reality, it is far greater the decline of the US in social economic, geoeconomic, and geopolitical terms in contrast with the powerful ascent of China to the position of the second strongest world economic power, ending in a few decades 100 years of humiliation by the predatory West.

The US debacle in Iraq and particularly its Waterloo in Afghanistan, reviving memories of its defeat in Vietnam in 1975, are clear symptoms of a historic decline that the military conflict in Ukraine cannot hide but rather emphasizes.

Zoltan Pozsar and Adam Tooze commenting on Pozsar's analysis stressed the following asymmetry in the world economy: the advanced capitalist economies in the Global North dominate global finance while the developing countries in the Global South, (where two-thirds of the world population live) produce about 60% of the world GDP. While Asia and China are the center of gravity of world manufacturing, North American and European firms still command the bulk of the profits embedded in global supply chains (Mona, 2022).

The "asymmetry" demonstrates clearly the dominance of the finance capital of the Global North on the manufacturing and productive activity in the Global South – or, to use V. I. Lenin's terms in his classical work on Imperialism the parasitism of Western capitalism dominating the world and the historical decay of capitalism itself in its highest and latest stage of historical development.

US capitalism is the highest point reached by global capitalism becoming its center- and the center of the current global crisis as well. US world hegemony, its rise in the 20th century and its decline, more and more obvious in the 21st century, has to be concretely situated within the world-historical context: the imperialist Age of protracted, nonlinear, and turbulent capitalist decline, of our transitional epoch.

Historically, even at the time of its undisputed supremacy, as in the aftermath of World War II, US capitalism "had to be base its equilibrium at home on a world equilibrium (Trotsky, 1926). For this reason, America needed always subordinate partners, particularly Europe and the imperialist Euro-Atlantic Alliance of NATO as well as an international system of dependent and vassal states all over the world.

The Bretton Woods settlement in 1944, including the fixed convertibility of the US dollar to gold as the cornerstone of a global monetary system, was based not only on the huge resources of US capitalism but also on its own structural need to rebuild Europe in ruins and Japan to avoid a social revolution in the European Continent, where fascism was defeated above all by the Soviet Red Army and the communist led partisans of the antifascist Resistance. Reconstruction and stabilization of capitalism in Europe was the basis to build the NATO military infrastructure for the "Cold War" against the Soviet Union and the so-called "communist threat."

The Keynesian edifice built on the Bretton Woods agreement did not eliminate the contradictions of capital accumulation. The fixed convertibility of the US national currency with gold as the universal equivalent was distorting the function of the law of value. Finally, the entire edifice together with the post-war monetary system collapsed, amid great international political upheavals. It followed the chaotic stagflation of the 1970s and, from the 1980s on-wards, the turn to neoliberalism and finance capital globalization leading, after a series of successive shocks to the 2008 world Crash and the global financial crisis.

The US dollar as the currency of the most powerful capitalist country kept its role as a global reserve currency. Nixon's Treasury Secretary John Connolly cynically declared to his Western foreign counterparts in G10 that the dollar is "our currency but your problem." On this "extraordinary privilege" to printing money for financing US deficits, the US dollar kept its centrality in international exchange relations, in what it was misnamed "Bretton Woods II," in the 1990s, particularly after the demise of the Soviet Union and the end of the Cold War. But the decline of a US economy more and more financialized and deindustrialized, in a globalized competitive environment, made it also the center of the implosion of finance globalization in 2008, with all its consequences and successive devastating shocks.

The escalation of the geopolitical crisis with NATO's eastward expansion, the military conflagration in Ukraine, the sanctions against Russia, above all the weaponization of the US dollar in the international financial system led to the upending of the fictitious "Bretton Woods II," the turn to de-dollarization, diversification of foreign exchange reserves in central banks, commodity-backed currencies in Asia, the search of alternative monetary systems of payments and financial swap lines, particularly by China, obviously by Russia, as well as by the BRICS and other countries in the Global South.

A "Bretton Woods III," with a weaponized dollar and within a rapidly worsening global geopolitical and geoeconomic crisis, is either impossible or it will turn into its opposite, a kind of an anti-Bretton Woods. An indication for this is the case for a 'New Washington Consensus,' advanced by the Biden Administration's National Security Adviser Jack Sullivan in his speech at Brookings Institution on April 27, 2023.

Replacing the previous neoliberal global 'Washington Consensus," the new one, according to Sullivan has to be based on "industrial policy" and "national security." The new "industrial policy" aims to revitalize US industry with subsidies of hundreds of billions of dollars, as it is already has been showed by the misnamed "Inflation Reduction Act" – provoking already the ire of the European Union recognizing it as a weapon of trade and economic warfare. Insofar the 'national security' of the (not so) "New Washington Consensus" is concerned its axis is aimed against China and Russia. In other words, it is serving the aims of US-led global "hybrid" war against what the renovated NATO doctrine calls" primary strategic rivals."

Already Western analysts have raised objections about the feasibility of such a strategy.

- First, the so-called "New Washington Consensus" cannot find a bipartisan consensus in Washington itself. The US political system is deeply split, and also the social body itself is divided transversely, in multiple directions, as it was manifested during the Trump Presidency, the George Floyd multiracial rebellion amid the pandemic disaster, the 2020 elections, and especially the fascist assault against the Capitol on January 6, 2021.
- Second, the European Union receives new blows by the huge subsidies provided to its US competitors by the Inflation Reduction Act, the new Industrial Policy and the policies for a so-called "green transition."
- Third, the Global South countries have been left out from the so-called "New Washington Consensus" or rather they become again its first victims under the crashing burden of their debt, energy, and food crises.

Under these conditions the "New Washington Consensus' does not contribute neither to a recovery of a world equilibrium nor to a stabilization at home. On the contrary, if implemented, it will destabilize further an already destabilized world environment, while it will deepen all splits and fractures at home. Inescapably a new round of social, economic, and political explosions will follow in Europe, in the Global South, and in the United States as well, while the global geopolitical crisis will escalate.

What is publicly acknowledged is that the "Biden Administration just declared the death of neoliberalism," with Sullivan's speech. It is rather a late official recognition, a post mortem, for the historic shipwreck of neoliberalism already took place in the 2008 Crash. The Global Financial Crisis followed by the Third Great Depression, demonstrated objectively that neoliberalism as an economic strategy of survival of the capitalist system after the collapse of post-war Keynesianism has failed as well. Both conflicting economic strategies advanced in the 20th century to avoid a repetition of the 1929 Crash and the Great Depression of the 1930s have failed, leaving a global social system objectively in a protracted, unresolved crisis and subjectively in a strategic impasse.

The US-led Western imperialist war drive is the desperate, futile, and catastrophic effort of the global system to overcome the gigantic obstacles blocking the road for its expanded reproduction. In these conditions, an international anti-imperialist, anti-war workers popular mobilization and struggle comes to the center to defeat the impeding global catastrophe. This is the primary strategic task for the international workers movement and, as in 1914, the strategic dividing line between Marxists and those social-imperialists claiming to be on the "Left."

7.3 BEYOND THE CRISIS OF TRANSITION: "FUTURE IS BOTH OPEN AND NECESSARY" (OLLMAN, 1993)

There is no exit from the labyrinth of the exploding contradictions of capitalism by remaining trapped within the same labyrinth, either by looking for another "world hegemon" within the labyrinth to replace the present Minotaur or to hope that there will emerge multiple "poles" while remaining within the deadly trap of the same declining global system of capital.

Not a dogma but a dialectical scientific method is needed to understand the ever-changing situation, to victoriously confront Minotaur and discover the orientation for an exit from the labyrinth before it is too late.

Humanity is in an epoch of a transition for more than a century. A transition is not a linear motion from one point to another but the unfolding of contradictions driving a nonlinear process, full of pitfalls, sudden turns and zigzags, leaps forward or regressions. When these contradictions enormously sharpen while remaining unresolved for a protracted period, they become extremely destructive, possibly leading to the "mutual ruin" of the conflicting class forces, as the Communist Manifesto had warned.

Global capitalism that brings now humanity to the brink of the abyss has at the same time created the material historic conditions for its overdue overcoming as well as its legendary gravedigger- the world proletariat.

Decline of an old formation does not solely manifests the exhaustion of the potential of a specific social organization to meet the growing needs. As Hegel pointed out (Hegel, 1940), it is also the negative appearance of an emerging new superior principle of social organization negating the previous one. Transition is not a process of partial alteration or a limited change of the already existing but the substantial transformation of it to its opposite, according to the deeper demands of the actual process of social life.

One most essential manifestation of this rising higher principle of social organization is the growing tendency of integration of science in the productive forces of social labor.

Karl Marx pays special attention on it and discusses this tendency, especially in the Manuscript of 1857–58/Grundrisse, in the famous a chapter on the General Intellect (Marx, 1973).

This chapter occupies an important place in recent theoretical debates, particularly during the height of finance globalization and the widespread introduction of rapidly developing high-tech Artificial Intelligence into social and economic life worldwide. Notions of "post-industrialism," a "4th technological revolution," or "immaterial labor" dominating and replacing material production were, and still are, debated across the entire spectrum—from the right to the left, from the elites at the World Economic Forum in Davos to the Italian school of *post-operaismo* and Antonio Negri, as well as the activists of the World Social Forum before the 2008 global financial crash.

Although confusion and disorientation prevail, the legendary "newborn baby" should not be rejected together with the "dirty waters of its delivery"!

The tendency of a growing integration of scientific knowledge in social production revealed by Marx in the *Grundrisse* has immensely developed in the 20th and 21st centuries, liberating unprecedented forces of creation as well as of destruction.

We have to keep in mind that the Marxian concept of the General Intellect has nothing to do with mechanical technological determinism. According to Marx this tendency reveals the potential and leads towards a new form of social metabolism between human society and nature. It drives a transition to a classless society where the separation of mental and manual labor as a source of alienation can be and should be superseded-aufgehoben. Thus, the rule of *homo economicus* in bourgeois modernity is challenged and ended.

Many thinkers internationally, in our epoch, under the relentless shocks of great scientific discoveries and their often-dramatic implications for humanity investigated the contradictory relations between technological progress, human life and human culture as a whole. They have stressed either the growing potential of science for emancipation or for catastrophe, or for both.

The problem raised by theoreticians in the West in the past century is quite known. On the contrary, less attention was paid or knowledge exists for the important contributions on this field made in other parts of the world.

Russia is a special case. Profound insights and research have been developed from the pre-revolutionary period to the early Soviet times, and even in investigations after the collapse of 1991, in post-Soviet Russia struggling with new problems in a changed world environment.

The Bodrum Seminar (August 30, 2023) gave us the opportunity to carefully think on the contribution by Sergey D. Bodrunov on the transition to *Noonomy* as a possible future of modern society.

Noonomy, a neologism (recalling Vladimir Vernadsky's development of a Noosphere beyond the limits of its basis, the biosphere) comes from the combination of two ancient Greek words: Νους (*Nous*, Intellect) and Νόμος (Nomos, law-governed regularity). The roots of the synthesis in Noonomy could be traced to Aristotelian philosophy. Its deeper understanding could be further acquired by the development of the concept of Intellect by the great medieval Arab Aristotelian philosophers. Particularly

Averroes (Ibn Rushd, 1126–1198), the Great Commentator of Aristotle from Cordoba in Andalus, advanced a re-elaboration of the Aristotelian concepts of *Νους Ποιητικός* (in Latin *Intellectus Agens, Active Intellect* and *Νους Υλικός* (in Latin *Intellectus Possibilis*, Material or Possible Intellect) (Averroes, 1998), extremely important to grasp the Marxian understanding of the General Concept in *Grundrisse.*

Bodrunov's Noonomy represents the vision of a society where technological progress permits a knowledge-based production focusing and driving the progress of human talent, capacities, and solidarity beyond the limits posed by today's social conditions of competition and private property relations. Joint production and social cooperation will have as a result diffusion of property and disappearance of private property, socialization, and improvement of all spheres of human life (healthcare, education, etc.) (Bodrunov, Desai, & Freeman, 2022).

The transition to Noonomy, according to Bodrunov, has as content and historical aim. the transition "through cognition to new needs and new values" (Bodrunov, Desai, & Freeman, 2022, pp. 101–115) from the homo economicus of the past and present to a homo culturalis in the future.

This insight of the character of the transition acquires special importance in understanding today's global transition, including its crisis.

In other occasions, we had explored the crisis of global transition. Our first approach was developed following the collapse of the Soviet Union (Matsas, 1992).

Later, we insisted that the global crisis in the early decades of the 21st century should not be reduced into an abstract economic crisis but to grasp its essential content as an anthropological crisis.

During the post-2008 world and euro-zone crisis, disastrously affecting Greece, we emphasized that the world is facing the death agony of homo economicus (Matsas, 2012).

Then, analyzing the socio-historical nature of the recent global pandemic shock of COVID-19, based on the scientific research presented by epidemiologists such as Wallace et al. (2020), we focused on the dramatic crisis of social metabolism between nature and human society under capital globalization (Matsas, 2020).

As the world is at crossroads and humanity faces the greatest challenges the alternative to a decayed system threatening to bury life on Earth under its ruins, is to theoretically comprehend the urgency and actively perform a tiger's leap, to use Walter Benjamin's expression, a leap of oppressed and dispossessed humanity to universal human emancipation, to the Realm of Freedom, through the Renaissance and victory of a renewed world Socialism.

KEYWORDS

- **capitalism**
- **crisis**
- **globalization**
- **Noonomy**
- **social metabolism**
- **transition**

REFERENCES

Averrois. (1998). *Mind and thought. Large commentary on volume III of Aristotle's De Anima.*

Bodrunov, S. D. (2022). *Anthology of noonomy: Fourth technological revolution and its economic, social and humanitarian consequences* (225 p.).

Bodrunov, S. D., Desai, R., & Freeman, A. (2022). *Beyond the global crisis: Noonomy, creativity, geopolitical economy*. St. Petersburg: S. Y. Witte INID Publishing.

Foster, J. B., & Suwandi, I. (2020). COVID-19 and catastrophe capitalism. *Monthly Review*, *72*(2).

Hegel, G. W. F. (1940). *Elements of the philosophy of right*. Tel-Gallimar Publishing.

Marx, K. (1973). *Grundrisse (Notes on economy)*. Penguin Books Publishing.

Matsas, S. M. (1992). *On the concept of the crisis of transition: A philosophical sketch.* Greece: Leon Publishers.

Matsas, S. M. (2012). *Greece in general*. Paris: Lignes.

Matsas, S. M. (2020a). *America zero hour*. Nea Prooptiki.

Matsas, S. M. (2020b). *Pandemic and crisis: The perfect storm*. Nea Prooptiki.

Matsas, S. M. (2023). Where is the world going? Report at the Assembly of the International Socialist Center 'Christian Rakovsky'.

Mona, A. (2022). Regime change. *Phenomenal World*. [Online]. URL: www.phenomenalworld.org/analysis/regimechange/ (accessed May 27, 2023).

Ollman, B. (1993). *Dialectical investigations*. Routledge.

Trotsky, L. (1926). Europe and America. *[Online]*. URL: https://www.marxists.org/archive/trotsky/1926/02/europe.htm (accessed May 26, 2023).

Wallace, R., Liebman, A., Chaves, L. F., & Rodrick, W. (2020). COVID-19 and circuits of capital. *Monthly Review*, *72*(1).

CHAPTER 8

The Transformation of the "Economic Man" into a "Cultural Man"

NATALIA YAKOVLEVA

Senior Researcher, Institute of Economics, Russian Academy of Sciences; Doctor of Economics; Associate Professor (Moscow, Russia)

ABSTRACT

In the light of the theory of noonomy, this chapter substantiates the need for priority development of human potential in the process of transformation of an "economic man" into a "cultural man." That person is becoming increasingly characterized by the creative content of work, the rejection of simulated needs, and the development of human qualities as the highest criterion of progress. This movement forces us to look at the goals and means of economic development in a new way and put the intensive development of a person and his potential as the main productive force of society and the values of social development in the center. It is shown that the category of "human potential" is qualitatively different from the narrow concept of "human capital." Using the example of the socio-humanitarian sphere, in particular, the scientific and educational sphere, it is considered how the goals and motives of activity in this area can change if they focus on a cultural person, a creative person. This chapter presents the main components of this process in the field of education.

Global Transformations of the 21st Century: The Future of Humans, Markets, and Capital.
Sergey Bodrunov (Editor)

DOI: 10.1201/9781779644022-8

8.1 INTRODUCTION

International scientific discussions have repeatedly expressed the view that humanity is undergoing profound technological and socio-economic transformations that affect both humans and society. The question arises: how exactly do technological and socio-economic transformations affect human beings, and to what extent are human beings, as active subjects of history, able to influence the transformation of society, the progress of technology, and the development of culture? This aspect is particularly crucial, as human development and the realization of individual potential are fundamental drivers of progress across all other spheres in contemporary society. This thesis has been consistently emphasized in the works of Russian and foreign social philosophers, political economists, and sociologists throughout the latter half of the 20th century. It still does today.

8.2 "ECONOMIC MAN" VS. "CULTURAL MAN," "HUMAN CAPITAL" VS. HUMAN POTENTIAL?

The history of societal development demonstrates the evolving role and significance of humans in the progress of social structures. In the modern world, from an economic—or more precisely, political-economic—perspective, the human has emerged as the primary productive force within society. This is primarily due to technological advances and changes in the content of labor. From a humanistic perspective, the human becomes the central value in social development, as they embody universal and cultural values and serve as the primary driver of social progress. All this determines the importance of formation and development of human potential.

The scientific initiatives of the Witte Institute for New Industrial Development introduced a comprehensive concept of the genesis of Noonomy[1]. This concept provides an innovative methodology, theoretical framework, and practical applications for addressing a variety of challenges, including

[1]"Noonomy (primary definition) – a non-economic approach to organizing economic activity, emphasizing the fulfillment of specific human needs based on rational criteria informed by the advancement of knowledge and culture." (Bodrunov, 2020, p. 175). "Noonomy (extended definition) refers to a non-economic social form of economic activity focused on meeting nooneeds, particularly those related to the development of human personality. This is achieved through the advancement of nooproduction—production that operates independently of direct human labor ('unmanned production') and manages the technosphere as an external domain where the human cognitive potential is realized" (ibid, p. 194).

the question of human progress as we transition from an economic to a post-economic space and time, where the traditional economic means of fulfilling human needs is supplanted by a post-economic approach[2].

It is crucial to note that within the theory of Noonomy, as well as in Marxism[3], and in some aspects of behavioral economics, as well as in various sociological theories (such as the concept of the socioeconomic man), there is a shared notion that in contemporary conditions, the "homo economicus" (rational economic man of the market system) is being replaced by a human with different qualities, values, and motivations. In particular, the principal works of Bodrunov, along with articles addressing human issues (Bodrunov, 2021, pp. 18–31; 2022, pp. 15–26), illustrate that a new set of values and motivations is supplanting the core characteristics of the "economic man"—such as the focus on maximizing utilitarian benefits, monetary income, and, in contemporary contexts, simulated benefits. This shift also reflects a change in attitude towards work, moving away from viewing it as a burden, and transitioning from purely competitive relationships among humans. This represents a shift towards a "cultural man," defined by the creative nature of labor, a rejection of simulated needs[4], and the development of human qualities as the ultimate measure of progress. This theoretical view allows us to take a new look at the goals and means of economic development, putting the issue of intensive development of human potential at the center of our attention[5].

We proceed from the fact that the category of *human potential* is qualitatively different from the category of "human capital." "The identification of these concepts is a product of the domination of capital as the main production relation of capitalism in all spheres of human existence"

[2]"Noonomy presupposes a different approach to evaluating needs—one based not on conventional rationality but on reason, or 'noo,' which emphasizes understanding the true consequences of economic decisions and the genuine value of the needs being met. Noonomy represents an organized way of life, a method of satisfying needs within a society where the 'light of reason' prevails, devoid of any connection to production or production relations, property, or ownership relations, and where the concept of an economy, as traditionally understood, no longer exists or is possible. This is a non-economic way of meeting needs" (ibid., p. 178).

[3]See, for example, the work of the representatives of the school of post-Soviet critical Marxism, Buzgalin and Kolganov (2019, pp. 18–28), as well as the work of E. Fromm (2020) et al.

[4]Simulative needs are illusory, fake needs imposed by the market system solely in pursuit of expanding sales volume.

[5]In Russian social science of the 21st century, the concept of "human potential" has gained renewed significance, and there is a growing body of research on this topic: (Verenikin, 2005; Verinikina, 2021; Ivanov, 2013; Soboleva, 2006).

(Buzgalin, Yakovleva, & Barashkova, 2023, p. 4–21). Since, in the context of the modern economy, wealth is predominantly manifested as capital, there is an appearance that human potential is invariably realized as "human capital." In our view, "human capital" is a distorted form[6] of human existence, and therefore also of the formation and utilization of human potential, within the context of capitalism. Recall that in economic practice and theory, within both classical political economy and modern economics, capital is interpreted as value that generates additional value through the process of profit creation. Whether or not we accept the Marxist theory of exploitation, this definition of capital allows us to view human capital as merely the capacity to enhance one's own value. It implies that a human is reduced to their ability to increase their market value by offering their skills and capabilities in various service markets.

Today, both foreign and Russian scholars frequently conduct theoretical and economic research on the role of individuals in societal economic development, often using the concept of *human capital* as a foundation. The introduction and widespread use of this concept, on one hand, acknowledges the human being as a crucial factor in contemporary economic development. On the other hand, it reflects a reduction of the complex nature of human existence in the economy to merely a factor of increasing monetary wealth. Human potential encompasses not only an individual's capacity for reproductive labor (labor force) but also their potential for creative activity and personal development. The importance of these aspects is expected to grow both in the modern economy and in the future (Buzgalin, 2022; Pavlov, 2022, pp. 88–97). Therefore, by *"human potential" we understand the whole range of creative abilities of a person, including the ability to work, personal qualities, as well as the ability to creative activity.*

[6]The meaning of this category of dialectical logic is that under certain social conditions, the nature of social processes is such that it objectively and inevitably manifests itself on the surface in the form of phenomena (these very transformed forms) that create an appearance of content different from the actual one. Examples of such forms are well-known from Karl Marx's Capital. This primarily refers to the phenomenon of commodity and money fetishism, which creates the illusion that commodities and money represent the highest values in human society and are the primary determinants of human life. The whole world of commodity relations proves that this is exactly so, although in fact money and commodities are nothing more than one of the specific historically limited forms of economic wealth" (Buzgalin, 2009, pp. 141–162).

8.3 THE SOCIO-HUMANITARIAN SPHERE: THE REALM FOR DEVELOPING A "CULTURAL MAN"

The reduction of human potential to the narrower concept of human capital is particularly evident in the socio-humanitarian sphere[7], especially in the field of science and education. As a result of the commercialization[8] of this sphere, the development of human potential (for scientists and educators) is increasingly being assessed through monetary valuation. This trend is evident in the growing commercialization of all aspects of the scientific and educational process—from setting goals and developing resources for organizations in this sector to evaluating the work of employees in science and education.

In turn, the recognition that the future belongs not to the "economic man" but to the "cultural man"—who possesses different values and motivations compared to "homo economicus"—allows us to reevaluate the goals and means of human progress. Thus, the inherent need for work in a creative person—stemming from the fact that creative work is intrinsically self-motivated—enables the orientation of scientific and educational organizations (and, consequently, their members) towards activities that are characterized by this self-motivation and can fulfill a genuine need. This does not imply that monetary motivation will vanish in the near future. However, it suggests that the material support for a creative man should, first, be adequate to enable comfortable engagement in creative activities, and second, should not become the primary objective. On one hand, emphasizing the "cultural man" or "creative man" in science and education aligns with the theory of Noonomy, which envisions a transformation from "economic man" to "cultural man." On the other hand, this perspective enables us to draw practical conclusions about potential directions for the development of the socio-humanitarian sphere.

In our research conducted over recent years (Yakovleva, 2022), we have demonstrated, using the example of higher education, the necessity

---

[7]By the socio-humanitarian sphere, we refer to the core of the social domain—including education, science, healthcare, and culture—where the formation and development of human potential occurs directly (author's note).

[8]Due to commercialization, the socio-humanitarian sphere is increasingly shifting towards converting the creation of public goods into the production of commercial services. This is characterized by mixed financing of the social sector (with a trend towards reduced public expenditure), the development of market-oriented models of relations (including competition between and within social sector organizations, and the evaluation of these organizations and their employees primarily by financial and economic criteria, etc.) (author's note). For more details on the commercialization of education, see (Yakovleva, 2020, pp. 412–421; Yakovleva, 2020, pp. 154–157; Yakovleva, 2021, pp. 146–157).

of shifting from commercialization to socialization[9] (and, in particular, de-commercialization) of this sector and education as a whole. The components of such a process may be:

- Formation of education as a universally accessible sphere in which humans are included throughout their life, which implies the dominance of the free form of consumption of relevant benefits with the support of the state;
- Formation of individuals with certain personal qualities, potential (mental, physical, creative), and social responsibility – as the main goal of the activity;
- Development of an egalitarian system of relations, which implies that society supports social groups with low incomes and other restrictions on access to quality benefits of education;
- Democratization of the system of relations in the sphere of education at all levels.

8.4 CONCLUSION

The theory of Noonomy, which offers an original methodological and theoretical foundation for characterizing the transformation of "economic man" into "cultural man," creates important prerequisites for solving a number of theoretical and practical problems of human progress. As demonstrated in this chapter, using the example of the socio-humanitarian sphere—particularly in education—Noonomy provides a framework for addressing these challenges.

KEYWORDS

- **cultural man**
- **economic man**
- **human potential**
- **Noonomy**
- **socialization**
- **creative labor**

---

[9]Socialization of the social sphere is, firstly, its orientation on the development of human potential of each member of society, rather than on profit-making by this sphere; secondly, predominantly public provision of the social sphere (author's note). For more details on the socialization of education and the development of its socially oriented model, see (27, pp. 183–197; 29, pp. 110–115).

REFERENCES

Ariely, D. (2010). *The upside of irrationality: The unexpected benefits of defying logic*. Moscow: Mann, Ivanov and Ferber Publishing.

Batishhev, G. S. (1969). The active essence of a person as a philosophical principle. In I. F. Balakina & B. T. Grigoryan (Eds.), *The problem of human in modern philosophy* (432 p.). Moscow: Nauka Publishing.

Bekker, G. S. (2003). *Human behavior: An economic approach (Selected works on economic theory)*. Moscow: HSE Publishing.

Benhabib, J., & Spiegel, M. (1994). The role of human capital in economic development: Evidence from aggregate cross-country data. *Journal of Monetary Economics*, *34*, 143–173.

Bodrunov, S. D. (2020). *Noonomy: The trajectory of global transformation*. Moscow: S. Y. Witte INID; Kul'turnaya revolyutsiya Publishing.

Bodrunov, S. D. (2021). From homo economicus to homo sapiens. *Questions of Philosophy*, *12*, 18–31.

Bodrunov, S. D. (2022). From economic interests to noovalues. *Questions of Philosophy*, *7*, 15–26.

Bodrunov, S. D. (Ed.). (2019). *Foresight "Russia": The future of technology, economy and man* (Vols. 1, 2, 3). Proceedings of the Plenary Congress SPEC-PSE-2019. St. Petersburg: S. Y. Witte INID Publishing.

Bodrunov, S. D. (Ed.). (2021). *The genesis of noonomy: STP, diffusion of ownership, socialization of society, solidarism* (Vols. 1, 2, 3). Proceedings of the Plenary Congress SPEC-PSE-2020. Moscow: S. Y. Witte Publishing.

Buzgalin, A. V. (2009). Practice and truth: Dialectics as a method of removing obsessions in the world of transformed forms. *Philosophy of Economy*, *4*, 141–162.

Buzgalin, A. V. (2022). A creative person in the economy of the future. *Economic Revival of Russia*, *1*(71), 48–57.

Buzgalin, A. V., Yakovleva, N. G., & Barashkova, O. V. (2023). Person, human potential, "human capital" in the mirror of political economy (Article 1). *Russian Economic Journal*, *1*, 4–21.

Buzgalin, A., & Kolganov, A. (2019). Transformations of the social structure of late capitalism: From the proletariat and the bourgeoisie to the proletariat and the creative class? *Sociological Studies*, *1*, 18–28.

Changli, I. I. (1973). *Labor: Sociological aspects of research theory and methodology*. Moscow: Nauka Publishing.

Fromm, E. (2020). *On being human. Karl Marx's concept of man*. Moscow: AST Publishing.

Il'enkov, E. V. (1991). *Philosophy and culture*. Moscow: Politizdat Publishing.

Ivanov, O. I. (2013). *Human potential (Formation, development, use)*. IRES RAS, SPbGU. St. Petersburg: Skifia-Print.

Kapelyushnikov, R. I. (2008). A note on domestic human capital (Preprint). Moscow: HSE Publishing.

Kosolapov, R. I. (1984). *Where does personality begin* (2nd ed.). Moscow: Politizdat Publishing.

Pavlov, M. Y. (2022). Definition of creative activity: An economic approach. *Philosophy of Economy*, *5*(143), 88–97.

Peccei, A. (1977). *The human quality*. New York: Pergamon Press.

Schultz, T. W. (1971). *Investment in human capital: The role of education and of research*. New York: Free Press.

Soboleva, I. V. (2006). *Reproduction of human potential: Theory, methodology, priority areas* (Ph.D. Dissertation). IE RAS, Moscow.

Spengler, J. J. (1977). Adam Smith on human capital. *American Economic Review*, *16*(1), 32–36.

Thaler, R., & Sunstein, C. (2017). *Nudge: Improving decisions about health, wealth, and happiness*. Moscow: Mann, Ivanov i Ferber Publishing.

Verenikin, A. O. (2005). *Human potential of economic development* (Ph.D. Dissertation). M. V. Lomonosov Moscow State University, Moscow.

Verinikin, A. O., & Verinikina, A. Y. (2021). *Human potential: The fetishism of capitalist relations*. Moscow: RUSAINS Publishing.

Yakovleva, N. G. (2020a). Socio-economic grounds for commercialization and financialization of education. In *Production, science and education in the era of transformations: Russia in a [De]globalizing world (PNO-VI)* (pp. 412–421). Moscow: Association "Non-profit partnership for assistance in scientific research to S. Y. Witte INID."

Yakovleva, N. G. (2020b). Marketization of education in the era of capitalism: Towards the formulation of the problem. In *Competitiveness and development of socio-economic systems: Proceedings of the 4th International Scientific Conference in memory of Academician A. I. Tatarkin* (pp. 154–157). Chelyabinsk: Chelyabinsk State University.

Yakovleva, N. G. (2021a). Transformations of education in the economy of post-Soviet Russia: The relationship of digitalization and marketization. *Problems in Political Economy*, *2*, 146–157.

Yakovleva, N. G. (2021b). Contradictions of transformation and the genesis of a socially-oriented model of education (political and economic approach). *Problems in Political Economy*, *3*, 183–197.

Yakovleva, N. G. (2022). *Contradictions of the transformation of education in the modern economy (Political and economic approach)* (Ph.D. Dissertation). M. V. Lomonosov Moscow State University, Moscow.

Yakovleva, N. G. (2022). What sprouts of post-capitalism are capable of ensuring the progress of human potential and technological modernization? *Social Studies*, *9*, 110–115.

CHAPTER 9

Re-Thinking the Institutions and Practices for a Better Future World

AL CAMPBELL

Emeritus Professor, Department of Economics, University of Utah (Salt Lake City, USA)

ABSTRACT

Looking at the title, many readers might assume that this work is intended as a contribution to the ongoing vital social debate about the various functional aspects of a future ideal society. However, this is not the main purpose of the chapter. Its primary goal is methodological, questioning how to determine which policies and practices are best for the desired future of society. First, there is a discussion of what is generally needed as a basis for deciding whether certain institutions and practices of a future society will be desirable, and, in particular, whether they will be more desirable than those currently existing when compared to alternative concepts of that aspect of the future society. Secondly, two underappreciated views of Marx and Engels on human nature are discussed, which became important foundations for their goals of creating the desired post-capitalist society. Thirdly, a partial list of the most commonly cited goals of socialism is provided as a basis for rethinking old ideas about the most appropriate institutions and practices for the desired future society. Finally, after establishing a transparent framework, the author reconsiders the six standard doctrines of 20th-century socialism about the institutions and practices of the desired future society.

Before beginning the first section of this brief work, it will be useful to avoid confusion to make clear how I will use four of the ten words in the title, "future better world" and "re-thinking."

Global Transformations of the 21st Century: The Future of Humans, Markets, and Capital.
Sergey Bodrunov (Editor)

DOI: 10.1201/9781779644022-9

Within today's society, there are many very different general concepts of what institutions and practices would be appropriate for a better future society, and then beyond that, there are a plethora of differences of details among the multitude of variations of each general concept. A very broad division among concepts of a future society that is better than today's is between remaining within capitalism and fixing the institutions and practices that one does not like ("reformism"), and moving beyond (or "transcending") capitalism to some new system of social production and related social organization ("revolution," be the change peaceful or violent) that does not have the objectionable problems. In this work, I will use the concept of "future society" to be a synonym for a subset of anti-capitalist alternatives, a "socialist society." Among the many varieties of concepts of socialist societies, the one discussed here is most strongly influenced by the ideas of Marx and Engels.

However, given the breadth and strength of the ongoing influence of the views of Marx and Engels on ideas about a socialist future, it is important to be clear that there is no single "Marxist concept of socialism." Rather, even with the restricting adjectives "socialist" and "Marxist," there remains an abundance of different concepts of the future that consider themselves, more or less, "Marxist socialist."

Too often in articles discussing thinking about concepts of the future, the word "re-thinking" is used to mean "finding new alternatives because the old concepts are not acceptable." In this work, to the contrary, the word "re-thinking" will be used in accordance with its dictionary definition, "thinking again about some concept." Concretely, what this means is that it will not be assumed a priori that the institutions and practices being reconsidered are inappropriate for a desirable future society. Rather, to the contrary, the result of re-thinking the ideas on a well-formulated basis could be that they are not valid, or that they are valid, or that they were valid but the world has changed and so they are no longer valid now, or many other possible conclusions.

9.1 THE GENERAL NATURE OF WHAT IS NECESSARY AS A BASIS TO BE ABLE TO DECIDE THAT SOME CONCEPT OF A FUTURE SOCIETY WOULD BE DESIRABLE

This first section is very short because the point it makes is obvious, if one stops to consider it. What is logically necessary for rethinking concepts of the future, for reconsidering old ideas about what institutions and social practices are preferable ("good") for a desirable future society, is to know what you want those institutions and practices to achieve. The measuring stick for deciding which institutions and practices among different possibilities are considered appropriate or inappropriate for a desirable future society can only be how they do or do not support and promote some specified goals for the future society. This idea is tersely captured by the folksy English aphorism:

"You can't pick what road you want if you don't know where you want to go."

Having established that to execute the purpose of this work of re-thinking institutions and practices appropriate for the future it is *necessary* to know[1] the goals for the society so that one can consider if the institutions and practices support and promote those goals or not, this work next needs to specify those goals.

9.2 TWO CONCEPTS ABOUT THE NATURE OF HUMANS THAT ARE ESSENTIAL UNDERPINNINGS FOR MARX AND ENGELS' GOALS OF SOCIALISM

Section 9.1 established that to reevaluate previous ideas about appropriate institutions and practices for a better future, we need to first determine what goals we want the future society to support and promote. Section 9.3 will indicate the goals of the concept of socialism that will be used to do this, which this author asserts are consistent with the concept of socialism of Marx and Engels. As background to Section 9.3, this section will argue that many of those goals of socialism strongly reflect two fundamental views of the nature of humans. These views on the nature of humans are often insufficiently reflected on when discussing rethinking the institutions and practices of future societies. This section will give five quotes by Marx and Engels (from scores of other possible ones), both because they clearly indicate these two views about the nature of humans, and also to support the previous claim that the considerations on rethinking the

[1]It is intellectually best to explicitly specify the goals, because that makes for the clearest comparisons. Too often in practice the specification of the goals that underly the comparisons being made are only implicitly indicated by the arguments made in the process of the comparison of which alternatives are better or worse.

institutions and practices given in this work are "strongly influenced by the ideas of Marx and Engels."

The first of the two views about human nature that are strongly reflected in many of the goals for a future society to be presented in what follows is that humans by their very nature are a collective and social species. Because of the importance of the false attack by defenders of capitalism that socialism involves the subordination of the interests of the individual to the interests of the collective, this same first point will also be discussed in terms the nature of human individuality. The second of the two views to be discussed is the importance of *human consciousness* to the nature of being human.

9.2.1 HUMANS BY THEIR NATURE ARE A COLLECTIVE AND SOCIAL SPECIES

Throughout human history, individual humans have always conducted their lives as differentiated parts of a human society, demonstrating that existing collectively and socially is part of the nature of being human. A society is organized "in a human way" if the participation in society by each person supports and promotes their potential development. All the class societies throughout history, which were not organized "in a human way," did not adequately support and promote the human development of the subaltern.[2] Such a class society then presents itself to these subaltern individuals as being opposed to their manifesting their nature as humans by participating in and collectively directing human society. In 1844, Marx wrote:

> Since human nature is the true community of men, by manifesting their nature men create, produce, the human community, the social entity, which is no abstract universal power opposed to the single individual, but is the essential nature of each individual, his own activity, his own life, his own spirit, his own wealth. ... as long as man does not recognize himself as man, and therefore has not organized the world in a human way, this community appears in the form of estrangement, because its subject, man, is a being estranged from himself (emphasis in the original) (Marx, 1844a).

[2]To be more precise, restricting the collective self-determination or self-governance (to be discussed more below) of the subaltern definitionally involves blocking at least these dimensions of their potential human development.

Since the time of the Russian Revolution and before, defenders of capitalism have attacked socialist concepts of a better world as requiring the subordination of the interests and rights of the individual to the interests and rights of society. The refutation of this false assertion rests on the rejection of the false understanding of the relation of the individual to society that is the necessary background assumption for capitalist economic theory (neoclassical economics), capitalist political theory (liberalism[3]), and beyond (and including) those, the false broad capitalist ideological worldview. Given the strength of the false capitalist view of the individual in the developed capitalist countries since WWII and particularly since the rise of neoliberalism, including its penetration into the ideas of many advocates of transcending capitalism to build a more human future, re-thinking the practices and institutions for a better future world requires careful consideration of the nature of human individuality and the relation of the individual to the society that it is part of.

Looking again at the preceding quote from Marx, one sees that the issue of the collective and social nature of humans and the issue of the relation of the nature of the individual human to the society that it is part of are actually just two ways of referring to, or naming, the same issue. Given the significant contribution of the false capitalist concept of the individual to the ongoing defense of capitalism, it will be useful to discuss again the issue of the collective and social nature of humans, now in its equivalent form of the nature of the human individual and its relation to the society that it is part of.

As will be indicated in the next section, the actions of "emancipation" or "liberation," or the conditions of "liberty" or "freedom" resulting from those actions, have been longstanding goals of socialism for all humans. Socialism's well-known goal of transcending capitalism comes from these goals, together with an understanding of the operation of capitalism as presenting barriers to the achievement of these goals for all individuals. Hence contrary to the false assertion that socialism subordinates the interests of the individual to anything, we see that it is exactly a concern for the interests of all individuals that is the driving force behind the fundamental socialist project of transcending capitalism.

But the misrepresentation of socialism's goals by capitalist ideology as requiring the subordination of the interests of the individual to the interests

[3]"Liberalism" in the political theory sense of Locke and Montesquieu, not the American English political meaning of the word.

of society goes far deeper than just simply asserting the misrepresentation. Capitalist ideology's formulation of its false assertion rests on a false understanding of the nature of human individuals in society. From the 1800s onward socialist theory has understood this.

The capitalist view of the human individual that underlies their economic and political theories, and more generally its capitalist worldview, is often appropriately referred to by its critics as that of the "isolated individual." With no consideration of the social processes (thus yielding the "isolated individual") by which individuals develop what at some point in their lives they consider their interests, this view starts with an individual simply having inherent interests. The capitalist view's concern is then to consider what "rights" it should provide to this individual to protect and promote its interests against the interests of any other person, or the interests expressed by any collection of people, which is its simplistic view of what society is. From this lack of social process, the theory then tends to yield individuals that, even beyond being "isolated," become conflictual (including between the individual and society), as soon as there are limited resources that all individuals want unrestricted access to in pursuit of fulfilling their interests. The capitalist theory then quickly bogs down because guaranteeing one person's rights to some things negates another person's rights to those things. Their theory of the individual then falls back to prattling about what are "inherent rights," "natural rights," "God-given rights," and so on, in their inherently conflictual misunderstanding of the human individual.

Conversely, the starting point of the socialist understanding of the individual is the collective and social nature of humans, and thus the development of the individuality of each human through a process of the interaction of their biological capabilities with the social process of their lives. The creation of one's individuality through the social process of an individual's life includes the obvious ways that one's individuality is shaped by parents and teachers and interactions with thousands of other members of society, both individually and through society's institutions. But beyond that, it is further modified by the way one learns to view oneself, and the rest of the world beyond oneself, through the worldview of the particular subculture of the particular culture that one lives in. Contrary to the claims of the defenders of capitalism, socialism indeed starts its whole project of social transformation from a concern with individuals and what capitalism does to them, but those individuals are correctly understood as "social individuals" ("social beings" in the following quote), rather than "isolated individuals."

Marx indicated his understanding of this inherent connection of the very nature of an individual and the society that they are part of (which connections we will see in the next section are built into many of socialism's well-known goals for the future) at the very beginning of his and Engels' oeuvre.

Above all, we must avoid postulating "society" again as an abstraction vis-à-vis the individual. The individual is the social being. His manifestations of life—even if they may not appear in the direct form of communal manifestations of life carried out in association with others—are therefore an expression and confirmation of social life. Man's individual and species-life are not different, however much—and this is inevitable—the mode of existence of the individual is a more particular or more general mode of the life of the species, or the life of the species is a more particular or more general individual life (Marx, 1844, p. 299).

He returned to emphasize the fundamental importance of this and to express it even more clearly in a number of places in his mature writings, including in his best-known draft of his masterwork Capital.

The point is rather that private interest is itself already a socially determined interest and can be attained only within the conditions laid down by society and with the means provided by society and is therefore tied to the reproduction of these conditions and means. It is the interest of private persons; but its content, as well as the form and means of its realization, are given by social conditions that are independent of them all (Marx, 1857, p. 94).

9.2.2 THE IMPORTANCE OF HUMAN CONSCIOUSNESS TO THE NATURE OF BEING HUMAN

The second understanding of human nature that underpins many goals of socialism is that a *differentia specifica* of humans is their possession of capabilities that no other animals have. Two of these capabilities, central to the concept of socialism and its goals, are that humans have the ability to imagine future states of reality different from the existing reality, and the capability to employ rational thought, or reason, to decide how to realize the desired future state. This understanding of human nature holds that beyond the ability to act, which is common to most animals, humans can act consciously. These characteristics could be called "specifically human" or, as in the second quote to follow, "truly human."

Although the direct topic in the following work from 1867 is human labor, this early modern socialist discussion brings out clearly this understanding of the nature of humans that underpins many of the goals of socialism:

We are not now dealing with those primitive instinctive forms of labor that remind us of the mere animal. ... We presuppose labor in a form that stamps it as exclusively human. A spider conducts operations that resemble those of a weaver, and a bee puts to shame many an architect in the construction of her cells. But what distinguishes the worst architect from the best of bees is this, that the architect raises his structure in imagination before he erects it in reality. At the end of every labor process, we get a result that already existed in the imagination of the laborer at its commencement. He not only effects a change of form in the material on which he works, but he also realizes a purpose of his own ... (Marx, 1867, p. 188).

A use of the words "human consciousness," which is closely related to the meaning of the inherent unique characteristic of humans as "awareness" discussed in the last quote but somewhat different, is as follows. Here, "to be conscious" roughly means "to be aware of and to understand." This usage indicates a condition that may or may not pertain to a specific human at a specific time, as opposed to the previous usage to indicate an inherent characteristic of all humans, an aspect of the nature of being human. However, the meaning of this usage is nevertheless strongly related to the earlier one. All human decisions and activities influence the operation of all human societies, but humans often do not know in advance what the effect will be. Then, similar to human consciousness in the previous usage distinguishing the work of humans from that of other animals, in this different meaning the words indicate being aware of and understanding how human societies operate. When one wants a specific social result, one "in the main and to a constantly growing measure" (see following quote) knows what actions will generate the desired result.

Engels laid out this use of the term "consciousness" as a goal of a human-centered future society that would replace capitalism, which it had throughout the works of Marx and Engels, in one place as follows:

> ... The struggle for individual existence disappears. ... The whole sphere of the conditions of life which environ man, and which have hitherto

> ruled man, now comes under the dominion and control of man, who for the first time becomes the real, conscious lord of nature, because he has now become master of his own social organization.
>
> ... Only from that time will man himself, with full consciousness, make his own history—only from that time will the social causes set in motion by him have, in the main and in a constantly growing measure, the results intended by him. It is humanity's leap from the kingdom of necessity to the kingdom of freedom. (emphasis added to highlight its addressing of the issue of consciousness) (Engels, 1878, p. 270).

9.3 THE GOALS OF A FUTURE BETTER WORLD

The methodological argument of this work on how to re-think the institutions and practices proposed for a future better world is that one needs to consider if they can be used to first create and subsequently operate a socialist society, which requires that they not contradict any of socialism's goals. To make this argument does not require a comprehensive (or even a "very extensive") list of the goals of socialism to be made.

The first two parts of this section will list 17 of the most frequently proposed goals for a future society that is better than capitalism: first nine "broad and abstract" goals, and then eight "specific and concrete" goals. They are listed as illustrations of the nature of the goals of socialism, to make the discussion that will follow less abstract. The third part of this section will then briefly consider an equivalent way of describing the purpose of a future better society in terms of a single goal instead of a plethora, an approach that many authors use sometimes because it can be pedagogically useful to do so.

9.3.1 NINE "BROAD AND ABSTRACT" GOALS

The quote by Engels above includes three of the plethora of broad goals for a future better world that were expressed frequently in the 19th and 20th centuries (and still are today). The first was that humanity (collectively) "makes its own history." This is tied to the concept of human nature that was considered above, that humans have the potential to act consciously, and from that gain increased collective self-determination over their own existence, and hence (over time) of their own history. Two other common expressions of this same goal for a more human future society are that "people collectively become the subjects of history as opposed to beings its objects," and that "people collectively become the masters of their own fate." The second goal for a better future society indicated in the quote by Engels is a part of the first. For humans to collectively be the masters of their own fate, one necessary aspect is that they "become the master of [their] own social organization."[4] Other roughly equivalent expressions commonly used to indicate this goal of socialism are "self-determination," "self-governance," or "socialist democracy."[5] The third commonly indicated goal of socialism in the quote is "freedom," often expressed roughly equivalently as "liberty," or by the act that freedom or liberty is obtained by, "self-emancipation."

Even though when discussing the goals of a future better society socialists for convenience often drop the prefix "self" when indicating self-emancipation, it is nevertheless important to underline the centrality of that prefix "self" to the concept of socialism. It is a profound misunderstanding of socialism to see it as only concerned with material well-being and material equality. Cows have great material well-being in that the drive for maximum profits under capitalism means that they get all the food they want, immediate care for any medical problems, housing suitable to protect their health and wellbeing, and maybe even air conditioning for milk cows to boost their production if that passes a cost-benefit analysis. But "being materially taken care of" by Plato's philosopher kings

[4]There are other things that contribute to humans being the collective masters of their existence besides being masters of their own social organizations. For example, when humans learned to cultivate plants and breed animals, that reduced the dependence of their existence on natural climatic conditions and thereby increased their control over that aspect of their existence. There are goals for a future better world generalizing this type of increased human mastery over human existence, but providing a comprehensive or even very lengthy listing of the goals socialism is not necessary or even useful for the purpose of this work.

[5]A politically important aspect of the ideology of capitalism since its inception has been its claim to not only be consistent with democracy, but to promote it. It is a historical fact that many capitalist societies have allowed broader social participation in social decision making than earlier class societies. But even in theory, "capitalist democracy" (also called "bourgeois democracy") is extremely limited by specifically recognizing the priority of the property rights to the means of production (necessary for the exploitation that is at the heart of the capitalist system) over the democratic rights of the entire society whenever they come into conflict. In practice, capitalist societies do not require capitalist democracy to operate, and those capitalist societies that do generally operate with capitalist democracy limit or abandon it whenever a threat to the continuation of the capitalist nature of the society makes it useful to do so. Socialists often say that a goal of their society is "democracy", but when they do so they are using the word "democracy" as a shorthand expression for "socialist democracy". Capitalist democracy which prioritizes property rights in the means of production to society's collective democratic rights is not a goal of socialism.

is inconsistent with the socialist goal of collective self-determination that we have just considered, of becoming the collective masters of all the institutions that we are part of. Developing our potential to be more fully human definitionally (by the socialist understanding of the nature of being human discussed above) requires our being the collective active agents in determining everything about our social existence, since such collective self-determination is, as argued, something specifically human.

Starting with these three, a list follows of nine of the most common "broad and abstract" goals from the discussions over the 19th, 20th, and 21st centuries, as illustrations of this type of goal for a future better society.

- i. Humans collectively make their own history (they are collectively the subjects of their own history; they are collectively the masters of their own fate);
- ii. Society collectively controls all its own institutions (social self-determination; social self-governance; socialist democracy);
- iii. (Self) emancipation or liberation (or equivalently indicating this goal by the results of these actions, freedom, or liberty);
- iv. Solidarity;
- v. Equality;
- vi. Elimination of exploitation;
- vii. Elimination of all types of oppression;
- viii. Meaningful work (work that supports and develops the workers' potential humanity);
- ix. Environmental and ecological sustainability.

9.3.2 EIGHT "SPECIFIC AND CONCRETE" GOALS

The category of "goals for a future better society" also includes another plethora of goals which are of a different kind from those just considered: "specific and concrete" goals. These have been formulated in particular in the political fight against capitalism over the last two centuries. Again, as illustrations of the multitude of goals of this type, a list of eight follows:

- i. Adequate healthy food;
- ii. Universal free healthcare;
- iii. Universal free education;
- iv. Humanly dignified housing;

v. Adequate time not working (adequate vacations, and limits on working hours per day and working days per week);
vi. Comprehensive social security;
vii. Abolition of child labor;
viii. Social control of production.

9.3.3 "THE GOAL" OF SOCIALISM

If one is to re-think the institutions and practices of a future better world in terms of whether they support and promote its multiple goals, a theoretical issue immediately presents itself. What if one proposed institution or policy supports and promotes one goal of socialism better than does some alternative considered institution or policy, but supports and promotes some other goal(s) less? From their origins humans have implicitly resolved such issues in practice by evaluating the value to them of the trade-off of the gain for the one goal to the loss for the other.[6] If one instead were to have a single goal for a future better society, then of course this problem with a multi-dimensional goal would not arise as choices could be made according to which of the alternative alternatives supports and promotes that single goal better.

This author, and many other advocates of socialism over the last two centuries, often find it convenient and pedagogically useful in some given situations to talk about socialism as having a single goal, human development. Marx and Engles often referred to human development as the goal of their concept of socialism. To randomly pick just two illustrations, in 1845 Marx and Engels wrote about the goal of "… 'free activity,' which is for the communists the creative manifestation of life arising from the free development of all abilities of the [whole person] …," while two years later Engles wrote about the goal of "… the all-round development of the abilities of all the members of society …."

Changing the form of expressing the purpose of a future better society from "goals" to "a goal" of course cannot change at all the nature of the real-world problem that this work is concerned with, choosing between

[6]For an extended discussion of this issue see "Evaluating Against a Multi-Dimensional Economic Goal: A Sustainable and Prosperous Socialism" by this author, *International Journal of Cuban Studies*, 13(1), 2021, 105–126. The *IJCS* is open source and so this article is can be accessed at www.scienceopen.com/hosted-document?doi=10.13169/intejcubastud.13.1.0105.

alternative institutions and practices. Having put a label of "human development" on the overall goal immediately poses the question of what one means by human development. For example, in line with, and stemming from, their differing concepts of the nature of humans discussed above, capitalist ideology and socialist ideology have very different concepts of what constitutes human development. The socialist concept of human development that has been developed over the last two centuries is in fact best reflected by the multitude of goals socialists have established for a desired future better society. Human development for socialists involves humans developing more collective conscious control over their institutions and their existence, and doing this is supported by working in ways that develops these; being fed, educated, sheltered, and medically cared for at levels that support and promote the development by humans of their potential capabilities; and so on. A way to present the relation between a single goal such as human development and the plethora of goals in the "many goals" understanding of a future better society is to consider the plethora of goals as subgoals of the central goal: they indeed are also goals of socialism, but now are not simply posited as goals, but rather achieve their status as subgoals from their contributions to the support and promotion of the single posited goal.

While "human development" is a common choice when presenting socialism as having a single goal as the label for that goal,[7] there are many other labels for the same concept that different people use at different times when indicating the goal of a desired better future society, and of course it is the concept and not its label that is important. One is "development of humans' potential." The "development of humans' capabilities" (or equivalently "abilities") is a way of formulating this idea that has become well-known and is associated in particular with the work of Martha Nussbaum and Amartya Sen.[8] Bringing in the historical element, Fromm wrote "the history of mankind is a history of the increasing development of man" (Fromm, 1961, p. 43).[9] There are many other ways one can label the same concept of human development. The expression that this author finds the most beautiful as well as rich (but slightly too long to gener-

[7]Note that for both "human development" and the various possible alternative ways of expressing the same concept, in line with the discussion above on the nature of humans, this concept is to be understood as simultaneously referring to both individual humans and the human collective (society).

[8]Who, note, are explicitly not Marxist socialists.

[9]Fromm expands this statement of the goal of Marx and Engels' socialism in his section "Marx's Concept of Socialism" (1961, 58–69).

ally be convenient) is by Paulo Freire: "man's ontological and historical vocation to become more fully human" (Freire, 1992, p. 40). Like Fromm, he indicates that this goal has always been a goal of humanity, but he goes on to also argue that it is ontological: humans have the goal of human development because they are humans, and the goal of human development is part of what being human is.

9.4 ILLUSTRATIONS: RE-THINKING SIX EXAMPLES OF 20th CENTURY "DOGMAS" ON THE SOCIALIST FUTURE

The penultimate section of this chapter will now use the methodology developed to reconsider six "dogmas" of 20th century socialism about a desired better society intended to replace capitalism. As indicated previously, the purpose of this work is to indicate an explicit methodology for the process that has always occurred in practice by some advocates of a post-capitalist future of re-thinking what have become the dominant ideas among socialists at a given time about a desired future better world. While the six institutions and practices reconsidered are among those most discussed by socialists today, in the context of this work they are being presented only as illustrations of the application of the methodology. And while there were always some people who considered themselves to be socialists who had alternative ideas to the dogmas being reconsidered here, these were the dominant ideas on these issues among socialists in the 20th century. Some of the ideas being reconsidered were near hegemonic among socialists while others were dominant but less so. In all cases the word "dogma" is being used only according to its dictionary definition to indicate that the idea was dominant, with no negative implications. As indicated in the introduction, the re-thinking methodology needs to be free of any a priori assumptions about the appropriateness or inappropriateness of these dogmas prior to their being reconsidered.

The following six dogmas from 20th century socialism will be reconsidered:

1. Socialist production needs to be socially planned.
2. While the state may well be necessary in the transition from capitalism to socialism to fight the remnants of the capitalist class and its supporters, by the nature of "a state" it will "wither away" under a socialist mode of production.

3. The use of any type of markets for any purpose violates the goals of socialism and is therefore incompatible with a mode of production being socialists. "Socialism with markets" is an oxymoron. This is equivalent to the dogma that all planning and the execution of that planning in a socialist mode of production must be done by some system of material balances.
4. "Market Socialism" in the sense that the term came to be used in academia in the Global North in the last part of the 20th century is not a form of socialism.
5. The use of some circuits of capitalist accumulation in some subordinate parts of the economy (in particular not in "the commanding heights") is incompatible with a socialist mode of production.
6. The use of some circuits of capitalist accumulation in some subordinate parts of the economy (in particular not in "the commanding heights") is incompatible with any process of constructing a socialist mode of production.

   i. The validity of the dogma that socialist production must be socially planned (for short – "a planned economy") for a mode of production to be socialist follows almost immediately from socialism's goals that humans collectively make their own history, or that society collectively controls all its own institutions (or that it has social self-governance, or socialist democracy in all aspects of society, including the economy). Note that capitalism fails to meet these socialist goals (and therefore needs to be transcended to achieve socialism) in two ways. First, as opposed to all society collectively controlling its institutions and the functioning of its society, the decisions and actions of some subsection of society (the capitalist class) very disproportionally influence how society functions.[10] Beyond that, while the decisions and actions of the capitalists are the primary determinants of the functioning of the society, they cannot said to be controlling their society or its institutions in the socialist sense of the word discussed above of developed humans controlling their institutions and society consciously, a priori deciding what results they want

[10]Note that to violate these socialist goals it is not necessary that part of society has *no* influence on how society functions, only that the ruling class has *disproportionate* power. In general, the desires and associated efforts of the subaltern will have some influence, but the ruling class rules.

to achieve and then making decisions and taking actions that approximately yield the desired results. The lack of understanding by capitalists and their agents of any except quite general relations between economic goals they might want to achieve and the actions that would yield those is a well-known fundamental characteristic of capitalism.

ii. The dogma that the state will wither away under a socialist mode of production violates the goals of socialism. If society is to collectively control its own history and all its own institutions, this cannot be done by a process of all members of society together discussing, deciding on, and then implementing those decisions for every social issue. One could say that trying to do so would not leave enough time for the development of any other dimensions of human development than collective self-governance, but the time constraint is actually more severe than that. There simply is nowhere near enough time in our 24-hour days to make all social decisions through a process of everyone participating in meetings of the entire society in which everyone directly presents their thoughts on every social issue. And even beyond this time constraint that makes it impossible, to think that only in this way could society "protect the interests of every individual" is to fall into the misunderstanding of individuals as isolated and therefore with inherently antagonistic interests, which only they can be the agent to defend since all other agents have antagonistic interests. The socialist understanding of humans as inherently collective and social, and the goal of society to support and promote the human development of everyone, changes the role of the state from "protecting as best as possible all the conflicting individual interests," to determining the existing collective interests of the social individuals and enacting corresponding policies in order to best promote human development for all. There is nothing inherent to the task of determining these social interests that requires the direct participation of every member of society in resolving every social issue. To the contrary, our social nature means exactly that subsets of society which society decides are appropriate for the social tasks that they are being selected for can work to determine the social interest involved, and then to build institutions and enact polices to promote them. These subsets are the "active agents of collective society for the social issues in their mandate." And these institutions with the determined practices created to determine and promote society's collective interests are "the socialist state."

Confusing this issue is that Marx and Engles repeatedly argued that the most fundamental characteristic of a state in all class societies is its role of oppressing the subaltern in the interests of the ruling class. That role of the state will not be present in a socialist society. Hence if the transition from capitalism to socialism, and thus the extinction of the capitalist class, takes place over some extended period of time, one could say that the fundamental role of the capitalist state will "wither away." But Marx and Engels were very clear that other aspects of the capitalist state would not disappear (although basically all of them would need to be transformed to greater or lesser extents). Marx stated this very explicitly.

In this sense it is possible to speak of "the present-day state"[11], in contrast with the future, in which its present root, bourgeois society, will have died off.

The question then arises: what transformation will the state undergo in a communist society? In other words, what social functions will remain in existence there that are analogous to present state functions? (Marx, 1875, p. 95).

Confusing the issue still more, Marx and Engles at times used the phrase "the withering away of the state" to indicate part of the process of the transition from capitalism to socialism. But taking into consideration their clearly stated position that socialist society will have a state, together with their understanding that the fundamental characteristic a capitalist state is its oppression of the subaltern, looking at all the places in their work where they used the expressions similar to "withering

[11]By putting this in quotes Marx indicates that he is referring to what he has just talked about in his preceding two sentences, that which is common to all capitalist states notwithstanding what he calls their "motley diversity of form".

away of the state" it is clear that in these they used the word "state" to mean "capitalist state," or "state as we know it."

iii. The dogma that using any type of markets for any purpose is incompatible with a mode of production being socialist is false. There is no goal of socialism that using markets necessarily violates. One common procedure that leads to this false dogma is to postulate markets and planning as opposites. If that were correct, then by the correctness of the first dogma considered in this section, this dogma would also be correct. But there is no reason that one cannot have markets operate as a tool for some economic interchanges within a socially planned economy. Even under capitalism planning and markets are not opposite. Capitalist economies were extensively planned during WWII in the US and the United Kingdom, and French Indicative Planning (especially the first Plan) involved extensive planning for capitalism. Going beyond these exceptional examples of the possibility of planning in capitalist economies, all government intervention into capitalist economies is planning. This is true for industrial policies, trade policies, infrastructure policies, and many more. The capitalist world today is actually shifting from the ideology of neoliberalism to an ideology in which they openly call for more planning of various types of government intervention and industrial policies (and protective trade barriers) in the interests of its country's capital. The correct observation that these types of planning differ "in degree" from the system of material balance planning developed in the USSR that spread in modified forms to many other countries that broke from capitalism in the 20th century is correct, but there was also different degrees and different forms of planning even among all these.[12] The issue of the form and degree of planning is a separate issue from the issue of if using some markets as economic tools to carry out some economic tasks in an economy immediately precludes the possibility of having a

[12]Note also that these economies all had markets even in the core sectors of the economy that had no capitalist circuits of capital. These markets operated differently in some ways from markets in capitalist circuits of capital, a point that will be expanded on in what follows, but there were markets in these material balances planned economies.

planned economy. "Socialism with markets" is a theoretically possible subgroup of the large variety of different possible socialist modes of production.[13]

iv. The dogma that "Market Socialism," in the senses the term came to be used in academia in the Global North since the last part of the 20th century, is not a form of socialism is correct. There are actually two different concepts of "Market Socialism" that have become popular in academia in the Global North since late in the 20th century.[14] The best-known advocate of the first is Alec Nove. Here the "commanding heights" of the economy would continue to be planned in something resembling the material balance way of the USSR, while secondary parts of the economy, and particularly parts where such planning did not appear to be either efficient or effective, would allow capitalist relations of production. This already existed in some countries to differing degrees above all in parts of agriculture, with Poland being a particular example of this. This planning concept was then extended both to more parts of the economy "of secondary importance" that were not performing well under some particular variation of a material balances planning system, and in addition allow some of this capitalist production to be organized as larger capitalist enterprises (even if not the behemoths that exist today in capitalist countries). The government would regulate the private sector and also build a safety net much as is done under social democratic capitalism. Such a system would, of course, be incompatible with the socialist goal indicated above of ending all exploitation, of ending the appropriation of the products of their labor from some people by other people.

---

[13]Analogous to the large variety of different capitalist modes of production that have existed over the course of capitalism's history and that exist in the world today, there is a large variety of different ways that a mode of production could be organized and be socialist.

[14]Discussions of "Market Socialism" sometimes have a few paragraphs talking about the system of Lange, Lerner, and Dickinson from the 1930s. That system operates entirely differently from either of the two systems of Market Socialism that will be discussed here. While one could at least reasonably argue that their system would not be inconsistent with the goals of socialism presented, it will not be discussed here because there is no discussion anywhere in the world today of implementing that sort of system.

Two particularly well-known advocates of the other concept of Market Socialism, popular in academia in the Global North, are Pranab Bardhan and John Roemer. In this model, each enterprise pursues maximum profits according to the normal rules of competition between enterprises, similar to capitalism. However, all profits are distributed among the workers of the enterprise. Hence, as a collective version of a self-employed worker in a capitalist economy, no one appropriates the products of others' labor, and there is no exploitation (a cooperative enterprise-based version of Marx's petty commodity production from Chapters 1 to 3 of *Capital*, before capital and exploitation were introduced to his theoretical presentation). This concept of Market Socialism, however, violates the correct dogma of having a socially planned economy, and thus undermines the goal of society having conscious control of all its institutions. It is often falsely asserted that markets necessarily lead to a lack of planning (this argument is countered in Dogma 3 above), and therefore to "economic anarchy." What is true, however, is that production determined by uncoordinated enterprises in competition, without overall social planning, does result in such "economic anarchy" and a lack of control by society over its institutions.

The list of advocates for some form of Market Socialism in both of these senses is extensive. For a collection of relatively short introductory pieces on various interpretations by about 15 different authors, including Nove and Roemer, see *Why Market Socialism* (Belkin & Roosevelt, 1994).

"Socialism with markets" and "Market Socialism," notwithstanding how often many people confuse or conflate the two, are entirely different things.

v. The use of some circuits of capitalist accumulation in some subordinate parts of the economy (in particular not in "the commanding heights") is incompatible with a socialist mode of production. This dogma is actually a restatement of one of the two forms of Market Socialism discussed in dogma 4, and so it has already been evaluated as correct. It is repeated here in this form to underline the difference of this correct dogma from the one that will follow, which despite sharing so many words in its statement with this dogma and therefore too often being used interchangeably with it in practice, it is entirely different. This distinction is extremely important to make in the world today because this correct dogma is too often brought up to oppose the very large social processes going on today in China, in Vietnam, and as of recently, in Cuba, to which in fact it does not apply. The following dogma does apply to those social processes, but will be argued to be false.

vi. The use of some circuits of capitalist accumulation in some subordinate parts of the economy (in particular not in "the commanding heights") is incompatible with any process constructing a socialist mode of production. This dogma is false. It has been argued in the last point that, in line with the goals of socialism, once constructed a socialist mode of production cannot have any capitalist relations of production in it. That does not logically preclude the use of capitalist relations of production in some parts of the economy during the process of constructing a socialist mode of production.

This is a specific example of the well-known issue of the relation between the means and the ends of any desired process. They are of course related in the sense that the means used will always affect one's ability to achieve the desired ends. But it is also well-known that it is not in general logically excluded that one can use means that are themselves incompatible with the ends to achieve those ends. If one does that, however, it remains logically necessary in order to actually finish the process of achieving the ends to, at some point stop, using those incompatible means.

To make this logical argument concrete, consider the relation of war to peace. It is very broadly socially accepted that sometimes to achieve the end of peace it is necessary to use the incompatible means of fighting a war.[15] If one has a process where that is true, it nevertheless remains definitionally true that to actually achieve the goal of peace one must stop fighting the war. Similarly, within the Marxist tradition itself it is

---

[15]The fact that in the world today arguably the majority of governments fighting wars claim that they are fighting for the goal of peace when in reality they are driven by some other goal, does not negate the logical point being made.

widely (and in this author's view correctly) argued that in a transition from capitalism to socialism where the latter has the goal of ending all class oppression, it is necessary to use the means of oppressing the still existing capitalists in the form of legally taking from them the powers that they still have, because of their economic power in the transitional economy. Again, definitionally the use of those means of oppression that are being posited to help the process of constructing socialism will have to stop at some point before one can claim to have constructed a socialist mode of production.[16]

China, Vietnam, and Cuba are all engaged in (significantly different) social processes with the goal of building some sort of socialism. Given the theoretical point that the future is not determined, and beyond that, the political point that powerful forces in the world are fighting against those countries achieving that goal, it is not certain if they will succeed. All three countries have made capitalist relations of production legal in some parts of their economy (Cuba doing so in 2021). The logical point of this section, that using some capitalist relations of production in a desired transition to socialism does not preclude the desired goal of a society free from those relations, of course says nothing about if the use of such relations in a given process at a given time will actually support and promote the goal, make it more difficult to achieve, or even contribute to the failure to achieve it. Supporters of a future better world then need to study these three real-world experiments to see how the allowed capitalist relations under the given restrictions on them in the three very different countries in fact do affect their transitions to socialism. In the first place, the processes need to be continually monitored to evaluate if the capitalist relations of production, in the given way they are employed, are actually contributing to the construction of a post-capitalist society, or if to the contrary they are harming or blocking that goal. Second, if they are found to be more beneficial than harmful as they are intended to be, these processes must still be studied to deepen our understanding of what dangers to the process of constructing socialism they nevertheless do generate, and from that what policies can be adopted to address those dangers. And finally, these processes must be watched as the process of constructing a better society

[16]Also, since a socialist mode of production will have no classes and hence no remnants of the capitalist class. the cause for maintaining the oppression in the process of building socialism will have disappeared.

advances, to see how in the future these capitalist relations of production will be transcended to complete the desired construction of socialism.

One final word on the use of "socialist mode of production" in this point and throughout this chapter concerning the socialist goal of eliminating all exploitation. All socialists refer to the US as a capitalist economy. In actual fact, some production occurs in the US by forms of production that are best characterized as feudal. One example is the survival of legal sharecropping and of some modes of production that in practice amount to sharecropping, albeit both in minimal amounts. Much larger amounts of production by sharecropping or sharecropping-like production occur in many countries of the Global South that socialists classify as capitalist due to the dominance of that form of production there. In the US some production occurs that is best characterized as slavery, in particular among some groups of current immigrants. Again, this happens to a much greater degree in a number of countries of the Global South that socialists classify as capitalist. In this sense, it would be possible to talk of a country achieving the construction of a socialist mode of production that still has some "pre-socialist production" in some parts of the economy. Analogous to what socialists do today referring to countries as capitalist, I would expect in the future they will refer to countries where the strongly dominant part of the economy is conducted by socialist relations of production as socialist economies, even if they involve some niches of remaining capitalist relations of production. Throughout this work, however, including for the six illustrations of the methodology for evaluation of past dogmas, I have used the term "socialist mode of production" (or "socialist production" or "socialist economy") to indicate a system in which all production occurs through socialist relations of production.

9.5 CONCLUSION

The point of this work is to discuss a logically meaningful methodology for re-thinking existing ideas about appropriate institutions and practices for a future better world. There are two parts to the re-thinking methodology proposed. First one must know what goals one wants the institutions and practices to achieve, or at least to support and promote. Then one must analyze if the institutions and practices being re-evaluated will in fact support and promote those goals, and if they will do so better or worse than some alternative existing or posed institutions and practices. With this as its purpose, this work then discusses some of the most commonly presented goals that it asserts inform the Marxist vision of socialism, including two discussions on two not-well-recognized assumptions about the nature of humans that serve as underpinnings for many of socialism's goals.

Finally, as illustrations of the methodology discussed, six major dogmas from 20th century socialism are reconsidered on the basis of whether they are consistent with the goals of socialism. The six dogmas and their concluded validity based on this re-evaluation follow:

1. Socialist production must be socially planned. Valid.
2. The state will wither away under a socialist mode of production. False.
3. "Market Socialism," in the sense the term came to be used in academia in the Global North since the last part of the 20th century, is not a form of socialism. Valid.
4. Using any type of markets for any purpose is incompatible with a mode of production being socialist. False.
5. The use of some circuits of capitalist accumulation in some subordinate parts of the economy is incompatible with a socialist mode of production. Valid.
6. The use of some circuits of capitalist accumulation in some subordinate parts of the economy is incompatible with any process constructing a socialist mode of production. False.

KEYWORDS

- **capitalism**
- **human nature**
- **Marxism**
- **socialism**
- **institutions**
- **social transformation**

REFERENCES

Belkin, D., & Roosevelt, F. (1994). *Why market socialism?* Armonk, New York: M. E. Sharpe.
Engels, F. (1984). Principles of communism. In *Karl Marx Frederick Engels collected works* (Vol. 6, pp. 341–357). Moscow: Progress Publishing.
Engels, F. (1987). *Anti-Dühring*. In *Karl Marx Frederick Engels collected works* (Vol. 25, pp. 1–309). Moscow: Progress Publishing.
Freire, P. (1992). *Pedagogy of the oppressed*. New York: Continuum.
Fromm, E. (1961). *Marx's concept of man*. New York: Frederick Ungar.
Marx, K. (1867). *Capital* (Vol. I). In *Karl Marx Frederick Engels collected works* (Vol. 35). New York: International Publishing.
Marx, K. (1975a). Comments on James Mill. In *Karl Marx Frederick Engels collected works* (Vol. 3, pp. 211–229). Moscow: Progress Publishing.
Marx, K. (1975b). Economic and philosophical manuscripts of 1844. In *Karl Marx Frederick Engels collected works* (Vol. 3, pp. 229–346). Moscow: Progress Publishing.
Marx, K. (1986). *Grundrisse*. In *Karl Marx Frederick Engels collected works* (Vol. 28). Moscow: Progress Publishing.
Marx, K. (1996). Critique of the Gotha Programme. In *Karl Marx Frederick Engels collected works* (Vol. 24, pp. 75–99). Moscow: Progress Publishing.
Marx, K., & Engels, F. (1976). *The German ideology*. In *Karl Marx Frederick Engels collected works* (Vol. 5, pp. 19–539). New York: International Publishing.

CHAPTER 10

Noonomy: A Platform for Strategic Development (Regional Aspect)

SVETLANA PYANKOVA

Professor, Department of Regional and Municipal Economics and Management, Ural State University of Economics; Doctor of Economics (Yekaterinburg, Russia)

ABSTRACT

The chapter focuses on the need for uniformity in methodological approaches to regional strategic planning. Recommendations from both Russian and foreign scientists on improving the quality of strategic planning have been compiled. A new methodology for enhancing regional strategic planning is proposed, with the aim of increasing efficiency, optimizing the management of strategic territorial development, and improving the socio-economic conditions and quality of life for the population. The core platform of the proposed methodology reflects key approaches from the theory of noonomy, which advocates for a shift towards increased knowledge intensity in production processes, while simultaneously reducing material, capital, energy, and resource intensity. The author suggests categorizing regional strategies into three areas: low, medium, and high "knowledge-intensive components."

10.1 INTRODUCTION

Currently, in the context of global transformations, geopolitical turbulence, and an unstable global socio-economic situation, close attention is being paid to the unification of methodological approaches for effective strategic

Global Transformations of the 21st Century: The Future of Humans, Markets, and Capital.
Sergey Bodrunov (Editor)

DOI: 10.1201/9781779644022-10

planning of territories (regions, municipalities) and the search for new vectors and pathways for the country's development. In their monograph, Bodrunov and Glazyev note that "the increasing level of uncertainty in the world… has led mankind to the need to actively search for ways and means to bring stability and ensure the sustainability of progressive socio-economic development" (Bodrunov & Glazyev, 2023, p. 9).

At the same time, as Kolganov (2021, p. 266) notes: "there is a clear lack of scientific concepts that would give us guidelines for making ambitious strategic decisions." Dmitriev also emphasizes that "it is necessary to develop a unified methodology for all stages of strategic planning" (Dmitriev, 2009). In this regard, the task of improving the efficiency of territorial strategic development becomes increasingly relevant.

In the article "*Noonomy in Monotowns: Forming Trends of a New Industrial System and Improving Institutional Capacity*," the author addresses the issue of enhancing the quality of strategic planning for single-industry towns (Pyankova, 2022). This chapter presents methodological approaches for more effective regional strategic planning.

10.2 RESEARCH METHODOLOGY

At present, strategic documents should be formed in accordance with structural normative documents regulating the procedure for forming strategic planning documents[1,2] as well as conceptual approaches to creating a strategy for the development of territories, developed by scientists and researchers (Animitsa et al., 2010, p. 56; Zinchuk, 2012, p. 101; Pulyaevskaya & Khristoforov, 2021, p. 70).

As stated in the monographs of Kvint: "Strategic approach to national development implies, first of all, the use of strategic ideas…" (Kvint, 2015); "In order to develop a strategy, as a first step it is necessary to orient national development projects on a long-term perspective…" (Kvint, 2020, p. 48)

In order to improve the quality of planning, scientists recommend a number of measures, in particular: "joint participation in the development of documents of the administration, business, and population" (Kosarev

[1]"On Strategic Planning in the Russian Federation" (as amended and supplemented) (2014). Federal Law No. 172-FZ. URL: https://base.garant.ru/70684666/.

[2]"On the Fundamentals of Strategic Planning in the Russian Federation" (2009). RF Presidential Decree No. 536. URL: https://crystalbook.ru/wp-content/uploads/2021/06/Указ-президента-Об-основах-стратегического-планирования-в-рф.pdf.

and Vetrov, 2010, p. 37; Ilyina, 2012); "development of normative-legal frameworks for regulating social standards"; and "linking the systems of strategic and territorial planning among themselves and with the budget process" (Dmitriev, 2009).

The methodology of improving strategic planning of regions is introduced for your consideration, aiming at increasing the efficiency and optimizing the process of managing the strategic development of territories, improving the socio-economic situation and the quality of life of the population.

The author believes that the key platform of the new methodology of strategic planning of regions should be the main approaches of the theory of noonomy, the founder of which is Doctor of Economics, Professor Bodrunov: the trends towards the growth of knowledge-intensity of production, the growth of knowledge intensity of its processes, the reduction of material/capital/energy/resource intensity, etc. (Bodrunov, 2018a, p. 57, 2018b, p. 72).

I should note that the monograph authored by Kvint and Bodrunov, has already presented the unification of unique concepts of strategy and the theory of noonomy (Kvint & Bodrunov, 2023, p.152). Sharing the authors' views, a universal methodology of strategic planning of regions is proposed.

As Bodrunov pointed out in his monograph: "For the transition to new stages of technological progress it is necessary to master more and more new knowledge and find ways of their technological application. It is the most knowledge-intensive technologies that become the most advanced" (Bodrunov, 2020, p. 65). It should be noted that under "knowledge intensity of material production technologies," Bodrunov, Desai, and Freeman indicate "the process that critically synthesizes the achievements of industrial and information economy..." (Bodrunov et al., 2022, p. 30). The main features of "knowledge-intensive production" are presented in Bodrunov's Noonomy (Bodrunov, 2018b, p. 70).

In one of his reports, Bodrunov (2021, p. 58) noted the main aspects of technology progress, among which are: "transformation of knowledge into the main source, resource and result of socio-economic development" and "transit to the sixth technological mode and so on." It is these aspects of technology progress that the author has included in the proposed methodology for the development of the industrial system and improvement of the institutional potential of the region.

Conventionally, the whole process of modelling the levelling of industrial voids of regions (Figure 10.1) can be divided into three stages:

- The first stage is the identification of industrial and institutional voids of the regions and their assessment;
- The second stage is the formation of the Strategy for the Development of the Industrial System and Improvement of the Region's Institutional Potential;
- The third stage is the organization of monitoring of the effectiveness of the Industrial System Strategy and Improvement of the Region's Institutional Potential.

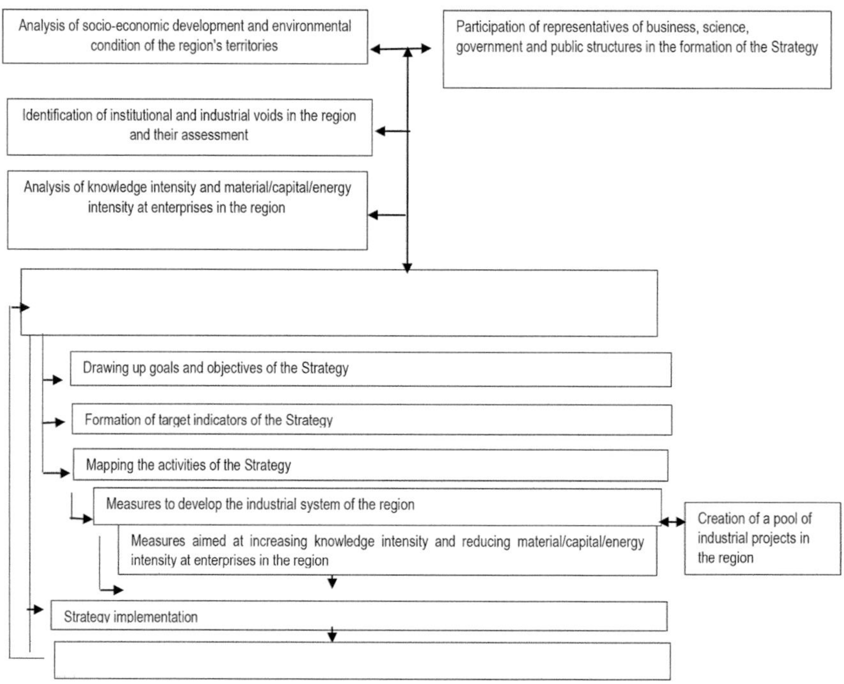

FIGURE 10.1 Methodology of industrial system development and improvement of institutional potential of the region.

I will focus on each stage separately:

1. One of the key indicators for assessing the development of the territory is proposed to determine the following: labor productivity of the region, investment in fixed capital, investment in staff

development, knowledge intensity of production, knowledge-intensity of production, coefficient of digital development of production, coefficient of technological development of production, coefficients of reduction of material/capital/energy intensity of production. That is, these are indicators that are key in the theory of noonomy, which is undoubtedly a platform for the formation and implementation of strategic documents.

Analyzing these indicators in cities and comparing them with the region-wide value allows us to identify the acuteness of some specific indicators. Of course, in this case, it is appropriate to introduce a criteria-based assessment scale, as well as the introduction of an integral level of indicator for the region, characterizing the policy of leveling industrial voids.

The analysis results in a cartogram of industrial renewal of the regions in the coordinates "acuteness of socio-economic problems" – "depth of industrial voids" (Figure 10.2).

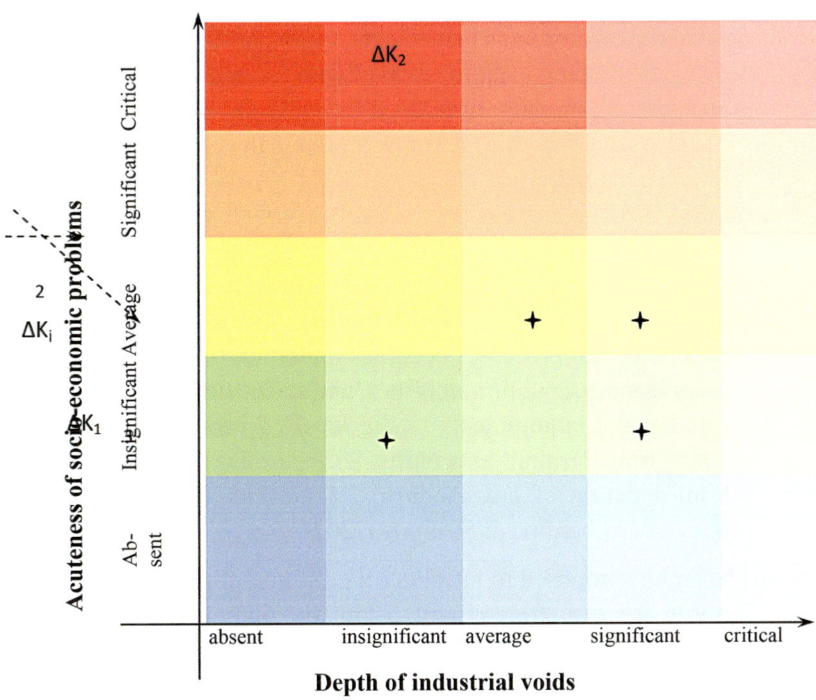

FIGURE 10.2 Cartogram of industrial renewal of the regions.

2. At the same time, among the important activities of the region's development it is proposed to approve two blocks of activities included in the "institutions of stabilization" and "institutions of strategic development."

   The latter institute is proposed to include such innovative measures as: in the troduction of digital "twins" in enterprises, the formation of continuous flow production cycles, the establishment of robotic/automated technologies, the introduction of nanotechnologies, the establishment of intelligent robots and systems, introduction of virtual production assistants, development of alternative energy sources. And I emphasize the important point that it is necessary to monitor the correlation between the implemented activities and the achieved indicators.

   Nowadays, innovation is the source of more progressive development of regions: the installation of robots for recycling waste, robots controlled by signals coming from the human brain, the creation of AI scientists (AI – artificial intelligence), the introduction of self-driving cars, nanorobots in medicine, the expansion of "green" technology, the automatic digitization of voice commands of controllers – all these are already introduced technologies in the world. And, of course, the strategic documents being developed should take into account global developments. And here it is the continuous improvement of the "knowledge" of all participants of the process, who prepare strategies and participate in their implementation, that should be emphasized. On this basis, the emphasis on the acquisition of intellectual, innovative knowledge and in-depth knowledge of technological processes becomes important both for representatives of business, public authorities, and scientific community. After all, today the requirements to the level of personnel knowledge are also transforming, as a particular example: must comply with the introduction of cross-industrial (inter-industry) technological processes (Akberdina & Smirnova, 2021).

   The author proposed to introduce a grouping of regional strategies in three areas: a strategy with a low, medium, and high "knowledge-intensive component." The choice of strategy will depend on the development indicators of the region and its resource investment base for the development of knowledge of employees of enterprises, state and municipal authorities and the population.

3. Further, quality control of production systems should be an important point in the strategies. In general, continuous automated quality control of the formation and implementation of strategic documents of the territories (indicators, implemented measures) is important, and it is open to the public.

   In 2006, the author defended her PhD thesis on “Investment Strategy of an Industrial City-Forming Enterprise” (Pyankova, 2006). The paper analyzed the strategic documents of 83 city-forming enterprises in the Sverdlovsk Region. It was found that over the period of 10 years of investment (from 2001 to 2015), 49.8% of investment in fixed capital was attributed to iron and steel industry, 29.4% to electric power, and 16.1% to non-ferrous metallurgy. And if we further track the dynamics of the development indicators of city-forming enterprises from 2015 to the present, it is the enterprises that previously made significant investments in fixed capital and in improving the educational level of their employees that have more effective development, especially during the sanctions regimes and the pandemic period. In particular, on the example of the city-forming enterprise Seversky Pipe Plant, a direct correlation between the educational level of employees (employees’ qualification) and the output of the enterprise was established (Figure 10.3).

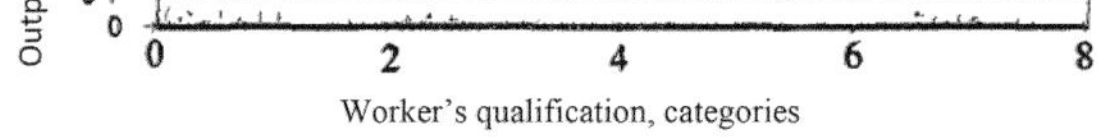

FIGURE 10.3 Relationship between the educational level of employees and their output.

The coefficient of determination, which characterizes the proportion of variation in the dependent variable explained by the regression equation, was 0.91. This practical case study also shows the importance of applying the theory of noonomy in the formation of strategic programs and concepts of industrial enterprises in the region.

The author also emphasizes that for more effective socio-economic development of the region it is important to apply an integrated approach to the formation and implementation of the strategy, including the consolidation of efforts of all actors of the territory (business, government, population, media, and others) (Figure 10.4).

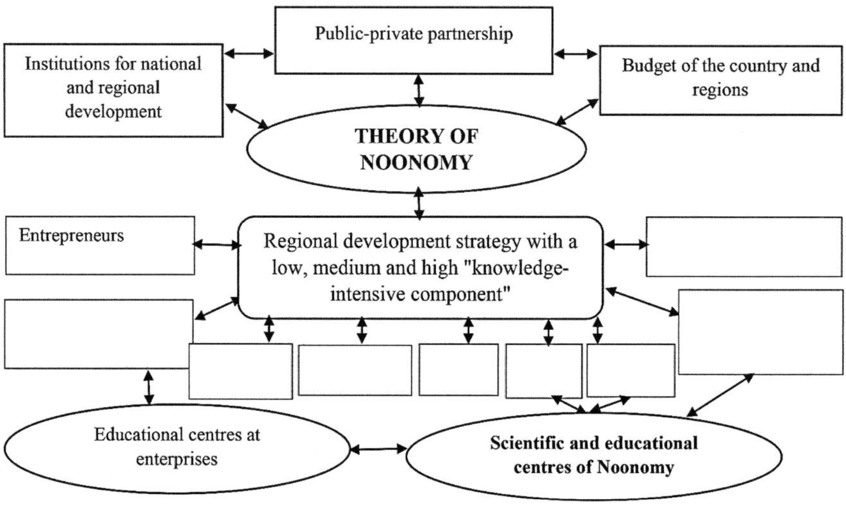

FIGURE 10.4 Key actors involved in the formation and implementation of the strategy of socio-economic development of the region.

In contrast to existing management approaches, the above proposed scheme takes into account such actors as entrepreneurs, media, scientific and analytical journals, universities, and the scientific community.

The scheme takes into account a set of financial resources aimed at implementing the region's strategies: development institutions, the budget, and funds from the business community.

The basic platform in the formation and implementation of the strategy is the theory of noonomy. The scheme takes into account the analytical, research, teaching, and advisory activities of the educational centers at the enterprises of the region and scientific and educational centers of Noonomy.

These scientific-educational centers of Noonomy will be the sources of advanced training of personnel in the general theory part of Noonomy, the basic platform for research solutions for more effective socio-economic development of regions, the periphery of implementation of key parameters of the theory of Noonomy, the key to consolidation of efforts of all authors of the territory (business, government, population, media, universities, scientific community, public organizations and others), the analytical center for studying key indicators of the region (the level of knowledge-intensity of production, knowledge intensity of its processes, material/capital/energy resource intensity of production and others), the co-organizer of the key projects of the region, the consulting body of management decision making.

Also, the scheme presents an important relationship characterizing the presentation of scientific results of Noonomy research and education centers in Russian and foreign scientific and analytical journals.

The author believes that the assessment of the effectiveness of strategy implementation should be taken into account in the evaluation indicators of Governors and public authorities, included in the system of additional bonuses for regional leaders, considered at public councils, published, and discussed in the media, and publicly presented to the population of the region.

Thus, the unification of unique concepts of regional strategy and the theory of Noonomy is an important, necessary step towards more effective socio-economic development of territories, improving the quality of their industrial development, improving the welfare of the population. Consolidation of the efforts of all actors in the territory will make it possible to take into account the positions of all stakeholders in order to avoid acute failures and include the necessary solutions.

KEYWORDS

- **knowledge-intensive production**
- **noonomy**
- **regional strategic planning**
- **socio-economic development**
- **territorial development**
- **technological innovation**

REFERENCES

Akberdina, V. V., & Smirnova, O. P. (2021). Cross-industrial transformation: Structural changes and innovative development. *Innovations and Investments*, *17*(7), 1238–1260.

Animitsa, E. G., Bochko, V. S., Peshina, E. V., Animitsa, P. E., Tatarkin, A. I., & Fedorov, M. V. (2010). Conceptual approaches to the development of a strategy for the development of a single-profile city. *International Journal of Experimental Education*, *11*, 56–57.

Bodrunov, S. D. (2018). Breakthrough strategy: Resources and opportunities. *Scientific Works of the Free Economic Society of Russia*, *214*(6), 52–70.

Bodrunov, S. D. (2018). *Noonomy*. Moscow: Kulturnaya revolyutsiya Publishing.

Bodrunov, S. D. (2020). *Noonomy: The trajectory of global transformation*. Moscow: S. Y. Witte INID; Kulturnaya revolyutsiya Publishing.

Bodrunov, S. D. (2021). The global transformation of modern society and the national development goals of Russia. *Scientific Works of the Free Economic Society of Russia*, *230*, 54–65.

Bodrunov, S. D., & Glazyev, S. Y. (2023). *Regularities of the noonomy foundations formation as future social order: To know and operate*. St. Petersburg: S. Y. Witte INID; Moscow: Tsentrkatalog Publishing.

Bodrunov, S. D., Desai, R., & Freeman, A. (2022). *Beyond the global crisis: Noonomy, creativity, geopolitical economy*. St. Petersburg: S. Y. Witte INID Publishing.

Dmitriev, M. E. (2009). Strategic planning system – A large-scale organizational experiment. *Territory Development Management*, *3*, 6–12.

Ilyina, I. N. (2012). Strategy of modernization of single-industry towns of Russia. In *Development of single-industry settlements in the Russian Federation: A collection of scientific works* (pp. 4–12). Moscow: Financial University Publishing.

Kolganov, A. (2021). Predictive potential of noonomy to justify the development strategy. In S. D. Bodrunov (Ed.), *Anthology of noonomy: Fourth technological revolution and its economic, social and humanitarian consequences* (pp. 4–12). St. Petersburg: S. Y. Witte INID Publishing.

Kosareva, N. B., & Vetrov, G. Y. (2010). Municipal strategy as a form of long-term social contract. *Territorial Strategic Planning*, *11*, 36–39.

Kvint, V. L. (2015). *Strategy for the global market: Theory and practical applications*. New York & London: Routledge, Taylor & Francis.

Kvint, V. L. (2020). *The concept of strategizing*. Kemerovo: Kemerovo State University Publishing.

Kvint, V. L., & Bodrunov, S. D. (2023). *Strategizing societal transformation: Knowledge, technologies, and noonomy*. Apple Academic Press.

Pulyavskaya, V. L., & Khristoforov, A. A. (2021). On strategic planning in industrial single-industry towns. *Development of Territories*, *24*(2), 69–73.

Pyankova, S. G. (2006). *Investment strategy of an industrial city-forming enterprise*. Ekaterinburg. URL: https://new-disser.ru/_avtoreferats/01002902189.pdf (accessed on 7th October 2024).

Pyankova, S. G. (2022). Noonomy in monotowns: Forming trends of a new industrial system and improving institutional capacity. *Noonomy and Noosociety: Almanac of Scientific Works of the S. Y. Witte INID*, *1*(4), 35–48.

Zinchuk, G. M. (2012). Formation of a development strategy in the municipal management system of a single-industry town. *Vestnik of the Plekhanov Russian University of Economics*, *4*, 96–102.

CHAPTER 11

The Role of Civil Society in the Transition to a New Economy

LEO GABRIEL

Director, Institute for Intercultural Research and Cooperation, University of Vienna; Professor (Vienna, Austria)

ABSTRACT

The author of this chapter addresses the importance of analyzing the contradictions and conflicts occurring in the world in terms of the transition to a more thoughtful study of socio-economic, geopolitical, national, and cultural processes through the prism of the interests and values of the social majority, rather than market fundamentalism. It is shown that under conditions of a multidimensional crisis of the market capitalist system (economic crises, pandemic, military-political confrontation), neoliberalism reaches a dead end, which can only be overcome if humanity shifts to another path of development – a non-economic in its nature.

Economists always have this vision from above, which reveals great insights most of the time. But when in their analyses they get down to the grassroots, where people and peoples really live, very often human beings are being transformed into figures, statistical data reflecting percentages of growth and curbs summarized by timelines. Being a social anthropologist, I want to invite you to do it the other way around and see first the people in their communities before talking about "societies" and nation-states.

Elizabeth (known as "Sissi"), the wife of the late and in fact the latest emperor of Austria, Franz Joseph, once said: "Without the people and peoples" – and she meant the plural, which was very important given the

Global Transformations of the 21st Century: The Future of Humans, Markets, and Capital.
Sergey Bodrunov (Editor)

DOI: 10.1201/9781779644022-11

pluri-national and multicultural nature of the Austrian-Hungarian Empire, "even the emperor would lose his power and his rights."

A few years later, the Austrian-Hungarian Empire collapsed and so did the Soviet Union about 70 years later. In both cases, this happened because the leadership of both Empires did not recognize in time that the people and peoples, their local and regional constituencies, had changed a rather long time ago and fought for their independence.

11.1 THE DAWN OF MARKET FUNDAMENTALISM

This is also the case nowadays, when in the present multidimensional crisis of the market-driven capitalist system, we can observe that neoliberalism is reaching its dead end. It has failed in the crisis of 2008, when the privatized financial markets had to recur to the umbrellas of the States and it has failed during the pandemic a couple of years ago (Gabriel, 2020), and it is failing nowadays, in our war driven times, due to its incapacity to guarantee economic stability as a peacekeeping force. In some ways, Manuel Wallerstein was right when he predicted already in 2003 at the eve of the wars in Afghanistan and Iraq that "militarism is the last stage of the neoliberal empire."

If we look at the world from below, there, where we can find the vast majority of the world population, we realize that some big countries like China and India, Brazil, Russia, and South Africa (the so-called BRICS) are popping up as a conglomeration of a great variety of different cultures. And if we look even closer into the universe of the people and peoples, we can see for example that the indigenous cultures of Latin America, which are so many that you cannot even count them, we realize that the overwhelming majority of the world population is not following, is not able to follow, neither the market system nor the systems of Nation States which the governments once praised as the incarnation of "progress" and "well-being." As a matter of fact, they always have been kept on their own and only a few could manage to rise up to the promised land of the so-called "American way of life."

And if we get even closer, we can see at the present moment that they have a choice between Scylla and Charybdis: either they are going up to the North in extremely precarious and dangerous paths till they are drowned in the Mediterranean or they are kidnaped and shot on the way between Mexico and the United States. Is this the way of "integrating" the people of the Global South into the "free market system" the Milton Friedman and his scholars have promised four decades ago?

11.2 FROM THE GRASS ROOTS TO SOLIDARITY ECONOMICS

Certainly not. Searching for an alternative to this unbearable situation our *Institute for Intercultural Research and Cooperation* has discovered, in the framework of one of the most ambitious socio-anthropological research projects of the European Union[1], that the relatively autonomous economic structures of indigenous cultures had inspired a great variety of NGOs, experts and social activists to present an alternative to the so-called "free market system."

Instead of creating top-down economic concepts and theories these people developed an alternative economic system from within the existing social structures. Considering that a majority of the world population, especially in Africa, Asia, and Latin America are still living on an extremely precarious subsistence level, in so-called "informal economies." Some Latin American economists like Marcos Arruda from Brazil and Ricardo Soto from Perú have developed a concept called "Solidarity Economics."

At the difference of the capital-driven market system grounded on competition and aimed at economic growth as its ultima ratio Solidarity Economics proposes an economic structure of "amplified subsistence" based on mutual cooperation of relatively autonomous urban and rural communities. In order to achieve this, the communities should cut the distance between producers and consumers following the "principle of subsidiarity" as it has been developed by the Christian, Muslim, and Buddhist tradition. This means to give preference to what can be produced on the local and to establish markets with their own currencies on the regional level.

This implies to invert the presently existing pyramid of production and distribution where global structures like the financial capital and big players like Blackrock dictate the markets. This not only favors the big transnational companies, but also destroy the environment.

By putting the human being and the earth as a whole in the center of the universe, Solidarity Economics creates new economic subjects, which

[1]Website for Multicultural Autonomies in Latin America. URL: www.latautonomy.com.

in Latin America are called "Prosumidores," meaning that producers become consumers and consumers valuable actors in the production process.

The "prosumidores" don't ship food from other continents when they can produce it in their own or their neighbors garden. The priority is given to the consumption on the spot where those who are selling the products many times are also producing them. That gives a completely different understanding to economy than the one we are used to into the market fundamentalism, but also to the state-driven concept of socialism, where we are condemned to be mere consumers without having any say about the production process.

11.3 NOONOMY IN THE GLOBAL SOUTH?

This kind of understanding of economy comes structurally quite close to the predicaments of Sergey Bodrunov's *Noonomy*. At a certain moment I had the honor to present the Spanish edition of Bodrunov's book on *Noonomy* in Mexico (Bodrunov, 2020). Among the most outstanding experts of political economy in Mexico's most prestigious University Center (right across the Russia Embassy) immediately some key questions arose: "How does *Noonomy* tackle with the marginalized people and peoples who also in Mexico represent the tremendous majority of the population?" and "How can you talk about an equalitarian knowledge society in an environment where more than one-third of the population cannot write and read?"

Since Bodrunov was not present it was me who tried to give an answer. I said: "*Noonomy* refers to a concept, where economy is based on culture. For many centuries the Mexican culture has been and still is based on the wisdom of its ancestors. And this culture consists of societal values like conviviality and cooperation, wisdom, and human dignity. What Bodrunov is heading for, is to design an economic system which is based on a common sharing of resources and goods."

11.4 WITHOUT PEACE NO ECONOMIC JUSTICE

Or, just to give another example: in the International Peace Movement I belong to and which I consider the most important social movement nowadays, we all agree that war and military conflict have to be substituted by ceasefires and political negotiations. Because we realized that wars destroy the economies as much as the environment.

When I talk about military confrontation, I don't talk only about the Ukraine. We have wars everywhere: in Western Africa, Sudan, the Middle East; in Myanmar and in Latin America, where there are many wars with and between the organized crime. Recently I had the honor to co-organize an international peace conference in Vienna[2].

Among the 600 participants from 35 countries, we could also count with the presence of David Choquehuanca, Vice-president of Bolivia, who also is a very renown indigenous philosopher. In his statement, he asked: "Why do these things happen in Europe and in other continents and why they don´t happen in the indigenous world? Because indigenous people are looking beyond the conflict. They see what's coming afterwards and that drives them to find means for political solutions, before the conflict comes to a point of no return."

And finally: what does all that mean for us intellectuals who are also living in a system of competition and confrontation many times? What can we learn from the Global South for the creation of a transition towards a new economic world order? And above all: what can we DO? I think, first of all, we should get involved in the communities surrounding us.

I remember a time when I wanted to study physics and have still in my memory the famous predicament of Werner Heisenberg who said that you cannot measure a physical phenomenon without interacting with this phenomenon; the observer always becomes an actor and transforms this reality. Well, let's take that as a goal as scientists, let's get involved in transformation of society, not only by writing books and developing wonderful theories as valuable as they are. In order to change reality, we have to go to the roots, looking for the gatherings of people who are, in my opinion, the main actors of history; not the market system and not the Nation States, but the people and peoples themselves who are involved in an ever-changing reality. And this reality will change, because it must change. And since I have been living through several revolutionary processes, I know that this is possible. Another world is possible!

---

[2]Website for the International Summit for Peace in Ukraine. URL: www.peacevienna.org

KEYWORDS

- **civil society**
- **neoliberalism**
- **noonomy**
- **solidarity economics**
- **socio-economic transition**

REFERENCES

Bodrunov, S. D. (2020). *Noonomia: Monografia*. Plaza y Valdes S. A. de C. V., Alfonso Herrera # 130, int 11, Colonia San Rafael 06470, Ciudad de Mexico.

Gabriel, L. (2022). Noonomy in the transition to a post-capitalist society: Perspectives from the Global South. In S. D. Bodrunov (Ed.), *Anthology of noonomy: Fourth technological revolution and its economic, social and humanitarian consequences: Technology and socio-economic progress: Traps and opportunities for the future* (pp. 195–200). Leiden; Boston: Brill.

CHAPTER 12

Cognitive Model of the Noonomy Concept in the Author's Discourse

EKATERINA KABAKHIDZE

Associate Professor, Department of Linguistics, Translation Studies and Cross-Cultural Communication, Faculty of Foreign Languages and Area Studies, Lomonosov Moscow State University; Candidate of Philosophy (Moscow, Russia)

ABSTRACT

Analyzing the terminological neologism "noonomy" that is borrowed from the economic sphere, the chapter depicts the cognitive model of the concept in the author's discourse, reveals language markers that signal about the shift of the socio-economic paradigm and transition to a new industrial society of the second generation.

12.1 INTRODUCTION

Today we are witnessing ongoing changes of the social world order caused by the global digitalization, change in the mode of information perception and its processing, as well as in the nature of cognition (cognitive deficits exemplified by clip thinking), humanistic ideals debacle and subsequent ignominious transition to a new state of public consciousness manifested in the ideas of transhumanism. To address these challenges, social sciences provide research aimed to resurrect authentic humanism on the basis of fundamental economic theories adapted to the present-day challenges and prerequisites of the evolutionary changes in ontological and anthropological spheres of the 21st century.

Global Transformations of the 21st Century: The Future of Humans, Markets, and Capital.
Sergey Bodrunov (Editor)

DOI: 10.1201/9781779644022-12

The present linguistic and philosophical investigation has been instigated by Sergey Bodrunov's scientific papers creator of the phenomenon of noonomy (Bodrunov, 2018, p. 432), which as the authors of the "Nezavisimaya Gazeta" newspaper article entitled "Russia is Turned into the Cradle of Noonomy" conquers minds of the growing number of researchers both inside and outside Russia. The significance and scale of the theory of noonomy as well as the speed with which the theory of noonomy is spreading around the globe prove the urging need to provide an in-depth analysis of the phenomenon integrating into the research methodology of different sciences including cognitive linguistics. The linguistic analysis of the emerging term requires prior discussion of the main theses that serve as starting point for the research and premises for the two key questions that will be answered in the chapter.

The first thesis states that noonomy as a scientific theory cannot be narrowed down to the economic theory, meaning that noonomy first and foremost is the means of human post-economic being and meeting its needs. Technological progress fueled by knowledge lies in the very foundation of noonomy. Being the main source and engine of progress, knowledge is becoming predominant over the material resources. Changes in the material production and evolution of industry result in shifts of socio-economic paradigm as well as socio-economic model of the society. As a result, one economic order is replaced by another one. Recently we have been reflecting on the 6th technological order whereas today we are witnessing the transition to the 7th accompanied by the fast-paced convergence of bio-, nano-, info and cognitive phenomena.

Sergey Bodrunov metaphorically compares the synthesis of technologies and their climax in noonomy with an Ancient Greek quadriga with four horses galloping through space and time, namely knowledge-based production, property diffusion, socialization, society solidarization and evolution of a man of culture represented in the annihilation of simulated needs (Bodrunov, 2022, pp. 5–13). Following this representation noonomy can be defined as a concept with explicit anthropocentric features or a theory of social and human evolution driven by the pursue for the ideals of humanism rather than merely new economic theory. The first question that requires linguistic and cognitive approach can be formulated in the following way – "What is noonomy? How is it conceptualized? How does one cognize the quadriga of noonomy and its place in consciousness?" Linguistic and cognitive analysis of the notion "noonomy" in the author's discourse will allow us to address these questions.

The answer to the question about the nature and essence of noonomy gives rise to another question – who is the rider of the chariot? Is it a noohuman? How can we know that the era of the new human being integral part of the new industrial society of the second generation has come? What are the ways to trace the human transformation? It needs to be highlighted that in the present chapter human transformation is regarded in the context of changing mental states, which can be witnessed and evaluated in human activities. To avoid such simplified approach more fundamental evidence are researched. Having said that, the evidence should be searched for in consciousness that are manifested in language practice. Thus, the second part of the chapter will be devoted to the issue of transition to noohuman and language indicators that stand behind these changes.

To approach the first question "What is noonomy?" it is worth starting with analysis of the terminological neologism "noonomy" coupled with a brief overview of the names for the emerging economic theories which complement rather than compete with one another for the sake of provision of a broader context serving a background for the concept of "noonomy."

The terminological neologisms representing new economic theories or aligned with transition period of the contemporary society encompass such terminological collocations, as "noospherical socialism" by Subetto (Subetto, 2019, pp. 27–41), "evolution of world economic order" by Glazyev S.Y. Glazyev, 2016, pp. 5–45), "positive feedbacks of economy" by Brian Arthur (Arthur, 2020, pp. 92–99), economic model "multiple equilibrium and diverse paradigm" by Vines and Wills (Vines, Wills, 2018 pp. 1–42), "creative economy" by Alan Freeman (Freeman, 2012, pp. 2–21). These theories explain to some extent laws, cycles, and stages of social-economic development driven by innovations, a combination of impulses and fluctuations of economic space, the evolution of world economic order along with technological and economic paradigms and crisis.

When comparing the newly emerging economic terms, one cannot avoid noticing that the term "noonomy" is single-component in contrast with the terms listed above that have two or more components in the name. Phonosemantic analysis of the notion "noonomy" shows that this word is perceived subconsciously as something "nice" and "smooth," which may take us to the conclusion that the terminological neologism will be easily absorbed by language and become part of its vocabulary. Etymologically the term "noonomy" comes from the Ancient Greek terms "nomos" (*νόμιμον*) which means 'tradition, law, rule' and "noos" (*νόος*) meaning thought, mind, reasoning, common sense, intention, heart, opinion, meaning, sense, world soul, etc. The etymological analysis proves that the semantic core of the notion 'noonomy' is represented by 'law,' 'reasoning,' 'thought,' 'heart,' 'subject,' 'value.'

To reveal mental correlates and images of language units as they are represented in consciousness along with emotional links, value components linguo-cognitive analysis is applied in linguistics. This method enables analysis and structuring of mental contents of the notion "noonomy." Apart from the fact that cognitive analysis of the concept "noonomy" aims to research conceptual aspects of the notion in the author's mental lexicon based on articles and monographs written by Sergey Bodrunov within 2020–2023. The conceptual analysis will be enriched with metaphorical models of the concept noonomy.

Since the notion of noonomy is not fixed by the specialized dictionaries due to the fact it is a terminological neologism, to outline its semantic fields we will render to the definition of noonomy stated in the words of its author – Sergey Bodrunov: "noonomy is a way of managing noosociety. At the same time noosociety is not the same as noosphere, not an abstract "noospherical society," it is a society, the material basis for the existence of which and the satisfaction of people's needs is noonomy… noonomy is a way of satisfying needs in a society where there is the "light of reason"; where there is no relation to production and production relations; where there is no relation to property and property relations; where there is no economy and where economy is impossible" (Bodrunov, 2021, pp. 19–92). From the definition above one can deduce the following conceptual aspects:

12.2 NOONOMY AS A CATEGORY OF REASON

- **Slot 1. "Rational Knowledge:"** *In noonomy, the new **nature of rationality** and, accordingly, the new definition of development goals acquires paramount importance.*
- **Slot 2. "Rational Consumption and Needs:"** *And when we talk about noonomy, we mean a transition to a fundamentally different criterial base, to some special **principles based on "noo" for forming a way to satisfy people's needs.** Yes, growing, changing, but "noo-"needs.*

Noonomy puts at the forefront not the private pursuit of profit or other income, which is achieved by the chaotic play of market forces, but the ***rational desire to satisfy specific needs, assessed as reasonable – truly reasonable.***

- **Slot 3. "Knowledge and Science:"** *One of the basic meanings of the concept of "noonomy" is that* ***scientific knowledge begins to play a major role in economic development****, replacing spontaneous economic development with conscious and goal-oriented activities of people.*

  Of course, the universality of man in noonomy will not lie in the fact that each person will know everything, but in the opening opportunity and acquired ability to master almost any ***necessary knowledge.***

  But in order for the system of noonomy to be workable, it is necessary that a new rationality be formed – ***the rationality of the scientific justification of goals and the subordinate choice of means.***

  And noonomy, and not economics, will become a ***knowledge-intensive and "smart" way of meeting the needs of both individual members of the noosociety and no-society as a whole.***

- **Slot 4. "Rational Attitude:"** *But since they themselves are not included directly in the production process, it will no longer be an economy, but, let's accept this term, noonomy – relations not within the framework of production carried out by a person directly, but* ***relations regarding nooproduction, developing without the direct participation of a person, but regulated and guided by the human mind.***

12.3 NOONOMY AS SPIRITUAL CATEGORY

- **Slot 1. "Ultimate Value:"** *And this is correct, because the main value for a person and society is time. Not profit, but time – this is the key meaning of the new economy NIS.2, which turns into an* ***"absolute" in noonomy.***

  After all, noonomy is based on the transition from a growth paradigm based on economic "rationality" focused on increasing volumetric cost indicators to a development paradigm based on achieving specific goals, satisfying various human needs, formed on the basis of higher values, in the future – ***noovalues.***

- **Slot 2. "Truth:"** *Noonomy – let us emphasize once again – presupposes a different way of carrying out economic actions and a different way of assessing needs – based not on the "old" rationality, but on reason, on "noo," based on an understanding of the true consequences of economic decisions and the* ***true value of the needs being satisfied.***
- **Slot 3. "Opposition to Material:"** *The basis of noonomy is a non-economic type of satisfaction of human needs, which will be formed through a new quality of production, where a person will become, in accordance with Marx's vision,* ***"beyond material production itself."***

  Namely (in noonomy), ***knowledge and cognition of the world as a world of culture*** *(in an extremely broad sense) and self-limitation of irrational (in the criterial base developing in the direction of "noo") needs.*
- **Slot 4. "Non-Economic (Spiritual) Being and Evolution of Human and Society:"** *Noonomy as a way of* ***non-economic (immaterial) human existence.***

  The opportunities created by modern technology create the prospect of a change in the ownership paradigm and a transition from economics to noonomy, which means a ***rejection of economic rationality, leading to an unbridled pursuit of increasing production and consumption.***

  By noonomy (clarifying the above definition) we understand a non-economic way of organizing an economy to satisfy needs, which is carried out by a person who ***has gone beyond the boundaries of material production.***

  How can one generally summarize the defining goals in noonomy if economic goals become a thing of the past? They can be defined ***as growth and development of a person.***

  The path to noonomy lies not only through the denial of the primacy of the "zoological" nature of man, but also through his elevation above his own creation – the technosphere. ***Its development ceases to be a spontaneous process, subordinated to the pursuit of the accumulation of material wealth, expressed in volumetric monetary categories.***

With the transition to nooproduction and noonomy, attitudes toward satisfying specific, reasonable needs become rational, and ***criteria of rationality replace criteria based on monetary gain. The needs for knowledge, trust, social recognition, and self-realization become dominant over the needs for the absorption of life's goods,*** *and the volume of goods absorbed no longer acts as the main goal of human activity – insofar as this need is already saturated within reasonable limits.*

- **Slot 5. "Cultural Revolution:"** ***With the transition to noonomy, all these categories and the real relations corresponding to them – market, money, capital – disappear.*** *In general, they, like everything that is "essentially formative" in the economy, will disappear along with the economy – this reflection of the biological principle in a person,* ***transferred from primary biological needs to society, to relationships, and yes! – into culture.***

12.4 NOONOMY AS AN INSTRUMENT FOR CREATION OF THE FUTURE STATE AND SOCIETY IMAGE

- **Slot 1. "Formation of the Future Society:"** *However, such a transition from current economy to noonomy should be based on a change in the entire set of social relations, and noonomy* ***can only be strengthened within the framework of an integral system of noosociety.***

  Noonomy needs to be built now, albeit in a very narrow segment, but to practically work out what will certainly ***become the future of economic activity and human development.***

- **Slot 2. "Transformation of the State Political System:"** *At the same time, obviously, as part of this process, the* ***state itself will be transformed,*** *gradually turning from an institution of coercion* *into an institution for coordinating public interests and human development, up to a complete change in its essence at the stage of transition to noonomy.*

- **Slot 3. "Knowledge Society:"** *Hence, noonomy is a way to satisfy needs in a* ***society where there is the "light of reason."***

  And here the following position should be put forward: this entire structure, provided for in the theory of noonomy, can develop only when ***a person, in parallel with some knowledge (in particular, technological and other scientific and natural) assimilates and masters other knowledge.***

- **Slot 4. "Knowledge-Intensive Production and Technological Progress:"** *From here it is just a step to transfer all production to full "autonomous navigation," to the creation of that same* ***technobase of noonomy,*** *autonomous from humans.*

  Here you can see a completely clear sequence of transitional steps to the ***technological basis of noonomy.***

- **Slot 5. "Fair Society, Equal Society:"** *One can assume the withering away of this type of social relations – in noonomy, the basis for splitting people by class, by profession (along with the withering away of the professions themselves), and in general –* ***by splitting by social status, disappears.***

  And therefore, when we talk about NIS.2, and even more so about the movement towards noonomy, ***we are not talking about just a technological change, but about a change in society as a whole****, about a change in those institutions that are entailed, so to speak, by changes in the technological base.*

12.5 NOONOMY AS ACTION

- **Slot 1. "Movement into the Future:"** *Noonomy tells us both the* ***target vector and the path to be taken****.*

  The theory of noonomiy predicts *that at the NIS.2 stage the sharing economy, the economy of split and blurred property rights, will dominate.*

Only those economies that can respond to the challenges of not only the NIS.2 bursting into our lives, but also the noonomy ***that is on the horizon, will be able to take worthy positions in the world of the near future.***

- **Slot 2. "Evolutionary Process:"** *Of course, the movement* ***towards noonomy is a long historical transition***.

  The concept "noonomy" has a frame structure comprised of the slots given below (Figure 12.1):

  1. Noonomy as a Category of Reason:
     - Slot 1. "Rational knowledge;"
     - Slot 2. "Reasonable consumption and needs;"
     - Slot 3. "Knowledge and science;"
     - Slot 4. "Reasonable attitude."
  2. Noonomy as Spiritual Category:
     - Slot 1. "Ultimate value;"
     - Slot 2. "Truth;"
     - Slot 3. "Opposition to material;"
     - Slot 4. "Non-economic (spiritual) being and development of human and society;"
     - Slot 5. "Cultural revolution."
  3. Noonomy as an Instrument for Creation of the Future State and Society Image:
     - Slot 1. "Formation of the future society;"
     - Slot 2. "Transformation of the state political system;"
     - Slot 3. "Knowledge society;"
     - Slot 4. "Knowledge-intensive production and technological progress;"
     - Slot 5. "Fair society, equal society."
  4. Noonomy as Action:
     - Slot 1. "Movement into the future;"
     - Slot 2. "Evolutionary process."

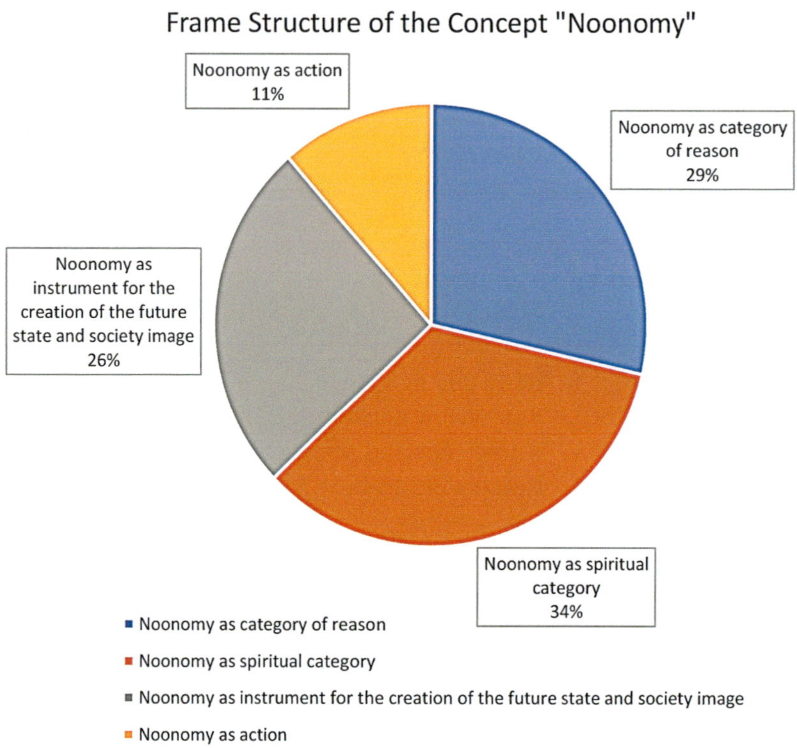

FIGURE 12.1 Frame structure of the concept "Noonomy."

Methods of cognitive linguistics were applied to study the frame aspects of the notion "noonomy," whose core is represented by the frame "noonomy as spiritual category" (34,2%) dominated by the slot "non-economic (spiritual) being and evolution of human and society." The conceptual space of the core is structured by the four slots: ultimate value, opposition to the material, truth, cultural revolution. The nearby periphery includes the slot "noonomy as category of reason" (29%) and another slot "noonomy as instrument for creation of the future state and society image" (26%). The remote periphery is represented by the slot "noonomy as action" (11%).

The predominant cognitive aspect of the concept noonomy in the author's discourse is spiritual sphere followed by the category of reason. Interestingly enough, the conceptual aspect of the state and its future image along with the image of nation is also marked in the verbal representation of the concept noonomy. Applied aspects of noonomy, such as "noonomy as action," are also constituents of the concept, although to a much lesser degree than ontological and epistemological aspects. Such a disproportion may be explained by the fact that noonomy is a fundamental theory with its practical forms and feasible outcomes still to be elaborated.

Let us address the second question of the research: how can we understand that the era of a new human, a new industrial society of the second generation, has arrived? Is it possible to observe the transformation of humanity through the mirror of language? Before we begin exploring the answer, we must examine the discourse elements typical of the retrograde mode of thinking in the capitalist system, identify distortions of meaning, meaningless language games, and empty concepts—in other words, those aspects embodied in language that noonomy, with its ethical potency, seeks to withdraw from speech practices. First, we must acknowledge the existence of simulacra in culture and language, beyond the economic sphere. For the purposes of this research, simulacra are defined as words that are not rooted in national consciousness and can be compared to "broken" concepts. These words have a "referent" but lack a "significant." According to J. Baudrillard, simulacra provide reference to a missing subject or event, stemming from the radical negation of the sign as value, thus creating hyperreality (Baudrillard, 2015, pp. 8–13). One of the most well-known examples of simulacra is the phenomenon of "educational service." According to dictionaries, the term "service" has two lexical meanings: (i) an action that brings benefit or helps others (to render service, to offer one's service to someone); and (ii) paid work done in the interests of another person. Etymologically, the noun "service" originates from the Latin word servus, meaning slave. Therefore, the semantic core of this notion is comprised of the sememe "to serve someone" or to be one's slave/servant. The other term in the phrase "educational service"—education—is represented by two lexical meanings: (i) the process of acquiring systemized knowledge and skills, enlightenment; and (ii) the sum of knowledge obtained as a result of education. When these two lexemes are placed together, one cannot help but experience cognitive dissonance. By no means can education—a matter of crucial importance for the individual, society, and state—be reduced to notions of servitude or paid service.

Another example of simulacra in language are discourse markers, such as conjunction "sort of" and the synonymic adverb "kinda." Let us give an example: "I kinda wanted to help you." What about the speaker's real intention – did the speaker really want to help or not? Was it a true desire or an imitation of it? There is another example: "Are you a sportsman? Sort of!" There are a lot more examples of the same nature resonating with social phenomena and attitudes towards consumerism, devaluation of true values and ideals, which are often replaced by simulacra signs.

If we look into the future and ask ourselves what changes in language may serve as evidence of human consciousness transformation, we may notice the changes as they are described below using the metaphorical image of quadriga. Thus, one of the horses of the chariot signifies the transition to knowledge intensive technologies. In language such a transition may be witnessed in the growing use of the word 'truth.' Sergey Bodrunov highlights in his works that the criterial base for knowledge is represented by the notion of truth. The historical National corpora of the Russian language allows to make up graph of the use of the word-form 'truth' in a diachronic perspective starting with the Medieval time until the present day. The graph shows that the use of the word 'truth' peaked at 98% of texts in the Medieval time as opposed to only 20% of use in the contemporary texts (Figure 12.2).

FIGURE 12.2 History of the use of the word form "truth" in the 12th–20th centuries.

One may deduce from this dynamic that in case the frequency of the use of the word 'truth' grows, it will mean that society is walking along the path towards knowledge and science. Another horse in the chariot is represented by the real estate diffusion and society solidarization. What changes in language may prove that the society is unifying? One of the typical markers in language which showcase the atomization of society, its disunity is represented by the dichotomy 'us vs them,' 'we vs. they.' In case these oppositions are used less frequently in a discourse, it will mean that social bonds are becoming stronger leading to society unification. One more horse in the quadriga represents annihilation of simulative needs along with evolution of the man of culture. In language one may see this change in the preservation of cultural and language variety around the globe. Researchers show concerns that language extinct is one of the key social issues in the 21st century. According to UNICEF there are approximately 6,000 languages in the world with at least one language vanishing per week. The loss of language means inevitable loss of unique world picture shared by the language users and unprecedented loss of unique national culture. The increase of cultural phenomena in language may be manifested in its creativity, which is a key component of noonomy. In language the level of creativity may be measured by the frequency of metaphors. This presupposition is proved by the Silver Age of poetry in Russia and emerging new movements such as futurism, avant-garde and many others that marked the transition to the new Soviet Russia. The poem of Velimir Khlebnikov with its eloquent style and exceeding number of metaphors is one of the best examples of it.

Cherry dew of your sword
Drying with wavy hair outpoured.
And here out of the executioner's laughter
The one whose laughter is rampageous comes after.
Sometimes you are a black-eyed fortune teller,
Multiverbal, keeping silent ever,
Other times you are a laughing mermaid
Sitting on a mammoth tusk deep-laid.

Khlebnikov along with other poets of the Silver Age created unsurpassed images of being painting it with metaphors which had never existed in language before or after picturing the emerging image of a new human born in the times of tectonic changes of social, political, and economic life featuring the shift from the tsar Russian Empire to the Soviet Russia. Once metaphors dominate the language of poets, writers, and painters again and create brave new historical images, it will prove the paradigm change in public consciousness.

12.6 CONCLUSION

Conceptual and phonosemantic analysis undertaken in the research shows that the terminological neologism "noonomy" is becoming an integral element of scientific economic discourse, capable of conquering other similar new terms reflecting economic reality of the present day due to its deeply meaningful contents. In Sergey Bodrunov's discourse, the following conceptual categories of the term "noonomy" have been underpinned: reason, spirituality, statehood, society, and action.

To conclude, the concept "noonomy" synthesizes spiritual and ethical, logical and rational, social, and political components in the context of the future world order of state, society, and human. The formation of post-economic reality, the birth of a new industrial society of the second generation—phenomena that are theorized in noonomy—will get its language manifestation through the diminishing or elimination of simulacra units in language, an increase in the use of the word "truth," the annihilation of the "us vs. them" dichotomy, and metaphors, as products of language creativity, becoming permanent residents of the discourse.

KEYWORDS

- **cognitive model**
- **discourse**
- **language transformation**
- **noonomy**
- **noosociety**
- **technological progress**

REFERENCES

Arthur, B. W. (2021). Positive feedbacks in the economy. *Scientific American, 262*(2), 92–99.

Baudrillard, J. (2015). *Simulacra and simulation* (A. Kachalov, Trans.). POSTUM Publishing House.

Bodrunov, S. D. (2018). *Noonomy*. Moscow: Kul'turnaya revolyutsiya Publishing.

Bodrunov, S. D. (2019). Noonomy: Ontological theses. *Economic Revival of Russia*, *62*(4), 7–9.

Bodrunov, S. D. (2021). What is noonomy? In S. D. Bodrunov (Ed.), *Anthology of noonomy: Fourth technological revolution and its economic, social and humanitarian consequences* (pp. 19–92). Brill.

Bodrunov, S. D. (2022a). Scientific and technological progress and transformation of society: Noonomy and noosociety. Part 2. *Noonomy and Noosociety. Almanac of Scientific Works of the S. Y. Witte INID*, *1*(2), 13–35.

Bodrunov, S. D. (2022b). Technological progress: Prerequisite and result of the socio-humanitarian direction of economic development. *Economic Revival of Russia*, *71*(1), 5–13.

Freeman, A. (2012). Is creation an industry? A constructive critique of the economics of the cultural and creative industries. *London Metropolitan University. SSRN Electronic Journal*, *3*, 2–21.

Freeman, C., & Soete, L. (1997). *The economics of industrial innovation* (3rd ed.). London: Pinter.

Glazyev, S. Y. (2016). Regularity of the change of world economic patterns in the development of the world economic system and related political changes. *Science. Culture. Society*, *22*(3), 5–45.

Glazyev, S. Y. (2022). Global transformations from the perspective of technological and economic world order change. *AlterEconomics*, *1*, 93–115.

Grinin, L. E., Korotaev, A. V., & Bondarenko, V. M. (Eds.). (2017). *N. D. Kondratyev: Crises and forecasts in the light of the theory of long waves. Modern point of view*. Moscow: Uchitel' Publishing.

Schumpeter, J. A. (1995). *The theory of economic development: An inquiry into profits, capital, credit, interest, and the business cycle*. Moscow: Eksmo Publishing.

Subetto, A. I. (2019). Noospherism: The new system of preservation and development of humanity on Earth. *Theoretical Economy*, *54*(6), 27–41.

Vines, D., & Wills, S. (2018). The rebuilding macroeconomic theory project: An analytical assessment. *Oxford Review of Economic Policy*, *34*(1–2), 1–42.

Index

A

Acceleration of,
  acceleration, 7
  diffusion, 9
  STP acceleration, 7
Afghanistan, 104, 158
Africa, 22, 158–161
Agency for strategic initiatives, 30
American military-industrial-security complex, 42
Antagonism, 2
Anthropological, 101, 110, 159, 163
  crisis, 101, 110
Antifascist resistance, 105
Anti-
  imperialism, 16, 22
  imperialist, 16, 107
Aristotle, 26, 110
Artificial intelligence, 5, 29, 45, 89, 108, 152
Asia, 104, 106, 159
Atomic bomb, 5
Autonomous innovation, 41

B

B2C, 79
Baumol
  fallacy, 91
  theorem, 91
Bifurcated world system, 43
Bifurcation, 7
Blackrock, 159
Blurring, 8, 9
Bodrunov, 1, 5–8, 12, 15, 17, 25, 34, 37, 38, 40–45, 47, 51, 59, 93, 101, 109–115, 121, 147–149, 157, 160, 163, 164, 166, 174, 176
Border of equilibrium, 7
Bourgeois
  economics, 102
  modernity, 109
Brazil, 71, 158, 159
BRICS, 18, 21, 43, 54, 106, 158
  countries, 18, 21
Buddhist, 159
Bukharin, 23
Bureaucratic class, 41
Business, 82, 148, 152, 154
Buzzing atmosphere, 10

C

Capital, 1, 8, 15, 19, 25, 37, 47, 59, 65, 101, 113, 116, 121, 127, 140, 147, 157, 163
  controls, 20
  owner, 4, 19
  ownership, 19
Capitalism, 15–21, 23, 25, 37–39, 45, 60, 64, 67, 73, 77, 95, 101, 104, 105, 107, 108, 111, 115, 116, 122, 124–126, 128–130, 131–142
  see also: Capitalist class; Capitalist system
Capitalist, 4, 15–22, 37–41, 43, 45, 64, 67, 73, 74, 84, 94, 95, 103–105, 107, 121, 122, 125, 126, 130, 133–135, 137–144, 157, 158, 173
  class, 16, 38, 134, 135, 137, 142
  ideology, 126
  state, 137, 138
  system, 4, 15, 39, 107, 130, 157, 158, 173
Carsharing, 8
Catastrophic
  consequences, 7
  predictions, 5
Celluloid, 76
China, 12, 18, 20–22, 28, 39, 40, 43, 53, 71, 77, 78, 102–104, 106, 141, 142, 158
Christian, 159
Civil society, 41–43, 157, 162
  associations, 41
  institutions, 42

Civilization, 2, 5, 11, 41, 45
 development, 5
Civilizational
 development, 7, 42
 ideology, 40
Classical philosophy, 2, 5
Cognition, 5–7, 9, 26, 69, 110, 163, 168
Cognitive, 114, 163, 164, 166, 172, 173, 176
 dissonance, 173
 model, 163, 176
Collateral, 8, 9
Commercialization, 117, 118
Commodities, 22, 65, 75, 78, 80, 116
Commonwealth, 39
Conceptual, 1, 148, 166, 172, 176
 analysis, 166, 176
Consumer protection, 25
Consumerism, 44, 45, 174
Consumption, 8, 49, 64, 77, 97, 118, 160, 168, 171
COVID-19, 110
Creative
 class, 41, 86
 economy, 64, 165
 labor, 59–61, 69, 85, 88–90, 95–97, 118
 nation, 87
 production, 59, 60, 82, 84, 86, 88, 91, 96, 97
Creatosphere, 45, 76, 84
Crisis, 7, 15, 17, 18, 20–22, 50, 81, 101–107, 110, 111, 157, 158, 165
Cuba, 141, 142
Cultural
 imperatives, 2
 man, 113, 115, 117, 118
 revolution, 169
 transformations, 8
 values, 1, 114
Cumulative reforms, 43

D

De-commercialization, 118
De-dollarization, 18, 102, 106
Deindustrialization, 38, 39
Deleterious effects, 41
Democratization, 118
Department of Culture, Media, and Sport (DCMS), 61, 87, 88
Detective story, 10
Developing countries, 48, 49, 51, 53, 54, 56, 104
Dichotomy, 175, 176
Diffusion, 9, 12, 40, 110, 174
Digital economy, 25, 29, 35
Digression, 9, 10
Discourse, 3, 67, 163, 164, 172, 173, 175, 176
Dogma, 108, 134–136, 138–141, 143, 144
Dominant capitalist, 16
Draughtsperson, 90
Drudge, 79
Dynamic mapping, 88

E

Ecological sustainability, 131
Economic, 1, 2, 4, 6–9, 12, 16, 18, 21, 25, 27–29, 37–40, 42, 43, 44–47, 48–50, 51–56, 63, 65, 68, 74, 102–104, 106–108, 110, 113–118, 125, 126, 136, 138, 140, 142, 147, 149, 151, 154, 155, 157–165, 167–169, 171, 173, 175, 176
 actors, 8
 being, 2, 164
 competitiveness, 54
 complexity, 55
 corporations, 38
 depression, 43
 development, 1, 25, 38, 40, 43, 47, 50, 51, 53–56, 113, 115, 116, 149, 154, 155, 167
 growth, 47–52, 56, 68, 159
 human, 9
 indicators, 27
 institutions, 40, 42, 43
 legal, 8
 man, 113, 115, 117, 118
 policy, 21, 41
 rationality, 168
 relations, 2, 6–8, 48, 50
 society, 9, 12
 system, 8, 40, 46, 50, 51, 159, 160
 territory, 16
 university, 34
 way, 9

Economy, 3, 4, 6, 8, 9, 12, 15, 17, 18, 23, 25, 29, 34, 35, 41–45, 47–49, 51–55, 61, 65, 66, 73, 74, 81, 84–86, 103, 105, 115, 116, 135, 138–140, 141–144, 149, 160, 165–170
  centered model, 9
Educational
  level, 153
  service, 173
Ego, 3
Egoistic, 3
Election campaigns, 25
Electronic communications, 38
Emancipation, 109, 111, 125, 130–131
Emotional links, 166
Energy resources, 45
Engels, 26, 60, 84, 121–124, 127–130, 132, 133, 137
Engineering products, 54
English aphorism, 123
Entrepreneurship, 41
Environmental sustainability, 51
Ethical, 173, 176
Etymological analysis, 166
Evils, 4
Evolutionary process, 171
Exhaustion, 1, 22, 101, 108

F

Fabian notion, 82
Fascism, 22, 105
Fascist, 18, 22, 106
Fashion industry, 94
Fetishism, 75, 116
Fetishization, 4
Financial
  repression, 20
  services, 54
  system, 38, 105
Financialization, 21, 22, 45, 81
Food technologies, 45
Foreign direct investment (FDI), 38, 39
Foundations, 1, 8, 121
Framework, 6, 10, 39, 43, 64, 89, 114, 118, 121, 159, 167, 169
Free market system, 159
Freelancer, 4
Fully automated luxury communism (FALC), 45
Future
  production, 9
  products, 9
  society, 121–124, 128–130, 133, 171

G

GATT (General Agreement on Tariffs and Trade), 77
Geopolitical economy, 15–18, 23, 59, 67
Glazyev, 7, 43, 148, 165
Global
  integration, 37
  neoliberalism, 43
  scale, 7, 38
  transformations, 7, 12, 147
Global South, 104, 106, 107, 143, 159, 161
Globalization, 7, 15, 37, 38, 43, 44, 48, 50, 102, 103, 105, 108, 110, 111
GOALS, 123, 129, 131
Government, 88, 138, 139, 154
Gross
  domestic product (GDP), 28, 40, 48–51, 53, 104
  national income, 30
Gucci, 93–97
Guillotine, 10

H

Hegemonic
  core, 37, 39
  Western countries, 38
Heightening inequality, 21
Hieroglyph, 26
Historical trajectory, 17
Homo
  culturalis, 101, 110
  economicus, 101, 109, 110, 115, 117
  sapiens, 12
Human
  capital, 8, 49, 113, 115–117
  community development, 3
  development, 2, 114, 124, 132–134, 136, 169, 170
  lives, 3

nature, 121, 124, 127, 129
needs, 2, 6, 9, 45, 114, 115, 168
potential, 55, 113–118
social creativity, 16
talent, 110
transformation, 9, 165
values, 9
work, 41
Humanism, 163, 164
Humanistic culture, 3
Humanity, 1, 6–7, 15, 16, 20, 44, 63, 86, 101, 102, 108–111, 114, 129, 131, 134, 157, 173
Hybrid world, 37
Hypothetical person, 3

I

Ideal influences, 6
Ideational
appeal, 45, 46
beliefs, 46
Immaterial labor, 108
Imperialism, 16, 20, 22, 23, 37, 67, 104
see also: Anti-imperialism
Imperialist nations, 16
Impetus, 22, 50
Individual private property, 8
Industrial
cooperation, 47, 67
digitalization, 54
infrastructure, 42
policy, 86, 106
product, 7, 64, 65, 72, 74, 79, 83, 84
production, 38
society, 41, 44, 48, 163, 165, 173, 176
state, 40, 44
Industrialization, 71
Inequality, 4
Inflation reduction act, 106
Information and Communication Technology (ICT), 60, 67
Institutions, 2, 6, 37, 41, 44, 45, 77, 87, 121–137, 140, 143, 144, 152, 154, 170
Intangible assets, 9, 65, 73, 78–80, 84
Intellectual property, 32, 77
rights, 9, 45
Intellectuals, 20, 161
Inter-imperialist rivalry, 21
International
Bureau of Weights and Measures, 26
economic
coordination, 43
governance, 18
order, 40
Electrotechnical Commission, 26
IMF, 39, 43, 71, 103
organizations, 25
power, 21
struggles, 17
systems of exchange, 102
trade, 39
Iraq, 104, 158
ISO, 26, 28, 31
IT industry, 54, 55
sector/services, 54, 55

J

Joint
production, 110
use, 8
Joint-stock companies, 19
Justified, 6

K

Key component, 7, 175
Knowledge, 1, 2, 5–7, 9–12, 23, 27, 34, 38, 42, 45, 51, 54, 63, 68–70, 77, 78, 82, 84–86, 101, 109, 110, 114, 147, 149, 151, 152, 155, 160, 164, 167–171, 173, 174
intensity, 7, 147, 149, 151, 155
intensive
material production, 1
production, 7, 12, 149–155, 170, 171
products, 1, 9, 51, 54

L

Labor
intensity, 51
productivity, 51, 150
intensive industries, 53
Landlord, 8
Language
creativity, 176
transformation, 176

Latin America, 158–161
Legal persons, 8
Legitimacy, 22, 23
Lender, 8
Liberal
  economic theories, 43
  principles, 43
Liberalization, 48
Liberation, 71, 125, 131
Life expectancy, 30
Linguistic, 164
  analysis, 164
Linguistics, 164, 166, 172
Loan, 8
Logical, 141, 142, 176
Lyricism, 11

M

Machine building, 55
Macroeconomic
  policy, 20
  problems, 49
Manual labor, 83, 84, 101, 109
Market
  fundamentalism, 6, 157, 160
  socialism, 135, 139, 140, 144
Marx, 5, 15–20, 41, 60, 63–65, 73, 74, 78, 94, 95, 108, 109, 116, 121–125, 127, 128, 132, 133, 137, 140, 168
Marxism, 16, 17, 21, 23, 115
Marxist, 20, 23, 68, 107, 116, 122, 123, 133, 141, 144
  concept, 23, 122
  socialist, 122, 133
  theory, 116
Material
  aspects, 12, 85
  foundation(s), 1, 9, 12, 63
  growth, 5
  objects, 5, 11, 79
  phenomena, 5
  things, 6
  wealth, 3, 30, 169
Mechanization Resistant, 90
Media, 38, 39, 154, 155
Medieval, 174
Mental
  objects, 5, 65, 76, 77, 85, 86
  productive capacity, 90
Metabolism, 101, 109, 111
Metamorphosis, 41
Metaphors, 175, 176
Methodological approaches, 147, 148
Metrology, 25, 28, 29, 35
Mexican, 62, 160
Mexico, 159, 160
Microscope, 5
Middle East, 161
Military-industrial-security complex, 42
Minotaur, 107, 108
Modernization, 7, 53
Mono-ownership, 8
Monopolistic Institution, 77
Monopoly phase, 19, 20
Moral Code, 9
Multilevel system, 25, 34
Multipolarity, 17
Muslim, 159
Myanmar, 161

N

NACE system, 70
NAICS, 70
National
  corpora, 174
  economies, 15, 38
  Endowment for Science, Technology, and the Arts (NESTA), 87
NATO, 39, 102, 105, 106
Need satisfaction, 9
Negative consequences, 6, 40
Neoclassical
  economics, 23, 74, 125
  growth theory, 85
Neoliberal
  model, 7
  principles, 43
  thinkers, 76
Neoliberalism, 7, 18, 21, 22, 37, 39, 40, 43–44, 105, 106, 107, 125, 138, 157, 158, 162
Neoliberals, 21, 77

NESTA, see: *National Endowment for Science, Technology, and the Arts*
NGOs, 159
Ninja mortgage, 81
Nomos, 165
Noocontrol, 10
Noo-development, 9
Noo-ego, 6
Noo-homo sapiens, 12
Noohuman, 2, 3, 12, 165
Noo-man, 12
Noonomic system, 93, 97
Noonomy, 1, 3, 5–7, 12, 15–17, 21–23, 37, 40, 43–46, 59–66, 74, 77, 85, 93, 95–97, 101, 109–111, 114–118, 147–149, 151, 153–155, 160, 162–173, 175, 176
  action, 170
  instrument, 169
  spiritual category, 167
  global south, 160
Nooproduction, 10, 114, 167, 169
Noosociety, 166, 167, 169, 176
Noovalue, 3
Noo-values, 6
Novel process, 90

O

Obsolete, 9, 55
OECD, 48, 52, 53
Oil refining products, 54
Ontological, 134, 163, 173
Orchestra, 63, 91, 92, 95
Ownership, 8, 19, 29, 38, 39, 43, 60, 77, 115, 168
  paradigm, 168
  rights, 8, 40, 130, 170
  splitting, 8
Oxymoron, 135

P

Paradigm, 6, 21, 63, 163–165, 167, 168, 175
Paradoxical, 10, 11, 60, 73
Partial transfer, 8
Paucity, 16
People-centered conception, 23
Periphery, 7, 154, 172
Philosopher, 44, 130, 161
Philosophical, 1, 26, 67, 164
Phonosemantic, 176
  analysis, 176
Physical quantity, 74
Policy
  autonomy, 16
  paradigm, 21
Political, 2, 3, 18, 21, 37–44, 46, 67, 68, 105–107, 114, 116, 125, 126, 131, 142, 157, 160, 161, 171, 175, 176
  atmosphere, 41
  economy, 3, 18, 67, 116, 160
Politics, 2, 18, 23, 43
Polycrisis, 18
Population, 43, 47, 49, 50, 74, 86, 95, 96, 104, 147–149, 152, 154, 155, 158–160
Post-economic
  space, 115
  way, 7, 9
Post-industrial development, 47, 51, 55, 56
Primary
  resource utilization, 52, 53
  resources, 47, 52, 53, 56
Production, 1, 5–10, 12, 16, 17, 19, 23, 29, 38, 41–45, 47–49, 51–54, 59, 60, 62–67, 70, 71, 73–75, 76–79, 82, 84–86, 88, 91–94, 96, 97, 101, 108, 110, 114–117, 130, 132, 134–136, 138–144, 147, 149, 151–153, 155, 159, 160, 164, 166–168, 170
Productive forces, 15, 16, 22, 23, 108
Progressive transformation, 7
Property
  diffusion, 8, 12, 164
  relations, 1, 9, 12, 40, 110, 166
  rights, 8, 40, 130, 170
Prosumidores, 160
Public
  authorities, 152, 155
  interests, 2, 3, 170
  ownership, 20

Q

Quadriga, 12, 164, 174, 175
  of noonomy, 164
Qualified, 20, 51, 73

Qualitative, 1, 27, 38, 47, 49, 52–54, 56, 59, 61, 89
accounts, 89
aspect, 61
change, 49
characteristics, 27
component, 52, 53
growth, 53, 56
level, 54
shift(s), 1, 38
Qualities, 26, 113, 115, 116, 118
Quality, 7, 25–35, 42, 44, 49, 50, 52, 78, 91–93, 97, 118, 147–149, 153, 155, 168
control, 153
Economics, 25, 27, 28, 35
lessons, 34
management, 25, 28–31, 34, 35
of life, 25, 30, 31, 34, 49, 50, 147, 149
problems, 27
related legislation, 25
Quantifying, 87
Quantitative, 26, 47, 52, 53, 61, 65, 74, 84, 91
aspect, 61
component(s), 47, 52, 53
gradations, 26
growth, 53
relations, 65
Quantum
by quantum, 11
leap, 19
level interactions, 69
Quarter, 37
Queensland University of Technology (QUT), 87
Quotation(s), 43, 94, 123, 125, 127–130, 137

R

Rational, 84, 114, 115, 127, 167, 169, 176
attitude, 167
consumption and needs, 166
knowledge, 166
Real
estate sector, 80
sector, 47, 51, 55, 56
Reference
framework, 28
standards, 28
Reflections, 2
Regional strategic planning, 147, 148, 155
Reindustrialization, 37, 40, 42, 45
Relative invariance, 12
Reproduction, 19, 54, 56, 84, 85, 92, 107, 127
labor, 116
Research
education, 155
R&D, 48, 50, 51, 54, 55
Reverse influence, 5, 6
Revitalization, 23
Revolution, 10, 64, 66, 125
devours, 10
RIA rating, 30
Ricardo Soto, 159
Rigid conflict, 6
Robotization, 40, 51
Rude mechanicals, 83
Russian
Federation, 31–33, 40, 44, 148
language, 174
military-industrial-security complex, 42
statism, 44

S

Saint Petersburg's experience, 25
Satisfying needs, 9, 115, 166
Scholars, 8, 28, 116, 159
Schumpeterian, 23
Science guy, 10
Scientific
cognition, 5
community, 4, 12, 152, 154, 155
Council for Metrological Support and Standardization, 35
paradigm, 27
research, 54, 110
technical progress, 4
technological
progress (STP), 4, 7, 10, 12
revolution (STR), 10
SCO (Shanghai Cooperation Organization), 43
associations, 43

Second generation, 40, 163, 165, 173, 176
Self-
  determination, 124, 129–131
  development, 41
  discover, 2
  realization, 96
Semi-
  core, 37, 40
  peripheral, 40
Service sector, 47, 55, 80–82
Seventh technological mode, 7
Seversky pipe plant, 153
Silver Age, 175
Simulacra, 173, 174, 176
Simulacrum, 89
Social, 2, 4–7, 11, 16–23, 25, 27, 29, 34, 37–43, 51, 55, 59, 60, 62–66, 68, 69, 71, 73–75, 77, 78, 86, 91, 93, 96, 97, 101, 104–111, 113–118, 121–131, 133–137, 139–142, 149, 157, 159, 160, 163–165, 169, 170, 174–176
  consciousness, 7
  cooperation, 97, 110
  development, 2, 25, 113, 114
  existence, 7, 69, 131
  instability, 51
  issues, 137, 175
  metabolism, 101, 109–111
  narratives, 11
  phenomena, 4, 174
  processes, 6, 116, 126, 141, 142
  production, 5, 109, 122
  productive capacities, 16
  structure, 40, 59, 114, 159
  transformation, 18, 62, 126
  welfare, 42
Socialism, 16–20, 23, 25, 42, 44, 60, 111, 121–130, 132–135, 137 144, 160, 165
Socialist
  China, 21
  production, 134, 144
  society, 93, 101, 122, 129, 137
  political parties, 41
Socialization, 9, 12, 16, 19, 60, 75, 110, 118, 164
  processes, 9, 12
Socially neutral mechanism, 4
Societal development, 49, 114
Society, 1, 2, 4–6, 9, 11, 12, 15–17, 26, 40–45, 48, 63–66, 68, 74, 77, 78, 85, 93, 94, 96, 101, 109, 110, 113–118, 121–131, 133–137, 140, 142, 160, 161, 164–167, 169–176
  solidarization, 164, 174
Socioeconomic, 1, 3, 25, 41, 102, 113–115, 148, 149, 154, 155, 162
  content, 1
  development, 1, 34, 149, 154, 155
  theory, 3
  transition, 162
Socio-humanitarian sphere, 113, 117, 118
Sociopolitical institutions, 42
Solidarism, 12
Solidarity, 6, 12, 37, 110, 131, 159, 162
  economics, 162
Soviet
  Red Army, 105
  school, 9
  socialism, 44
  Union, 20, 65, 102, 105, 110, 158
Specifically human, 128, 131
Sphere, 2, 9, 11, 55, 77, 78, 84, 85, 88, 113, 117, 118, 128, 163, 172, 173
Spiritual, 1–3, 11, 30, 171, 172, 176
  category, 171
  development, 2, 11
  needs, 2
  principles, 1
  world, 3
Spirituality, 176
Sportsman, 174
Stakeholders, 42, 155
Standardization, 25, 26, 28, 29, 35, 60, 64, 70, 97
State
  institutions, 41
  revenues, 48
  socialism, 42
STEM industries, 79
STP, see: *Scientific and technological progress*
Structural transformation, 56
Subaltern, 40, 124, 135, 137
Sudan, 161
Supra-state forces, 41

T

Technocrats, 41
Technological, 1, 4, 5, 7–12, 40–42, 53–55, 63, 66, 67, 77, 78, 84, 85, 97, 108–110, 114, 149, 151, 152, 155, 164, 165, 170, 171, 176
  determinism, 5, 109
  development, 7, 10, 40, 54, 55, 84, 151
  innovation, 66, 97, 155
  lag, 53
  modes, 7
  process, 5, 152
  progress, see: *Scientific and technological progress*
  revolution, 10, 40, 108
Technology, 2, 4–8, 10, 45, 55, 65, 78, 90, 96, 114, 149, 152, 168
Technosphere, 114, 169
Terminological neologism, 163, 165, 166, 176
Territorial development, 147, 155
Tigers of Wrath, 82
TNCs (transnational corporations), 7, 49
Training system, 35
Transatlantic community, 7
Transition, 1, 3, 6, 7, 11, 19, 42, 54, 60, 92, 101, 102, 106, 108–111, 115, 134, 137, 142, 149, 157, 161–168, 170, 171, 174, 175
Transnational corporations, see: *TNCs*
Trident, 61, 88
Troglodytes, 11

U

Unemployment, 43
UNESCO, 34
UNICEF, 175
Uniform income growth, 49
Uniformity of measurements, 25, 28
Unifying interests, 2
Unionization, 79
United Kingdom, 138
Utilitarian needs, 3
Utopian vision, 44

V

Values, 1, 3, 6, 7, 9, 11, 45, 110, 113–117, 157, 160, 168, 174
  value-based aspects, 9
Victorian-era, 86
Vienna, 157, 161
Vietnam, 104, 141, 142
Virtual reality, 41
Viruses, 5
Visible, 9, 53

W

War, 18, 21, 22, 65, 68, 78, 84, 101, 105–107, 141, 158, 161
Washington Consensus, 106, 107
Weakness, 21
Wealth, 3, 61, 63, 78, 86, 96, 116, 124
Weight reference, 28
Welfare
  state provisions, 43
  states, 20, 22
West-centric globalization, 7
Western
  Africa, 161
  governments, 21
  prosperity, 23
  sanctions, 42
Withdrawal, 8
Witnessing, 9, 163, 164
World, 17, 22, 26, 39, 43, 51, 59, 77, 102, 105, 108, 121
  Bank, 39, 43
  Economic Forum, 108
  economy, 21, 38, 43, 48, 53, 61, 67, 103, 104
  hegemon, 102, 104, 107
  Intellectual Property Organization (WIPO), 77
  system analysis, 7
  Trade Organization (WTO), 28, 39, 43, 77
  wide web, 81, 92
  WWII, 51, 105, 125, 138
Worldview, 10, 125, 126

Y

Yachts, 96
Yield, 62, 80, 126, 136
Yoked, 83
Youngest, 26
Youth, 44

Z

Zeitenwende, 102
Zeitgeist, 102
Zenith, 103
Zero, 2, 51
Zigzags, 108
Zoo, 6